LOADED WITH
DYNAMITE

UNINTENDED CONSEQUENCES
OF WOODROW WILSON'S IDEALISM

French Premier Georges Clemenceau, American President Woodrow Wilson, and British Prime Minister David Lloyd George during the Paris Peace Conference in Paris, France, June 28, 1919.
Photo by Mansell/The LIFE Picture Collection via Getty Images

LOADED WITH
DYNAMITE

UNINTENDED CONSEQUENCES
OF WOODROW WILSON'S IDEALISM

H.D.S. Greenway

TIDEPOOL PRESS
Cambridge, Massachusetts

Copyright © 2021 by H.D.S. Greenway
Published in the United States in 2021 by TidePool Press

All rights reserved.
No part of this book may be reproduced in any manner whatsoever without written permission.

TidePool Press, LLC
6 Maple Avenue, Cambridge, Massachusetts 02139
www.tidepoolpress.com

Printed in the United States

Library of Congress Cataloging-in-Publication Data

Greenway, Hugh Davids Scott, b. 1935
    Loaded with Dynamite: Unintended Consequences of Woodrow
      Wilson's Idealism
    p.cm.
    ISBN: 978-0-9978482-7-4
    1. Greenway, H.D.S.
    2. Politics—International 3. Woodrow Wilson—United States
    4. Gabriele d'Annunzio—Italy, Mussolini 5. Abd el-Krim—
    Morocco, Franco 6. Sun Yat-sen—China, Chiang Kai-shek
    I. Title.

2020950309

FOR JB

NOTE ON ROMANIZATION

Many authors have used different transliterations for Berber and Arabic names and places when writing about Morocco in the 1920s. For consistency's sake I have followed the spelling used by David S. Woolman, whose book, *Rebels in the Rif: Abd el-Krim and the Rif Rebellion*, I found very helpful. The only exception is that I have used a more recent translation of Abd el-Krim's full given name.

For Chinese names and places, I have used the old Wade-Giles system, which was in use during the period about which I am writing. But in the first reference, after every name in parentheses, I include the modern, pinyin romanization that came into common use in the 1980s. For example: Peking (Beijing). The notable exceptions are Sun Yat-sen and Chiang Kai-shek, whose names reflect the Cantonese dialect and are familiar in the West, as well as V.K. Wellington Koo, who habitually used his western name in the many offices he held. I also spell the Yangtze River in the pinyin romanization.

Contents

Introduction		IX
CHAPTER ONE	Wilson	3
CHAPTER TWO	d'Annunzio	45
CHAPTER THREE	Abd el-Krim	81
CHAPTER FOUR	Sun Yat-sen	139
Appendix		183
Endnotes		189
Bibliography		199
Acknowledgments		207
Index		209

When the president talks of self-determination what unit does he have in mind? Does he mean a race, a territorial area, or a community? ... The phrase is simply loaded with dynamite. It will raise many hopes that can never be realized.

—Robert Lansing
    Secretary of State (1915-1920)

Introduction

THIS IS THE STORY of an American president who, for a brief moment one hundred years ago, was the best-known and best-loved man in the world. His inspiring Fourteen Points, his call for self-determination and consent of the governed, seemed to promise a brand-new world to those who had just suffered through the Great War of 1914–1918, the most destructive war the world had ever seen. It also gave hope to those longing to be free from colonial rule in the years when almost all of Africa and much of Asia was under foreign rule.

People came to Paris to see him during a peace conference that would decide the fate of millions, people representing nationalist causes the American president did not know existed. When the conference was over, Woodrow Wilson came to be reviled by many in Asia, Africa, and Europe because of decisions made and promises not kept.

This is the story, too, of three remarkable individuals who were affected by Wilson's decisions and inspired by his words on three continents. Gabriele d'Annunzio was a poet, war hero, Italian nationalist, author, playwright, and serial seducer of some of the most beautiful women in Europe. He lived in an age when poetry could still move the masses. He defied Wilson and his French and British allies when they denied Italy the right to take over the Austro-Hungarian port of Fiume when World War I was over, by taking it over himself with a band of Italian war veterans. For fifteen months he ran a revolutionary state with its own postage stamps, its own army, navy, and air force. His political theories, a mixture of left and right, attracted utopian dreamers, nationalist misfits, advocates of free love, bohemian idealists, and revolutionary outcasts who joined him in his never-never land until the Italians threw him out. Although he was never a Fascist, Fascism was born in d'Annunzio's Fiume, now called Rijeka in the Republic of Croatia. The malignant nationalism, the straight-armed salute, the stirring rallies, the bullying tactics and theatrics of politics, that Mussolini and Hitler were soon to adopt as their own, were all born in d'Annunzio's Fiume.

This is the story of Morocco's Mohamed ibn al-Karim al-Khattabi, known in the West as Abd el-Krim, who took the doctrine of self-determination literally, and for almost five years led the most successful revolt against a colonial power in the period between the two world wars; a leader whose guerrilla tactics were studied by Che Guevara, Mao, and Ho Chi Minh in the years to follow. He fought for his homeland in the Rif Mountains against his Spanish colonial masters, and later against the French, who threw every modern weapon available against him. Spain became one of the first to use poison gas against a civilian population during its war against Abd el-Krim. In the 1920s, he caught the imagination of the world, appearing on the cover of *Time* magazine. His revolt became the inspiration for a long-running Broadway musical and at least three Hollywood movies. For nearly five years, until defeated by the French and Spanish combined, he ran his own country with its own flag and its own government in an age when colonial powers were saying that backward natives were not civilized enough to be independent.

The Rif War, all but forgotten today, savaged democracy in Spain. Its colonial army of Africa under General Francisco Franco, after finally defeating Abd el-Krim in Morocco, turned on Spain's democratically elected government in Spain itself, sparking the Spanish Civil War, the curtain-raiser to World War II. Abd el-Krim set the standard for every war of national liberation that eventually ended colonialism in North Africa and everywhere else by the century's end.

This is also the story of Sun Yat-sen, the Chinese nationalist leader who fought to overturn an age-old monarchy and then unite China against warlord anarchy and foreign imperialism. Sun admired Wilson and American democracy, but after what was seen as an American betrayal of China at the Paris Peace Conference, selling out China's interests in favor of Japan, Sun, although never a Communist himself, turned his gaze toward another light: Lenin and Soviet Russia, the consequences of which are being felt to this day.[i]

In a sense, all four were failures. Sun Yat-sen never did unite China. That would be left to Chairman Mao and his Communist armies in 1949. But Sun is seen today as the father of modern China even by the ruling Communist Party. Abd el-Krim was finally defeated and exiled to an island in the Indian Ocean. But he inspired those who would eventually end colonialism, and he lived to see independence come to all the countries of the North African littoral. D'Annunzio failed to push Italy into annexing Fiume as he so desired. That was left to Mussolini to achieve. But d'Annunzio inspired Fascism, and in the mass rallies, slogans, and repetitive chants of his time, we can see the origins of nationalist movements in our own time. Woodrow Wilson failed to get the United States into his League of Nations to ensure world peace. But Wilson's words did not die with him. Self-determination and consent of the governed, concepts that were thought revolutionary a hundred years ago, have today become accepted everywhere people aspire to rule themselves.

---

i As recently as 2019, China's Xi Jinping brought up China's 1919 humiliation at the Paris Peace Conference in conversations with President Donald J. Trump. Trump had no idea what Xi was talking about. See Bolton, John; *The Room Where It Happened: A White House Memoir* (Simon & Schuster, New York, 2020).

What I seem to see—with all my heart I hope that I am wrong—is a tragedy of disappointment.

> —Woodrow Wilson
> President of the United States (1913-1921)

CHAPTER ONE

Wilson

EVEN BEFORE THE United States entered World War I, President Woodrow Wilson had begun reaching out to the principal belligerents: the "Entente" allies, Britain, France, Italy, and Russia, as well as to the "Central Powers," Germany, Austria-Hungary, and the Ottoman Empire. By the end of 1916, all the warring powers were looking at the unprecedented butcher's bill that modern, twentieth-century war was presenting, and were willing to consider a way out. Alone among the major industrial countries, the United States had stayed out of the horrific conflict. In 1916 Wilson won reelection to a second term, a Democrat after a string of three Republican administrations, partly on his campaign slogan that he had kept his country out of war. Now he wanted to bring peace to the world.

The first president to be born in the South since John Tyler left office in 1845, Wilson had made his name as president of Princeton University, then serving only two years as governor of New Jersey before being elected to the presidency in 1912. A longtime student of government, Wilson was an intensely private man, incapable of the bonhomie usually associated with politicians. He was rigid and inflexible when his mind was made up, impatient with negotiations and adamantine when it came to compromise. A strict Presbyterian, the son of a minister, Wilson was "almost childlike in his faith, seeking guidance from reading the Bible, church and prayer," according to one of his biographers.[1] Wilson believed that moral force could and should be the dominant factor in international affairs. He was extremely confident in his oratory to sway the masses, and he was good at it. But he was noticeably less good at other forms of winning people over. Backs were not slapped in Wilson's White House. "He was incapable of schmoozing," as another biographer put it.[2]

To this role of trying to broker an end to the slaughter in Europe, Wilson brought a big idea: a League of Nations to which the conflicts and disagreements of the world could be brought before a world parliament endowed with enforcement powers; a system that would replace the old balance-of-power politics that had so spectacularly failed. It may not have originally been his idea. Others had suggested such an international organization, notably the British, but Wilson made it his own and became its greatest advocate. Wilson the idealist spoke of a world in which small nations could have equal voice with big nations. He was an internationalist in a country that had only recently begun to look beyond its borders. He was a confident believer in the power of an American president to get things done—too confident, as it turned out.

Along with his Fourteen Points, Four Principles, Four Ends, and Five Particulars, his blueprints for a new world order, Wilson suggested a "peace without victory," saying that "peace imposed upon the vanquished" would leave a "sting of resentment, a bitter memory upon which the terms of peace would rest, not permanently, but only upon quicksand." And furthermore, he said, "No peace can last or ought to last, which does not recognize and accept the principle that governments derive all their just powers from the consent of the governed, and that no right anywhere exists to hand peoples about from sovereignty to sovereignty as if they were property."[3]

Peace without victory would come as music to the ears of the Central Powers. Hemorrhaging blood and treasure, by 1918 Germany was beginning to see its path to victory fading. For the ethnic minorities of Europe, and colonized peoples of the world, it was Wilson's "consent of the governed," which was enshrined in the Declaration of Independence as well as his call for "self-determination"[4] that electrified them, giving hope and expectation that Wilson, now the head of the undisputedly most powerful country in the world, would lead them to the promised land of national independence. Self-determination, he said, "is not a mere phrase. It is an imperative principle of action which statesmen henceforth ignore at their peril."[5] Lenin had asked, "What is meant by self-determination?"[6] But Wilson adopted that powerful phrase as his own four years later. Wilson would go on in the weeks and months ahead to make a series of pronouncements along a similar vein:[i]

> We feel ourselves to be intimate partners of all governments and peoples associated together against imperialism.[7]
>
> No gathering of peoples and provinces as mere chattels and pawns in the game.[8]
>
> Every territorial settlement is to be made in the interest of the populations concerned.[9]
>
> An evident principle runs through the whole program I have outlined. It is the principle of justice to all peoples and nationalities and their right to live on equal terms of liberty and safety with one another, whether they be strong or weak.[10]

These were promises that gave great comfort to colonized peoples of the world, and on the wings of twentieth-century communications they flew to the remotest corners of the globe. The tragedy was that Wilson was making promises that he either could not, or would not, deliver.

"We have no selfish ends to serve," Wilson declared. "We desire no conquest, no dominion. We seek no indemnities for ourselves, no material compensation for the sacrifices we shall freely make." His only goal, he said, was to make the world "safe for democracy."[11] Thus did Wilson announce the purity of his motives, trying to

---

i See Appendix, p. 193, for Wilson's Points, Principles, Ends, and Particulars.

distance himself and his country from the squabbling, greedy Europeans who had brought catastrophe upon themselves. Never mind that the United States, allegedly disinterested in the spoils of war, would eventually receive "through one channel or another four-fifths of the reparations paid by Germany" to the allies; such was the debt the allies owed to the United States, as Winston Churchill would later complain.[12] Before the last of Wilson's pronouncements were made, however, the war that Wilson had tried to avoid engulfed the United States in the spring of 1917. Some, such as former president Theodore Roosevelt, were delighted. It was Germany's unrestricted submarine warfare and the Zimmerman Telegram,[ii] in which Germany tried to get Mexico to make war on the United States, that pushed Wilson to war. But another consideration had to be that if the United States remained neutral it would have a lesser role to play sculpturing the peace at war's end. And that was a role Wilson very much wanted to play. By the time war was over in November of 1918, all Wilson's notions of peace without victory were no longer on the table.

Wilson's secretary of state, Robert Lansing, saw the flaws in his president's call for self-determination:

> When the president talks of 'self-determination' what unit has he in mind? Does he mean race, a territorial area or a community? Without a definite unit which is practical, application of this

---

ii British Intelligence had decoded and passed along to the Americans the text of German Foreign Minister Arthur Zimmerman's telegram to Mexico inviting the Mexicans to invade the U.S. should the U.S. enter the war against Germany. Perhaps in concert with Japan, Zimmerman said Germany would help Mexico recover Texas, New Mexico, and Arizona, which had been lost to Mexico in 1848. Since Wilson had recently sent troops into its southern neighbor's territory, Zimmerman hoped that Mexico might be receptive. But neither Mexico nor Japan, which was already at war with Germany, were interested. The telegram's interception and decoding was one of the most consequential events in the history of code-breaking espionage.

> principle is dangerous to peace and stability. ... It is bound to be the basis for impossible demands ... create trouble in many lands ... the phrase is simply loaded with dynamite. It will raise hopes that can never be realized. It will, I fear, cost thousands of lives. In the end it is bound to be discredited, to be called the dream of an idealist who failed to realize the danger until it was too late to check those who attempt to put the principle into force. What calamity the phrase was ever uttered. What misery it will cause.[13]

Indeed, uprisings were about to alight and spread like forest fires as nationalists around the world took heart at Wilson's words only to be crushed. Wilson thought of self-determination applying mostly to the ethnicities of vanquished enemies, rather than the colonies of his allies. Koreans were about to rise against their Japanese masters as were Egyptians against the British—uprisings that were ruthlessly suppressed. The darker-skinned peoples of the world would have to wait until another world war before their dream of throwing off the yoke of colonial rule would be realized.

Wilson himself had little concept of what his brave words would mean in practice. In due course, as the peace conference did its work, toxic disappointments would follow one upon another for those who had believed in Wilson's words. Peoples and provinces would be bartered about from sovereignty to sovereignty as if they were mere "chattels and pawns" in the game of power politics with little more justification than one great power had promised them to another. Even in Europe, Hungarians suddenly found themselves to be Rumanians. Austrians became Italians without being consulted. Africans and Pacific Islanders who had been German subjects found themselves British, Australian, or Japanese. Chinese, who had been under German jurisdiction, came under Japanese control. Toward the end of 1919, Wilson would confess to Congress that when he gave utterance to the words self-determination, "I said them without the knowledge that nationalities existed which are coming to us day after day."[14]

As for democracy, Wilson believed it was a "stage of development … built up by slow habit … Immature people cannot have it …" but no race or nation was incapable of democracy.[15] Wilson shared with many Americans then, and today, the belief that a morally superior United States stood at the pinnacle of political development. Wilson thought of himself as an anti-colonialist, and he worked hard to gain autonomy leading to eventual independence for the Philippines, an American colony since 1898. But the colonial subjects of his European allies and Japan would not get his attention no matter what encouragement they had taken from his words. Nor was he against armed intervention or regime change when it suited his moral sense of what was best. Under Wilson's administrations, American troops intervened in Cuba, Haiti, Panama, the Dominican Republic twice, Mexico twice, Honduras five times, and Russia after the Bolshevik revolution. No American before him had sent so many Americans to fight in foreign lands.

Much of this was in the future in December 1918 when Wilson sailed from New York to France to take his place at the peace conference in Paris where he hoped to reorder the world. However, Wilson's party had lost control of both the Senate and the House of Representatives in the mid-term elections, an event that would have fatal consequences later when he tried to sell his peace plan to a Republican-controlled Senate. He also failed to take a single Republican with him to Paris, thus ensuring enmity from his political opponents.

Five days before Wilson sailed, his old political enemy, Theodore Roosevelt, whom Wilson had defeated in the election of 1912, tried to rain on Wilson's parade. Roosevelt issued a public statement saying, "Our allies and our enemies and Mr. Wilson himself should understand that Mr. Wilson has no authority whatsoever to speak for the American people at this time. His leadership has been emphatically repudiated by them. His Fourteen Points … and all his utterances every which way have ceased to have any shadow of right to be the accepted will of the American people."[16] Given that technically the United States was still at war with Germany, Roosevelt's attempt to undermine the Commander in Chief could be considered close to treasonous. It was one of Roosevelt's last pronouncements. He died nine days later of a heart attack.

But none of that dampened the enthusiasm as Wilson's ship slipped down the Hudson River to the sea. "A thousand whistles screamed, a million onlookers cheered, and a great city rocked to the waves of exultant patriotism,"[17] recalled George Creel, journalist and Wilson's propagandist, who had been tasked with selling the war to the American public as well as Wilson's values abroad.

Wilson's reception in Europe was no less ecstatic. Everywhere he went he was met with rapturous crowds hailing him as the savior of mankind. In France crowds turned out in numbers that had never before greeted a foreign leader. In England he met the king, in Italy the Pope, and Italian cities competed with one another to rename streets and public squares in his name. At that moment he "enjoyed a prestige and moral influence unequaled in history," wrote one of his severest critics, the economist and member of the British delegation, John Maynard Keynes. "How the crowds of European capitals pressed about the carriage of the president! With what curiosity, anxiety, and hope we sought a glimpse of the features and bearing of the man of destiny, who, coming from the west, was to bring healing to the wounds of the ancient parent of his civilization and lay before us the foundations of the future."[18]

The French foreign minister, Stephen Pichon, thanked Wilson for coming "to give us the right kind of peace."[19] Is it any wonder that this austere, reserved Presbyterian elder, looking more like a stern frontier preacher in his frock coat than a conquering hero, succumbed to a touch of arrogance? Wilson's words had so affected the cities of the Great Powers that their leaders had to pay at least lip service to Wilson's ideals or face retribution at home. But that was a status that soon began eroding when dashed against the hard rocks of allied intransigence and the bold coasts of reality. When nobody got completely what they wanted at the peace conference, and when practicality and compromise trumped Wilson's lofty principles, "the disillusion was so complete that some of those who had trusted most hardly dared not speak of it," Keynes wrote. "What happened to the president? What weakness or what misfortune" had led to what many would consider "extraordinary" and "unlooked for" betrayals?[20]

Keynes thought Wilson intellectually inferior to his interlocutors at the Paris Peace Conference. But Keynes missed the point. Being British, he didn't grasp the essence of American exceptionalism, the belief that Americans are exceptionally endowed with virtue, that has influenced American foreign policy to this day. Coming from a new continent uncorrupted by the old, Wilson saw himself as bringing fresh, shining, new ideas just as the American Republic had itself been a fresh, shining, new idea 143 years before. Armed with moral certitude, Wilson didn't need to know the ins and outs of history or the complicated arrangements of a Europe that had so recently imploded. He was an American coming with new, idealistic, American solutions. It was all very well to know what had gone before. He himself had written history books. But history was irrelevant when up against moral certainty. And Wilson's moral certitude was as strong as any crusader knight before the gates of Jerusalem.

The Paris Peace Conference opened on the January 18, 1919, in the splendor of the French foreign ministry on the Quai d'Orsay. The conference was attended by more than thirty countries, with dozens more suppliants who wanted the status of their regions, religions, and nationalities recognized. Notably uninvited were the war losers: Germany, Bulgaria, the Ottoman Empire, and Austro-Hungary, which had already begun to disintegrate into squabbling nations before the congress even began. Also uninvited was the former ally, Russia, now that it was under Bolshevik control and wracked by civil war. Neither the British nor the Americans wanted the conference to be in Paris. Wilson's right hand man, Edward House, wrote in his diary, "It will be difficult enough at best to make a just peace, and it will be almost impossible to do so while sitting in the atmosphere of a belligerent capital."[21] But the French carried the day.

Dominating the conference were the Big Four, consisting of the starched and upright Wilson, Britain's wily Welshman, David Lloyd George, Georges Clemenceau, known as "The Tiger" by his countrymen, and the silky Sicilian, Vittorio Orlando of Italy, who always felt with some justification that he and his country were being treated as an inferior by the other three. The primary purpose of the conference was to forge a peace treaty with Germany, but there was other business, such as deciding new boundaries in Europe, as well as disposing of Germany's colonies overseas. Wilson had little knowledge of Europe and even less of the world beyond, and although he had brought a team of experts, he rarely consulted them. He leaned instead on his long-time aide, House, who went by the honorary title of Colonel House and had become personally acquainted with many of Europe's leaders at Wilson's request during the war. House's translator and right-hand man, Stephen Bonsal, said of Wilson, he "almost invariably ignored the expert who could have told him that his belief in 'easily recognizable frontiers of nationality' was not based on accurate knowledge; that frequently they did not exist ... "[22]

But then Wilson believed there was a certain virtue in ignorance and lack of experience in statecraft. America is the "prize amateur nation of the world," he had said in a speech during the war. "Now when it comes to doing new things and doing them well I will back the amateur against the professional anytime because the professional does it all out of the book and the amateur does it with his eyes open upon a new world and with a new set of circumstances. He knows so little about it that he is fool enough to do the right thing."[23]

Harold Nicolson, a member of the British delegation, thought that Wilson's one-track mind was an "intellectual disability" that rendered him "blindly impervious, not merely to human character, but to shades of difference. He possessed no gift for differentiation, no capacity for adjustment to circumstances. It was his spiritual and mental rigidity which proved his undoing."[24] But then Wilson had not come to Paris to engage shades of difference or to adjust to circumstance. He had come to save the world.

Keynes found Wilson to be more Presbyterian minister than statesman. "He could have preached a sermon" on any of the commandments which he had thundered from the White House, "but he could not frame their application to the actual state of Europe."[25] But then, Wilson was less interested in the actual state of Europe than he was in Europe and the world's future. And that meant a League of Nations above all else. Once the allies became aware that Wilson's bottom line was always going to be his League of Nations, and that he would make almost any compromise to achieve it, they knew how to outmaneuver the American president. Wilson's great prestige, based on American power while all of post-war Europe was destitute and indebted, was melting away as the conference got down to business away from the cheering crowds.

In the last years of, and immediately following, World War I when empires were collapsing all over Europe, scores of little countries sprang up like spring flowers declaring their independence. Even before the war had ended in September 1918, the allies had organized a Congress of Submerged Nationalities in Paris to come to grips with new and sometimes conflicting aspirations of nationhood. In 1919 their representatives were flooding into Paris, and most wanted to see Wilson in order to "explain their pathetic ambitions," wrote Ray Stannard Baker, Wilson's press secretary.[26] The correspondent for the *Telegraph*, E.J. Dillon, described the scene:

> Waning and waxing powers, vacant thrones, decaying dominions had, each of them, their accusers, special pleaders and judges in this multitudinous world center [Paris] in which tragedy, romance, and comedy rained down potent spells. An Arabian Nights touch was imparted to the dissolving panorama by strange visitors from Tartary, Kurdistan, Korea, and Aderbeijan [sic], Armenia, Persia and the Hadjaz-men with patriarchal beards and scimitar

shaped noses, and others from desert and oasis, from Samarkand to Bokhara. Turbans, fezzes, sugar loaf hats and headgear ... old military uniforms devised for embryonic armies of new states on the eve of perpetual peace, snowy white burnooses, flowing like mantles, and graceful garment like the Roman toga, contributed to create an atmosphere of dreamy unreality in the city while the grimmest of reality were being faced and coped with.[27]

Among them, on the sidelines of the conference, were the colonized of empires—Egyptians, Indians, Koreans annexed by Japan, Irish wanting to be free from Britain, Indochinese. Ho Chi Minh, who would later play such an outsized role in American history, donned a cutaway hoping to present Wilson with a long list of French abuses in Vietnam. He never got in to see Wilson, nor is there any record that his list of grievances was ever seen. It was the first of many missed chances for the United States to come to an agreement with Ho.

A plea from the Koreans, whose revolt against the Japanese would be put down with exceeding brutality, did reach the State Department in Washington. It was filed away under the notation "Do not acknowledge."[28] Japan had been an ally in the war, and Wilson needed Japan for his League of Nations. Self-determination could not be allowed to get away in the way of that goal.

Stephen Bonsal estimated that there were some thirty or forty "discordant peace delegations" entrenched in Paris, and many more that had not been invited to participate. Bonsal feared these "doves of peace" were fast developing into "virtual fighting cocks."[29] "Almost everywhere the war drums were still throbbing," Bonsal wrote in his diary in the spring of 1919. "There are battles along the Baltic and everywhere in the Balkans. Misery and starvation prevail almost everywhere in Eastern Europe."[30] Baker "counted up fourteen small wars ... Bolshevism was everywhere spreading like an infection from Russia," as its own civil war raged. "The new German government was scarcely able to maintain itself against the attacks of radicals. It seemed as if the world was in a race between peace and anarchy—with anarchy winning."[31]

Hatreds were brimming over in Paris too. A would-be assassin, a French anarchist, fired seven shots at Clemenceau as he came out of his house on the Rue Benjamin Franklin. Only one bullet struck home, wounding him in the ribs in a place from which it was too dangerous to remove the bullet. Clemenceau quickly recovered, remarking that no Frenchman, after such a long and terrible war, should be so poor a marksman as to fire seven shots while hitting him only once. The wound bothered him for the rest of his life.

India, unlike so many other colonial dependents, actually had a seat at the table in Paris, along with South Africa, Australia, New Zealand, and Canada, as part of the British Empire. Many Indian nationalists hoped for independence, but short of that they were asking for dominion status and home rule such as the white dominions enjoyed. Some thought that Wilson's Fourteen Points and self-determination were going to play midwife to a new era. Wilson put the Indians off by saying that India's case, as with so many other problems, could be taken up by a League of Nations, if and when it came into being.

The way the victorious allies were deciding the fate of millions in 1919 was often haphazard and hasty. When the British foreign minister, Arthur Balfour, wished to call Mark Sykes[iii] to testify on carving up the Middle East, Balfour was told that Sykes had a bad cold and could not attend. "Oh dear, how provoking," said Balfour, "I had hoped we could get on with this business today. Tell him it will go over to the eleventh, but he must not fail us then. I suppose

---

iii In 1916, before the Turks had been defeated, Britain's Mark Sykes and the French diplomat François Georges-Picot negotiated the secret Sykes-Picot agreement dividing up the Ottoman Empire between them. Italy and Russia were to inherit pieces as well. The secret was revealed by the Bolsheviks in 1917. Wilson, who felt boxed in by all the secret agreements the British and French had made during the war, tried to maintain that all of them were null and void because the allies had accepted his Fourteen Points which, he maintained, should supersede any previous agreements. His argument did not prevail.

we must take up the next item on the agenda. What's that? Oh yes, those islands in the Baltic. I can never remember their names."

When the appointed day rolled around, not on the eleventh, but on February 16, 1919, Balfour was told that Sykes had died that very morning of septic pneumonia caused by the so-called Spanish flu pandemic of that time. "Oh dear," said Balfour, "it seems we will never get on with the problem. What's the next item on the agenda?"[32]

Baker described the tension over territory well. "When an Englishman has a fancy fixed on some islands, or a Frenchman wants some billions more francs than there is any show of getting, or an Italian covets a town which was Italian in the days of the Venetian doges, there is difficulty afoot."[33]

The most vexing problem the conference had to face, because it concerned one of the Big Four, was Italy's demand for the Adriatic city of Fiume (Rijeka today). In the days of the Roman Empire, it had been called Flumen. It was an important port of the Austro-Hungarian Empire, and Italy wanted it. In yet another secret treaty, the Treaty of London, the British and French had promised Italy much of the eastern shore of the Adriatic if Italy would come into the war on the allies' side. Austria's most important port, Trieste, was promised to the Italians, but not Fiume. The Italians themselves, when the secret treaty was drawn up, had recognized that Fiume, on the other side of the Istrian Peninsula from Trieste, "must remain, as it had always been—the outlet to the great hinterland reaching back to Hungary."[34] But now the war was over and the Italians had been on the winning side. Now, they wanted Fiume, despite what they had agreed to before. The Croatians on the Adriatic shore thought differently. In the summer of 1918, before the war had ended, groups of Balkan Slavs met to discuss how the Serbs, fighting on the side of the allies, could join in a post-war union with Slovenes and Croats who were fighting on the Austrian side. Not only had these Slavic peoples been on different sides, they spoke different languages and practiced different religions. However, these southern Slavs were able to put these differences aside and form a new state to be called the Kingdom of Serbs, Croats, and Slovenes—all before Wilson had set sail for France. Later this union came to be called Yugoslavia, and would last until the 1990s when it came apart on linguistic, ethnic, and religious grounds. But in 1919 they were all trying to make the new union work.[iv]

The new kingdom could accept losing what had been promised Italy in the Treaty of London, but not the kingdom's most important remaining port, Fiume. The eleventh of Wilson's Fourteen Points held that Serbia should be granted "free and secure access to the sea," and now that meant not just Serbs, but Croats and Slovenes as well. But Wilson's ninth point had stipulated a "readjustment of the frontier of Italy" along "recognizable lines of nationality," and for the Italians that meant Fiume. But as Secretary of State Lansing had seen, lines of nationality were not always recognizable. Fiume had an Italian populated center, but the suburbs and hinterland were overwhelmingly Croatian—a vivid example of the difficulty in defining self-determination. Italy's Prime Minister, Vittorio Orlando, argued passionately that Fiume was as Italian as Rome, and that the Italians of Fiume wanted their city annexed to Italy as soon as possible. The Yugoslav population was just as adamant that this should not happen. Orlando argued that gaining the eastern shore of the Adriatic would "at last be the completion of Italian unification" begun half a century before by Giuseppe Garibaldi. Without it, Orlando said, "Italy would lack the territory necessary for a united and independent people." When asked by Lloyd George what he might take in exchange for Fiume, Orlando asked him what he might ask in exchange for "cutting off his hand."[35] The Italian did not think it fair that the Croats of Croatia should be favored

---

iv   Today there are six separate countries in the former Yugoslavia: Serbia, Croatia, Slovenia, Montenegro, Kosovo, and Northern Macedonia.

now that the war was over, when they only recently had been in the trenches fighting in the Austrian army against Italians.

The Italians feared that the new Yugoslav state was inherently unstable, and therefore, a danger to Italy. "For instance, you must know that the Serbs and Croats are culturally miles apart," an Italian diplomat, Giacomo de Martino, said to Bonsal. A peasant Croat is intellectually superior to the average statesman of Belgrade (Serbia), the Italian said, displaying his prejudice for Roman Catholic Croats as opposed to Orthodox Serbs. "It seems to us that what your president—whom we greatly revere—has in mind is to place these two fighting wild cats in a bag and expect them to act as kittens."[36] Whatever Wilson may have felt about the future of Yugoslavia, he was adamant that Fiume should be given to the new Balkan kingdom.

Douglas Johnson, one of Wilson's experts on boundaries, described the American position thus, "A few Italians were scattered here and there along the eastern Adriatic coast, but they formed remote Latin islets in the midst of a great Slavic sea, the most noticeable of which were Fiume and Zara" (further south down the coast from Fiume). If Fiume were to be linked to Italy by land, "about half a million" Yugoslavs would have to be annexed to reach about 24,000 Italians in Fiume. Italy was already about to get thousands of non-Italians in accordance with the Treaty of London, but that same treaty had excluded Fiume, which had been "specifically reserved for Croatia."[37] "That might all be very well," said de Martino. "We recognize that self-determination is applicable to many regions, but not the shores of the Adriatic, and we can never consent to placing the strategic positions indispensable to our safety in the hands of strangers who have been our enemies and who are even now acting in a hostile manner."[38]

The Fiume question came to the fore at the peace conference in the crucial month of April 1919. The Italians made their impassioned demands for the alpine Brenner Pass, Fiume, the Dalmatian coast, and the Adriatic Islands. The British and French were opposed to giving Italy anything more than what had been promised them. Clemenceau said, "I will live up to our treaty pledge ... but I will give no extras."[39] Both Clemenceau and Lloyd George feared that Italy might go Communist, or become pro-German as they were to do a generation later. Lloyd George tried to reason with Orlando, saying, "all of Europe needs America. Without America Europe cannot continue to live ... Wilson, as always obstinate, is greatly irritated now ... Can't we smooth things over?"[40] But Orlando could not be placated. He insisted he must have Fiume, so Clemenceau and Lloyd George stepped back and let Wilson take the heat. And heat there was. At one point, Orlando shouted, "Mr. Wilson, there are at least 30,000 Italians in the city. We cannot abandon them to the by no means tender mercies of the Yugoslavs, treaty or no treaty."[41] Wilson, aware that Orlando was inflating the number of Italians living in Fiume, countered by saying, "Mr. Orlando, there are at least a million Italians in New York, but I trust you will not on this score claim our Empire City as Italian territory."[42] Wilson had his back up now. He didn't like the whole idea of promises made by secret treaty, and he thought the Italians were too greedy. He readily saw the sense of giving the Yugoslavs a major port, and with Trieste, just to the north, going to Italy, Wilson saw no reason to go an inch further. With the Germans coming in May to sign a peace treaty, the allies were under pressure to get these other matters settled quickly. Bonsal thought Fiume might be the "rift in the foundation all which may bring down the whole peace edifice."[43] But the very first of Wilson's Fourteen Points had called for "open covenant ... openly arrived at." So Wilson felt justified in saying no to the Italians. After all, he was giving Italy defeated Austria's principal sea port, Trieste, as well as Austria's South Tyrol. Enough was enough.

There was another reason to say no. Before the war ended, the Italians and the Slavs of Serbia and those Slavs still in the crumbling Austro-Hungarian Empire had met to draw up the Pact of Rome. Accordingly, the Italians and the Slavs had agreed to "solve amicably their various territorial controversies on the basis of nationalities and the rights of people to determine their own fate in such a way as not to injure the vital interests" of either.[44] The Pact of Rome had been used as propaganda to pry Croats and Slovene soldiers away from loyalty to Austro-Hungary. This contributed to the collapse and defeat of the Austro-Hungarian army in the autumn of 1918. But now that peace had come, Italy seemed to be reneging on the deal.

Popular opinion in Italy was on the boil. Had not Fiume once belonged to the Roman Empire, and had not Venice once controlled the Adriatic? No power other than Italy should be allowed to close the Adriatic in the event of another war, the Italians argued. That Fiume in modern times had always been part of Croatia, and therefore, part of Austria-Hungary, was beside the point. Croatia had fought against the allies. The heart of Fiume was Italian. Therefore, it was argued, Fiume should be handed over to Italy, a country that had lost more than half a million men fighting on the allied side. Justice demanded no less.

Orlando was right that Wilson, Lloyd George and Clemenceau did not consider Italy as an equal partner in the Big Four. Wilson thought Italy greedy. Lloyd George thought the Italians unstable, and Clemenceau failed to conceal his contempt for the Italian position. Orlando was at another disadvantage as well. He alone of the Big Four knew no English. So Orlando was not able to speak to either Wilson or Lloyd George without a translator, nor could he understand their conversations with Clemenceau.

Growing tired of Orlando's protestations and theatrics, Wilson decided to take his case directly to the Italian people over the heads of Orlando and his government. In a manifesto to the people of Italy, to be widely printed in the world's press, Wilson argued his case. Wilson, as always, counted on his reasoning and his moral force to carry the day. He thought the adoration the Italian people had shown him during his visit to Rome just a few months earlier would suffice. It was a major miscalculation. Wilson badly underestimated the depth of Italian nationalism. Fiume was not a question of reason.

Fiume was pure emotion—not a commodity in which Wilson dealt.

Orlando stormed out of the conference and returned with his delegation to Rome. Although he would return to Paris briefly, it was too late. Orlando's inability to secure Fiume for Italy spelled the end of his career. He resigned as prime minister in June 1919. Whereas Wilson was once adored, now he was vilified. Cartoons showing him in a German uniform appeared in the Italian press. Streets and squares that had but recently been renamed for Wilson were renamed again. As for Wilson, he "will agree to no arrangement which gives any people away totally without their consent," said his press secretary.[45] Yet Wilson had just given Austria's southern Tyrolean population away without seeking the consent of its German-speaking people. He was about to give away another population in China without their consent. But when it came to Fiume, Wilson looked upon Italy's claim as a form of colonialism.

During this time, Italy did not help its case by ordering its troops to the Turkish port of Smyrna, now Izmir, to forestall a Greek invasion. Lloyd George, who favored a Greek invasion, was determined not to let "people as turbulent as the Italians into Asia Minor," and Wilson backed him up.[46]

After Orlando and the Italian delegation departed, Wilson faced a dilemma. Could he afford to lose another important power if he was going to have a meaningful League of Nations, his number one priority? This was on the president's mind when the conference turned its attention to the Shantung (Shandong) Question: What to do with the German concessions on the China Coast and the German colonies in general? In this, Wilson was not quite the disinterested peacemaker he imagined himself to be. As Orlando put it many years later, "At the conference it was emphasized that while America had over the other great nations the advantage of not having its own interest to defend, the only exception was precisely that of Shantung, since the equilibrium of the Pacific was an American interest."⁴⁷

Shantung Province, jutting out from China into the Yellow Sea toward Korea, was considered by the Chinese to be the cradle of their civilization, the birthplace of both Confucius and Mencius, two of their most revered sages from before the birth of Christ. It turned out to be Wilson's biggest headache and most consequential compromise. On the southern side of the peninsula is Kiaochow (Jiaozhou) Bay, the best harbor on the north China coast. In 1897, when the colonial grab for China was at its apex, two German missionaries, Richard Henle and Franz Nies, were killed. This was just the excuse the Kaiser was looking for, as he did not want to be left out of the colonial game in China. German warships sailed into Kiaochow Bay, under the command of Admiral Otto von Diederichs.ᵛ Putting troops ashore, the Germans seized 213 square miles of surrounding territory.ᵛⁱ An article in the *North China Daily* summed up China's weakness at the time, "A foreign power with three ships and 600 men finds no difficulty effecting a descent of a country with 300 million peopleᵛⁱⁱ and establishing herself without opposition within 300 miles of the capital."⁴⁸

The following year Germany demanded that the weak Ch'ing (Ching) Dynasty grant Germany a ninety-nine-year lease, similar to the one negotiated by the British to extend Hong Kong's territory

---

v Admiral von Diederichs entered into a confrontation with Admiral George Dewey and the American fleet in Manila Bay the following year. Germany stood ready to pick up the Philippines from the dying Spanish Empire should American resolve falter, or so the Americans believed.

vi China had been about to lease Kiaochow Bay to Russia when Germany seized it. Kaiser Wilhelm II, on a visit to Russia, casually asked his cousin, Czar Nicholas II, while riding in a carriage, if he would mind if Germany had Kiaochow Bay. The Czar, having no idea where Kiaochow Bay was, consented. When Russia's admirals protested, the Czar said the Kaiser had tricked him.

vii The population of China was closer to four hundred million in 1897.

into its "New Territories" that same year. The Germans lost no time in building a modern European town called Tsingtao (Quindao)[viii] by the bay, as well as a railroad into the interior. In due course most of the Shantung Peninsula was recognized as a German sphere of influence.[ix]

Japan, having seen the need for modernization and industrialization before other Asian countries in the nineteenth century, and never having been colonized itself, had transformed itself from a semi-feudal state into a constitutional monarchy with a Westernized economy and industry. The Japanese developed a modern army based on the German model, and built a navy along British lines. A sharp, short war with the decaying Chinese Empire in 1894–1895 established Japan's military superiority and whetted its colonial appetite. As a result of that war Japan annexed Taiwan and joined with the Europeans in carving up China into concessions, treaty ports, and spheres of influence that had been going on for the past six decades. In 1900 Japan joined an eight-nation coalition to put down the Boxer Rebellion, a primitive, anti-foreign, anti-Christian outburst of violence, encouraged by the Dowager Empress, Tz'u Hsi (Cixi), that convulsed northern China. Christian missionaries were slaughtered, as were thousands of Chinese Christians. The Legation Quarter in Peking (Beijing) was put under siege. Ironically, the coalition that fought the Boxers, so named because they called

---

viii   One of the first things the Germans did was build a brewery, the first in China, which still exists. Tsingtao beer is exported all over the world.

ix   The year 1898 was one of great colonial expansion in the Pacific. The Germans got Tsingtao, the British got the New Territories and Wei-hai-wei (Wehai), a tiny enclave on the Shantung Peninsula, the United States annexed the Hawaiian islands and took the Philippines as well as Guam from Spain, and the Japanese expanded their influence in Manchuria. The following year Germany would buy the Caroline and the Mariana Islands from Spain.

themselves the "Righteous and Harmonious Fists," included countries that later fought against each other in World War I: Germany, Austro-Hungary, Great Britain, France, Italy, Russia, the United States, and Japan.

In 1905 Japan performed an even more impressive feat of arms by beating Russia in a Far East war, destroying a Russian fleet that had sailed from the Baltic halfway around the world to meet its end in the Tsushima Strait near Korea. The victory marked "the first time since the Middle Ages that a non-European country had vanquished a European power in a major war."[49] The German Kaiser called it the most important naval battle since Trafalgar, while Lord George Curzon, the viceroy of India, worried that such a humiliation of a European power might reverberate "like a thunderclap through the whispering galleries of the East."[50] Curzon was right. Colonized people everywhere took heart. Mohandas Gandhi, then an obscure Indian lawyer in South Africa, saw the roots of the Japanese victory spreading so far that "we cannot now visualize all the fruits it will put forth."[51] Jawaharlal Nehru, who would later become independent India's first prime minister, heard the news while on a train going up to his English boarding school, Harrow. Only a boy in his teens, he had been dreaming of his own role in achieving "India's freedom, and Asiatic freedom from the thralldom of Europe."[52] Sun Yat-sen, thought of as the father of modern China, was passing through the Suez Canal at the time and found himself being cheered by Egyptian workers who thought he was Japanese.

Ever since 1896, Japan had been trying to integrate Korea's economy with its own, and in 1905 Japan declared Korea a Japanese protectorate. By annexing Korea in 1910, Japan acquired a land border with Manchuria, a Chinese territory over which Japan had declared a special interest. Japanese imperialism was on the march. At the same time, Japan became a model for modernization, especially in China. Hundreds of students joined others from the colonized world, traveling to Japan for inspiration and guidance. Sun Yat-sen would later say, "Men thought and believed that

European civilization was a progressive one in science, industry, manufacturing and armaments and that Asia could never resist Europe; that European oppression could never be shaken off," but "... the effect of the victory [over Russia] instantly spread over the whole of Asia." The lesson of Tsushima Strait was "certainly not a blessing for white people ... "[53] The carnage and self-destruction of Europe during the Great War would further discredit the concept of European superiority in the eyes of Asians and Africans.

When that war broke out in 1914, Japan, having formed a naval alliance with Britain in 1902, saw an opportunity and joined the allies to wage war on Germany. The opportunity was to gain control of the German concessions in Shantung and some of Germany's Pacific islands. With Britain's approval and token help, the Japanese landed troops on the Shantung Peninsula where the German garrison was weak with no chance of reinforcement from Europe. In a foretaste of what was to come in the next war, Japan launched the world's first naval air attack on Tsingtao with planes from a seaplane carrier. China had asked to be part of the Shantung takeover, fearing Japanese intentions, but Japan would not allow it. Shantung was about to pass from one colonial master to another. In addition, Japan took control of Germany's island colonies north of the equator. By arrangement, Australia and New Zealand took over Germany's island possessions south of the equator. The thinly stretched British were grateful to their Japanese allies for help combating German warships in the Pacific. Germany's Grand Admiral Alfred von Tirpitz would later write that the "entry of Japan into the war wrecked the plan of war by our cruiser squadron against enemy trade and British war vessels in those seas."[54] Winston Churchill agreed: "The entry of Japan into the war enabled us to use our China squadron to better advantage in other theaters."[55]

Later in the war when trench warfare began to eat up so many troops, Britain and France asked Japan to send soldiers to the Western Front. Japan said no, but did send destroyers as far away as the Mediterranean to help combat German submarines. At Britain's request, Japanese sailors in the harbor of Singapore helped put down a mutiny by Muslim Indian Army troops who thought they were being shipped off to fight their co-religionists, the Turks. In gratitude for all of this, the allies made yet another secret agreement that when the war ended, Japan could keep what it had taken from the Germans in the Far East. At the same time, the Chinese government entered into a secret commitment to the Japanese that they could keep what they had taken from Germany on the Shantung Peninsula, an arrangement that China would later say was made under duress. The British reply of February 16, 1917, to Japan's request for diplomatic support for Japan after the war shows the strength of Britain's imperial interests in Lloyd George's thinking, "His Britannic Majesty's government accedes with pleasure to the request of the Japanese government for assurance" that Britain will support Japan's claim to Germany's Shantung concessions and islands north of the equator, "it being understood that the Japanese government will, in the eventual peace settlement, treat in the same spirit Great Britain's claim to Germany's islands south of the equator."[56] It was *quid pro quo* time.

Lloyd George was aware that the rising power and influence of Britain's dominions who helped fight the central powers should be rewarded. Australia's Prime Minister, William "Billy" Hughes, had taken great exception to the fact that neither Australia nor New Zealand had been notified, let alone consulted, when Japan took over Germany's islands north of the equator with Britain's encouragement. In 1917 Britain's foreign secretary, Arthur Balfour, said that his predecessor, Lord Charles Grey, "held the view that if you are going to keep Japan out of North America, out of Canada, out of Australia, out of New Zealand, you could not forbid her to expand in China. A nation of that sort must have a safety valve somewhere …" Balfour went on to praise Japan for helping the allies to the best of her ability "with an eye to her own interest."[57]

Japan made no such request for diplomatic support from the United States, but an agreement signed in November 1917 between

Secretary of State Robert Lansing and Japan's special envoy, Viscount Ishii Kikujiro, committed both countries to maintaining the Open Door policy in China. In a secret protocol, they agreed not to take advantage of World War I to advance their positions in China at the expense of any of the other Entente Powers. Lansing did, however, commit the United States to acknowledging that Japan had a special interest in Chinese territory adjacent to Japanese territory. There was an obvious contradiction, as recognizing a special interest contravened the Open Door policy by which every country was to have equal access to exploiting China. Japan was encouraged that its goal of dominating Manchuria was thus furthered. Wilson and Lansing stopped short of officially recognizing that Japan had a paramount interest in China, or that Japan should have anything similar to what the United States had claimed in the Monroe Doctrine. However, the wording of the exchange of notes was sufficiently fuzzy to allow Japan to believe that, as far as China was concerned, it had a far greener light than the Americans had intended. The U.S. ambassador to China, Paul S. Reinsch, saw the danger. He reported to Washington that the arrangement with Japan was "quite generally interpreted as indicating a withdrawal of the American government ... from any desire to exercise any influence over China," and was favoring Japan.[58]

When the war was over and the peace conference addressed the Shantung Question, the only thing that stood in the way of Japan's ambitions might be President Wilson. Although Britain might worry about Japan's ambitions, it was the United States, despite the Lansing-Ishii exchanges, that saw itself as China's protector. Cynics might say that because America had come late to the colonial exploitation of China, the Open Door policy meant that the United States could exploit equally with everybody else. But Wilson would not have seen it that way. With missionary connections in China of his own, Wilson had been impressed that Sun Yat-sen, the first provisional president of the Chinese Republic, had converted to Christianity—a big plus in Wilson's book. Wilson was elected president the same year China shed its thousands-of-years-old monarchy to become a republic in 1912. Wilson recognized that the "awakening of the people of China to the consequences of their responsibilities under free government is the most important, if not the most momentous event of our generation."[59] He was not the last American to believe that China was destined to become more like America.

Wilson believed the Japanese had overplayed their hand in 1915 when they presented China with a list of twenty-one demands that would have extended Japan's economic influence over China and cemented its control of Manchuria. Both Wilson and Great Britain opposed Japan's ultimatum to the Chinese, and although Britain was deeply involved with fighting the war in Europe, they succeeded in getting Japan to lessen its demands. The United States and Japan were now in competition over who would become China's primary mentor and guide in a postwar world. Wilson believed he had been betrayed by Japan in 1917 when, as a reaction to the Bolshevik takeover of Russia, both had sent troops to Siberia. Wilson thought they had both agreed to send about 7,000 men. America ended up sending 9,000, but Japan sent 72,000 and deployed them farther west into Russia than Wilson thought necessary or desirable.

Wilson, along with most of his delegation, instinctively favored long-abused China over Imperial Japan. China had been picked and pulled apart by European powers for most of the nineteenth century by means of unequal treaties and concessions in which foreigners were in charge of great chunks of the country. And although China was slow to join the allies in the war against the Central Powers, China did enter the war in 1917 following America. China had neither the will nor the wherewithal to send troops to Europe, but even before China joined the war, it allowed the recruitment of 140,000 laborers, called "coolies" in those days, to work digging trenches, unloading ships and other non-combatant work to ease the acute manpower shortages the allies were facing. The British organized them into a Chinese Labour Corps, while the French formed a *Corps de Travailleurs Chinois*. Many were killed or died of disease. Several hundred were lost on a French ship torpedoed in the Mediterranean. Every Chinese working behind the lines freed up a Briton or a Frenchman to fight in the front lines. Chinese studying in Europe often acted as translators for their countrymen. Nonetheless the allies believed that China contributed much less to the war than had Japan.

At the peace conference Japan was granted Great Power status, although not at the same level as the Big Four. With three out of the Big Four committed by secret treaty to Japan's position concerning Shantung, it is no wonder that the Chinese delegation felt outgunned. Wilson seemed to be the only holdout in favor of China. Chinese nationalism was running high. Given Wilson's position on self-determination, and provinces not being traded away like chattels, the Chinese expected that Germany's concessions would promptly be given back to China. The original German lease had no provision for transfer to another country, so it seemed like an open and shut case. But the Chinese delegation did not know about the secret agreements promising the Japanese that they could stay in Shantung after the war as partial repayment for Japanese loans. China was at another disadvantage, because when compared to Japan, China did not appear to be master of its own fate and did not command the same respect. For many in the West, and in Japan too, China was a vast, phlegmatic, and backward country that had lost out on the nineteenth century's progress. The Chinese were looked down upon with some contempt. Consider the entry in the 1911 edition of the *Encyclopedia Britannica*:

> If the Chinese character is inferior to the European, this inferiority lies in the fact that the Chinaman's whole philosophy of life disinclines him to change or to energetic action. He is industrious, but his industry is normally along the lines marked out by authority and tradition.[60]

Although the Chinese had been making efforts to reform, clearly the word "modern" was not a word used in the West to describe China in 1919. Its government had "lost control of its own finances and tariffs and was dotted with foreign enclaves, ports, railways, factories, mines, and foreign troops to guard them," as historian Margaret MacMillan notes, "The great powers threw a cloak of extraterritoriality around their subjects on the grounds that the Chinese courts were too primitive ..."[61] China's first provincial president, Sun Yat-sen, complained to his bodyguard that "any foreigner could shoot a member of my own cabinet, and my government would have no jurisdiction over him. That is what we've got to change before we can hold up our heads."[62]

Besides the foreign-controlled treaty ports, China's largely foreign-built railroad system was yet another tool for foreign expansion, because foreigners wanted to control the railroad rights of way, injecting their control into the bloodstream of China. As Wilson's first secretary of state, William Jennings Bryan, had put it, China's foreign-owned railway systems will "deprive China of her own country."[63] Foreign gunboats, especially on the Yangtze River, brought European, American, and Japanese firepower into the very heart of China from the mid-nineteenth century on. And China was in the unique position of having not just one colonial master but, as Sun Yat-sen said at the time, "We are being crushed by the economic strength of the power to a greater degree than if we were a full colony. China is not a colony of one country, but of all. I think we should be called a hypo-colony."[64] At least a country with only one colonial master could count on help in a crisis, because the colonial power "is bound by morality and by treaty to assist," Sun said. "China, on the other hand, has many foreign masters but none of them are under any obligation to us."[65]

Perhaps even more harmful to China's reputation was the fact that the country was split between two competing factions, Sun's based in Canton (Guangzhuo) and another government in Peking, with war lords scattered about who did not really answer to either. The Chinese delegation at the Paris Peace Conference was made up of some who answered to Peking, while others answered to Sun in Canton—a compromise delegation that merely signaled a unity that did not exist. Ever since the Ch'ing Dynasty had been overthrown eight years before, China had been in chaos.

Such was the situation when it came time for China to make its case in Paris. One of the stars of the Chinese delegation was Koo Vikyuin (Gu Weijun), a graduate of Columbia University and a star of the debating team. Known in the West as V.K. Wellington Koo, he was Ambassador to the United States when he was in his twenties. He had a friendly relationship with Wilson and thought Wilson would support his cause. Koo gave a memorable and impassioned speech to the Conference, emphasizing that Shantung was the cradle of China's civilization, and then of vital importance, "a holy land to the Chinese." Germany's original lease had been "wrung out of China by force," Koo said, and if it were to be transferred to another power it would be "adding one wrong to another." He also pointed out that control of the German concessions meant control of Shantung Province, which would provide "a strategic gateway to all of north China."[66]

Koo's case was undermined by the fact that, although Germany might have taken Tsingtao by force, China subsequently and willingly reaffirmed that Japan could keep the German concession, a fact that Koo was unaware of when he made his presentation. In an exchange with Japan's Baron Makino, Koo argued for the direct restitution of Tsingtao to China citing *rebus sic stantibus*, a concept in international law under which treaties should be voided if the conditions when written had changed. Koo said that China's declaration of war against Germany in 1917 "had in itself put an end to the leases obtained by Germany in Chinese territory."[67] Although China was grateful to Japan for ridding China of the Germans, Koo said his delegation would be "false to their duty to China and the world if they did not object to paying their debts of gratitude by selling the birthright of their countrymen, and thereby sowing the seeds of discord in the future." It was a question of whether "we can guarantee a peace of half a century to the Far East, or if a situation will be created which will lead to war within ten years."[68]

Koo's speech was described as brilliant, especially when compared with the more clumsy presentation of the Japanese. Wilson himself was impressed, and said he was in a minority in regard to "captured colonies" because the other powers just wanted to "divide the swag ..."[69] The British and the French wanted to stand by their promises to Japan, while Wilson's delegation, with the possible exception of Colonel House, favored China's claim. The president's Fourteen Points and the principle of self-determination argued in favor of China.

There followed a discussion on whether Japan could have a Monroe Doctrine for China similar to America's claim regarding the Western Hemisphere. Britain's Lord Curzon put the case for Japan, and against China, well when he said, "Within sight of its shores you have this great helpless, hopeless, inert China, one of the most densely populated countries in the world, utterly deficient in cohesion or strength, engaged in perpetual conflict ... destitute of military capacity ..."[70] In Curzon's view, China was the natural prey for a country as well organized as Japan. Ambassador Reinsch in Peking, however, thought that any special relationship awarded to Japan over China would result in "forces set in action that will make a huge armed conflict absolutely inevitable within one generation."[71]

By 1919 America and Japan were highly suspicious of each other's expansion in the Pacific Ocean. America had the Philippines and Hawaii; Japan had Shantung and the string of former German Pacific islands that lay athwart America's lines of communication to the Philippines, bringing Japanese closer to Hawaii than Hawaii was to the West Coast of America. Wilson tried at the peace conference to reduce the effect of Japanese control over the former German islands by saying they should be mandated to Japan by the international community, and not just given to Japan as part of their empire. The colonial powers had little interest in Wilson's suggestion and thought enemy territory should just be given to the victors. Australia's objections led to a heated exchange between Prime Minister Hughes and Wilson, after which Wilson described Hughes as a "pestiferous varmint."[72] For Wilson a mandated territory was less permanent than an outright annexation, especially if granted by a concert of countries, his League of Nations, rather than just taken as spoils of war. Sadly, as with so many of Wilson's noble sentiments, the difference was more significant in theory than in practice.

Hughes was to play another role in the drama taking place in Paris. The Japanese wanted a racial equality clause written into the covenant of the proposed League of Nations. Ever since Japan started industrializing, and seeking her place among the great powers—all of them white—Japan had bridled under the racial superiority so evident in the affairs of nations. Japan wanted the covenant to make no distinction in law or in practice, on the basis of race or nationality. There were plenty of objections, however. The foundations of imperialism were predicated on the assumption that the white man knew best. The Japanese assured the powers that a yes vote would not require them to take steps to implement racial equality anytime soon. It was just a matter of principle. Australia's Hughes was adamant that support for the measure would undermine his White Australia policy, designed to keep immigrants of color out of Australia. No matter how worded, any draft of a racial equality clause would "throw Hughes into a berserker rage of uncontrolled fury."[73] Having been born in Virginia and brought up in Georgia during the American Civil War, Wilson was not a big fan of racial equality either. He had allowed large swaths of the civil service to be re-segregated on the basis of race during his presidency in order to get southern support for his wide-reaching domestic programs. There were Californians too, who favored laws against Japanese and Chinese immigration into the United States. Wilson knew that if he were going to get his League of Nations ratified by the U.S. Senate, he would need these votes.

The British were hesitant, committed as they were to the white man's burden in colonial affairs.[74] When the vote was taken, eleven of the seventeen delegates present voted for it, a clear majority including two of the Big Four, Italy and France. The nays were not recorded, but it was clear that those who voted against racial equality or abstained were the United States, the British Empire, Romania, Portugal, and Belgium—all colonial powers with the exception of Romania. Wilson ruled that although the yeas represented a clear majority, on such an important matter to which there had been strong objection, the vote needed to be unanimous for the measure to be passed. Thus by such legerdemain did Wilson avoid having a racial equality clause written into the covenant of the League of Nations. This was not his finest hour, and he was happy to hide behind Billy Hughes. Racial equality would have to wait until the United Nations rose to take the place of the League of Nations after World War II.[x]

The failure to pass the racial equality clause infuriated the Japanese public, but the Japanese delegation in Paris took it in stride, saying they would be willing to forgo racial equality if they could have their territorial ambitions met. Physical possession Shantung was less important than economic dominance of the province, including the railroads. Sovereignty might be negotiable. Economic interests were not. Japan made it clear that unless they got their way, they would not sign a peace treaty with Germany, and would not join

---

x   A good example of the anti-Japanese feeling in the United States at the time can be found in *Seapower*, the official magazine of the Navy League, September 1919. In an article entitled "Showing Our Teeth to Japan," E.B. Johns wrote that Japan's request for a racial equality clause in the League of Nations Covenant amounted to a "declaration of war upon the white race and particularly upon the United States where the convention of racial equality is being resisted ... Certain it is that the people of this country will plunge into another conflict rather than submit to the present demand of Japan for racial equality ... The American fleet will be a sentry on the furthermost outpost of Caucasian civilization. It is more than the white man's burden—it is his salvation."

a League of Nations, as the latter was to be incorporated into the Treaty of Versailles. The League, of course, was Wilson's first priority. He said to Colonel House, "If we fail to get a perfect peace ... at least we must not let the world slip back into anarchy," which Wilson was sure it would if the League of Nations did not come into being.[75] With Italy having walked out, and Japan threatening to do so, Wilson worried that his League might be a failure before it began. Wilson and House believed that unresolved problems, injustices, and other loose ends could be put right once the League came into being.

Wilson's colleagues began to notice how tired the American president looked and how much stress the proceedings were causing him. Remote, austere, and wracked with insomnia, Wilson seemed unable to delegate his responsibilities except occasionally to House. Wilson's face had begun to twitch, at times uncontrollably, "like a man due for a complete breakdown unless he is relieved of his burden," Bonsal noticed.[76] He began forgetting things and was uncharacteristically inarticulate at times. He seemed irritable even to the point of incipient paranoia. Wilson had had a history of small strokes going back to 1896 when he temporarily lost the use of his right hand. In 1906 he became temporarily blind in his left eye and lost feeling in his right arm. As president he often had to take to his bed with various nervous disorders after stressful moments back in Washington. In Paris he was finding the obsessions of his interlocutors, when they opposed his own, overwhelmingly stressful. In the critical month of April, when so many big decisions had to be made, Wilson came down with a virus, and most probably another small stroke.

To this day we cannot be sure how much these health issues affected his decision making, but it would be naive to assume they were negligible. Wilson's personality seemed to change under the pressures he was under; his forgetfulness seemed to accelerate as did his stubbornness. At one point he threatened to leave the conference and go home if he could not get what he wanted, an Orlando-style walk out. Happily, he was talked out of it.

American presidents were not under the same medical scrutiny as they are today. But we know Wilson was a very sick man at the Peace Conference. He got no exercise, but he soldiered on with a single-mindedness, believing as he did that the fate of the world was in his hands. When his doctor, Admiral Cary Grayson, urged him to slow down, Wilson said, "Give me time. We are running a race against Bolshevism and the world is on fire."[77] He was not wrong. Communist insurrections had broken out in several European countries, and the doctrine that Lenin was fomenting was spreading west out of Russia. There would be time to rest when the peace was secured, he said.

As the conference wore on, the allies began to find each other annoying. The Europeans viewed Wilson as prickly and sanctimonious. Clemenceau, who felt that Wilson spoke "like a college professor criticizing a thesis,"[78] said, "I never met a man who could talk so much like Jesus Christ and act so much like Lloyd George."[79] As for Lloyd George, he found Wilson "even-tempered and agreeable," but he also thought the American president stiff and unbending. Lloyd George characterized Wilson as "an extraordinary mixture of real greatness thwarted by much littleness."[80] As for Wilson, he thought Lloyd George "had no guiding principles."[81] Wilson sensed that few of his interlocutors liked him. "Indeed," he told House, "I am not sure that anybody does."[82] Wilson's headaches were becoming unbearable when Shantung was being discussed, and no wonder. No matter how he came to the problem, he met the solid wall of secret promises that the British and French had made to Japan during the war. Wilson tried and failed to get Japan's approval to turn the Shantung concessions over to the Big Four and Japan in a joint League of Nations trusteeship. The Chinese were prepared, if necessary, to accept that compromise as a temporary measure as long as it meant that all the German concessions would eventually be returned to China.

In terms of history and demography, China's case seemed to exactly fit Wilson's framework of a just cause. Japan, however, made it clear that it would not join the League of Nations unless it could keep Shantung. To be sure, the Japanese had hinted at a willingness to give *de jure* sovereignty back to China one day as long as they could keep all the economic privileges, including control of Shantung's railroads. Wilson's delegation felt that the president should stand by China even if Japan did walk out and refuse to join the League. Ray Stannard Baker put it more forcefully, saying that Japan's giving back sovereignty to China while maintaining its economic stranglehold would be like "offering China the shell and securing for Japan the oyster."[83] Some in the American delegation submitted their resignations rather than be part of what they thought would be a shameful betrayal.

Colonel House felt differently. "My feeling is that while it is all bad, it is not worse than the thing we're doing in many of the settlements in which the Western Powers are interested," he told the president, and that it would be best to just get along with it and "let the League of Nations and the new era do the rest."[84] But as Bonsal explained, throughout Wilson's agonized deliberations, "the argument that prevailed although never spoken is that with Italy withdrawn ... with Russia absent, and the Central Powers at least temporarily excluded, should the Rising Sun Empire [Japan] withdraw, our world congress, or whatever it is, would dwindle to the proportions of a rump parliament."[85] Never mentioned was the fact that, although the allies had an army in the field ready to break the armistice and march on Berlin if the Germans did not come to heel, there was no similar force in the Far East that could have ousted Japan from Shantung. If Wilson had broken up the conference by going against the British and the French on the Shantung question, it would not have lessened Japan's hold on Shantung, neither politically nor economically. No one was willing to go to war over Shantung.

In the end Wilson came down on the side of Japan. Japan would be allowed to keep the German concessions in China. When the final decision was made on the last day of April 1919 and the final wording of the Treaty of Versailles was written, there was no language about Japan ever returning anything to China in the future. The articles said only that Germany would agree to turn over to Japan all that Germany had acquired by treaty from China in 1898. Secretary of State Lansing wrote in his diary, "China has been abandoned to Japanese rapacity. I am heartsick over it because I can offer no adequate explanation to the critics. There seems to be none." In another entry he wrote, "I could say nothing in support of so iniquitous an abandonment of China."[86]

William Bullitt, who would later become America's first ambassador to the Soviet Union, was as disappointed as Lansing. Bullitt later wrote that Wilson's reaction to the demands of the allies became stereotyped, "surrender, regret, self-justification."[87] Wilson's self-justification was that the only hope of keeping the world together was to get the League of Nations with Japan in it, and then try to secure justice for the Chinese, Bullitt wrote. Wilson "... knew his decision would be unpopular in America, that the Chinese would be bitterly disappointed, that the Japanese would feel triumphant, that he would be accused of violating his own principles, but nevertheless he must work for world order and organization against the anarchy and a return to the old militarism."[88] How giving Japan such an important piece of China was going to serve the cause of anti-militarism was anybody's guess.

According to Baker, "Wilson was striving to forget that he had made a peace which could not be reconciled with his Fourteen Points, and he could not bear to have anyone tell him he had broken his word. He knew well enough what he had done, knew that the settlement had been agreed to which did not conform to his standards ..."[89] Bullitt promptly resigned, saying in a prescient letter to the president, "Our government has consented now to deliver the suffering peoples of the world to new oppressions, subjections, and dismemberments—a new century of war."[90] But perhaps the strongest condemnation of what had been done in Paris came from the tortured Wilson himself, for "... no issue at the peace conference disturbed the president to a greater extent ... or pleased him less," according to a historian of those times.[91]

A worn-out and discouraged Wilson turned to his doctor when the Shantung Question had at long last been answered, and said it was "the best that could be accomplished out of a dirty past."[92]

Attempts were made to persuade the Chinese delegation to sign the Treaty of Versailles, but China refused to sign because of the Shantung decision. Indeed, so unpopular was the decision among Chinese that Chinese students in Paris were prepared to physically prevent the delegation from signing. Wellington Koo told Colonel House that if he signed the treaty, even under orders to do so from Peking, "I shall not have what you in New York call a 'Chinaman's chance.'"[93] There was some fear among the American delegation that Wilson might be assassinated before he could board the ship that would take him home. China would eventually sign its own peace treaty with Germany in 1921.[xi]

Only three years later, at the Washington Naval Conference of 1921–1922, after Wilson had left office, the Japanese returned the shell of Shantung's sovereignty to China, but they kept the oysters and the pearls of their economic interests for themselves. The larger armed conflict that Ambassador Reinsch had predicted began when Japan went to war against China in 1937, and then to war against the United States with the bombing of Pearl Harbor in 1941.

The League of Nations did come into being and established its headquarters in Geneva, Switzerland. But when Wilson tried to bring his own country into the League, he failed. Sacrificing China's fundamental interest on the altar of Japanese expansionism did not sit well with the Republican-controlled Senate. It promptly passed a Shantung amendment to the Versailles Treaty, which would have reversed Wilson's Shantung decision favoring Japan, but the amendment was rendered moot when the Senate refused to ratify the

---

xi Wellington Koo would live to sign the United Nations Charter on behalf of China in June 1945.

treaty or commit the United States to membership in the League of Nations. Wilson's nemesis, Senator Henry Cabot Lodge, chairman of the Foreign Affairs Committee, called Wilson's Shantung decision the "robbing of China," the betrayal "of a friendly people who were our allies in the war."[94] The greater Senate objection to joining the League was the fear that the United States would be committed to join in a collective action against an aggressor, and that would infringe on American sovereignty—a fear that has dogged American foreign policy ever since. As Lodge, certainly no isolationist, put it, "We would not have our country's vigor exhausted, or her moral force abated, by everlasting meddling and muddling in every quarrel, great and small, which afflicts the world."[95]

There was a moment when compromise might have been possible. Lodge wanted to make some formal reservations if the Senate were to ratify the treaty. The British and French let it be known that they would not object. But Wilson had the bit in his stubborn teeth and refused all compromise. As he had with the Italians, Wilson decided to take his case directly to the American people. As always, he trusted his oratory and his reasoning to persuade. He left Washington and traveled by train across the country, 10,000 miles and twenty-nine cities in three-and-a-half weeks, amid pounding headaches, to sell his League of Nations to the American people. But by now he was in steep physical decline, and his old gifts of oratory were no longer what they had been. His inclination toward arrogance got the better of him, and he began insulting the very people he needed to ratify his treaty. The rigors of his train journey, and the strain of giving so many speeches across the country, caught up with him in Pueblo, Colorado, where he fell ill. The train was ordered to speed immediately back to Washington.

In early October he suffered a serious stroke that paralyzed his left side and impaired his vision. Then there began one of the most audacious cover-ups in American history. As Wilson lay incapable of fulfilling the duties of his office, his wife Edith and his most intimate advisors withheld the extent of his illness to Congress and to the American people for several weeks. Edith Wilson was *de facto* running the country. When he partially recovered, his reasoning slipped its mooring when he insisted that, despite his condition, he could run for a third term, something that no president had ever done before.[xii]

Having refused to ratify the peace with Germany, or join the League of Nations, the United States signed its own separate peace with Germany in 1921.

Wilson's great dream of the United States leading a world organization to keep the peace was shattered, and America sank back into isolationism. The Republicans swept back into office in 1920 with the election of Warren G. Harding. Wilson died in 1924, as did his old rival Lenin. It was a rivalry that would continue between the two ideologies until the end of the Soviet Union in 1991 and would continue between the two countries to this day.

The League did its best to settle international disputes, but the big powers were unwilling to step in together to halt the dreams of conquest of Germany, Japan, or even Italy. Mussolini's dictum that "the League [of Nations] was very well when sparrows shout, but no good at all when eagles fall out," was proven right. Wilson saw with absolute clarity that should the world fail to take collective actions against an aggressor, another world war, more terrible than the first, was inevitable.

A great admirer of Wilson, the then under secretary of the navy, Franklin D. Roosevelt, sailed home from Europe with the president in 1919. After World War II, in making his case for a United Nations to replace the failed League of Nations, President Roosevelt avoided many of Wilson's and the League's shortcomings. The United Nations may not be perfect, but it is still with us. As for

---

xii   Franklin Roosevelt is the only American president to ever have run and won a third term as president, and then a fourth, in 1940 and 1944. The 22nd Amendment to the Constitution now restricts presidents to two terms only.

preventing another world war, the fear of nuclear weapons may warrant more credit than the United Nations, but the world organization has helped keep the sparrows from shouting too loudly.

Few presidents have fallen so far from grace as Wilson has in the minds of his countrymen during the last hundred years, but it seems that Wilson had an inkling of how his brave words about self-determination and the rights of small nations might excite and ultimately disappoint. He had a foreshadowing of how American exceptionalism might ultimately fail to cure the world of its ills. When he was at sea, steaming to Europe in that December of 1918, on his way to the Paris Peace Conference, he turned to his public relations chief, George Creel, and said he knew that "these ancient wrongs, these present unhappinesses, are not to be remedied in a day or with the wave of a hand. What I seem to see—and I hope with all my heart I am wrong—is a tragedy of disappointment."[96]

———◆———

Gabreill [sic] d'Annunzio does not mince words about Woodrow Wilson in his new book: 'Let us have a new Crusade to re-establish true justice, which a cold, foolish man crucified with fourteen blunt nails ... ' he says.

    —*Chicago Tribune*, December 3, 1922

Levo la faccia, mentre il cor mi duole,
e pel rossore dè miei chiusi cigli
veggo del sangue mio splendere il mondo.

I raise my face, while my heart aches,
and by the redness of my closed eyelashes
I see the world shining with my blood.

    —Gabriele d'Annunzio
    From *Il Vulture Del Sole*

CHAPTER TWO

d'Annunzio

THE CONSEQUENCES OF the Paris decisions made by France, Britain, and above all by the United States had an immediate and negative effect on their closest ally, Italy. Denying Italy Fiume may have been a right and fair decision, but it undoubtedly contributed to Italy joining Germany against the allies in World War II. Britain and France had made far-reaching commitments to lure Italy into the first world war, but giving Fiume to Italy was not one of them. The question of how self-determination should be applied in Fiume's case was murky, with the Italians forming a majority in the city center, but not in the Croatian suburbs or the surrounding countryside. None of this lessened the shock and resentment in Italy of being told "no." Italians saw it as a national insult. They had made it clear that they considered Fiume to be part of the *Risorgimento*, the historical gathering of unredeemed Italians into one Italian nation, a process that had begun with Giuseppe Garibaldi's unification campaigns in the mid-nineteenth century.

Wilson was having none of that. Both Lloyd George and Clemenceau joined him in opposition to Italy's ambition. "The present Italian government was unable to make itself obeyed by the army or the navy, and therefore should not properly be called a government at all," said Clemenceau, who saw an opportunity to expand French influence in supporting Yugoslav claims.[1] But the British and French feared pushing Italy too hard. The fear of Communism shadowed the deliberations of the allies. Wilson, who wanted nothing to do with secret treaties in the first place, was the most adamant that Fiume should belong to the new Kingdom of Serbs, Croats, and Slovenes[i] which made up the two former Austro-Hungarian provinces of Croatia and Slovenia and the independent Kingdom of Serbia that had fought on the side of the allies in World War I. The new Balkan kingdom had declared itself a new nation even before Wilson had landed in France. Since the great port of Trieste to the northeast of Fiume was being transferred from Austrian to Italian control, Wilson reasonably believed that Fiume should become the new Slavic kingdom's principal outlet to the sea. The most that Wilson would consider was that Fiume might become a free port, an independent entity, but certainly not one annexed by Italy. Wilson did not want to give Italy the power to block most of central Europe's access to the sea. Italy, however, wanted nothing less than the entire eastern shore of the Adriatic so that no foreign power could impede its access to the Adriatic and to the Mediterranean beyond. Wilson, however, remained determined that Fiume should not be given to Italy. When it came to the question of who should rule Fiume, Secretary of State Lansing's prophesy was coming true. Wilson's soaring proclamations on self-determination were "loaded with dynamite." They were "bound to be the basis for impossible demands and create trouble in many lands."[2] Italians had embraced Wilson and his Fourteen Points. Now they perceived that the Fourteen Points were being used against Italy.

Did ethnic prejudice influence Wilson's decision? According to historian John Woodhouse, "Wilson shared with many of his fellow Americans a prejudice towards and distrust of Italy and the Italians. This was motivated partly by what conservative America saw as egalitarian political views expressed by recent immigrants,

---

i   After 1929 the Kingdom of Serbs, Croats, and Slovenes was officially called the Kingdom of Yugoslavia.

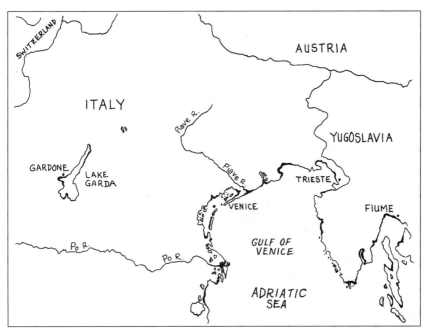

Areas of the Northern Adriatic where Gabriele d'Annunzio's war exploits, his Regency of Carnaro, and retirement on Lake Garda took place.
Map drawn by Julia L. Greenway

Fiume 5 lire stamp with portrait of Gabriele d'Annunzio, overprinted "Governo Provvisorio," issued in 1921.

partly by the corruption and violence later associated with criminal organizations such as the Mafia."[3] Wilson himself had written disparagingly about the "alteration of stock" that immigration from southern Europe had brought to America. In his *History of the American People*, published in 1902, Wilson wrote:

> Throughout the nineteenth century men of the sturdy stock of the north of Europe had made up the main strain of foreign blood … But now there came the multitudes of men of the lowest classes from the south of Italy and men of the meaner sort out of Hungary and Poland, men out of the ranks where there was neither skill nor energy nor any initiative of quick intelligence; and they came in numbers which increased from year to year, as if the countries of the south of Europe were disburdening themselves of the more sordid and hapless elements of their population.[4]

In the three decades before Wilson's arrival in Paris at least forty-six Italians had been lynched in America, and Italians found themselves in the cross hairs of the Ku Klux Klan.[5] Indeed, the Immigration Act of 1924, after Wilson had left office, specifically limited southern and eastern Europeans from immigrating to the United States in the furtherance of preserving the country's racial homogeneity.

Wilson, though, admired the Chinese, writing that "the Chinese were more to be desired as workmen, if not citizens, than most of the 'coarse crew' coming into the country on the Eastern Seaboard." The Chinese had their faults, in Wilson's view, but it was "their skill, their intelligence, their hardy power of labor, their knack of succeeding had driven their duller rivals out, rather than their alien habits, that made them feared and hated."[6] Yet Wilson's favorable view of the Chinese did not stop him from turning China down at the Paris Peace Conference.

Wilson's prejudices against southern Europeans would have included the Balkan Slavs whom he favored in the Fiume matter, not just the Italians whom he did not favor. In Wilson's Fourteen Points the defensible borders of Italy had already clashed with self-determination in the German-speaking alpine regions of Austria that were now going to Italy. But in the case of the eastern Adriatic littoral, Wilson wanted it to go as much as possible to the Slavic majority rather than recognizing the isolated Italian-dominated urban centers along the Dalmatian Coast. The city of Fiume itself had an Italian majority in 1919, but the outskirts and the surrounding suburbs were clearly Croatian. Indeed, trying to draw the boundaries along linguistic or ethnic lines in a polyglot territory such as Fiume and its surrounds showed the weakness in trying to draw borders in concert with self-determination. In the end, Wilson's desire to give the Yugoslavs an outlet to the sea probably had more to do with his position on Fiume than any anti-Italian prejudice. The French and the British were far more condescending toward the Italians than Wilson.

As part of the Austro-Hungarian dual monarchy in the eighteenth century, Empress Maria Theresa decided that Croatia would fall under Hungarian jurisdiction. Thus, Fiume became Hungary's principal seaport with a direct rail line to Budapest. Despite being but a small fraction of the population, Hungarians ruled the city. In 1910 six of the seven secondary schools in the city were Hungarian, and the seventh Italian. None was Croatian. The empress had also granted Fiume *corpus separatum* status—a separate political body—which added to the city's sense of entitlement and a certain sense of separation from the rest of Croatia. When the last Hungarian governor, Count Zoltan Jakelfalussy, left with his administration on October 29, 1918, he turned over the keys of the Governor's Palace to the new Kingdom of Serbs, Croats, and Slovenes. Soldiers of the new kingdom infiltrated the city soon after.

Fiume's Italian community, believing that their hour had struck, immediately formed a National Council. On the very next day the Council announced its allegiance to Italy at a public rally in the Piazza Dante near the port. Thus, for a while, Fiume had two mutually hostile administrations. The Croats held the Governor's Palace, high on the hillside overlooking the port like the royal box at an opera, while the Italians held city hall and the port below, with fighting in the streets separating them. On November 4, 1918, an Italian warship, *Emanuele Filiberto*, entered the harbor demanding that the Croat flag be lowered from the Governor's Palace. The Croats refused. French troops arrived on the fifteenth, and on the seventeenth Italian Marines attacked the Palace, hauling down the Croat flag and raising the green, white, and red *tricolore* of Italy. Sardinian Grenadiers entered the city and took charge. Demonstrations broke out across Fiume. Croatian shops were attacked and Croatian newspapers banned. American and British ships arrived in an attempt to restore order, but the Italians were clearly gaining the upper hand.

The Peace Conference began in Paris on January 18, 1919, and, as we have seen, Woodrow Wilson was very firmly against any idea that Fiume should become Italian, to which the Italian delegation took great objection. The Yugoslavs lobbied with equal fervor that Fiume should belong to them. From then on the fate of the city was supposed to be left to the powers deliberating in Paris. But the allied soldiers in Fiume were split among themselves, as were the allies in Paris, leading to violence between French and Italians that left nine French soldiers dead in June of 1919. Many of the French troops were colonial Vietnamese soldiers who were subjected to racial slurs.

The incident led Clemenceau to call the Italians "no more than a nation of assassins."[7] At this, the Inter-Allied Commission of Control intervened, dismissing Fiume's National Council, sending fresh British, French, Italian and American troops into the city, and ordering the Sardinian Grenadiers out. This caused great lamentations among the Italian community in Fiume, with church bells ringing and crowds begging the Sardinians to stay in order to protect them from the Croat population. It was not until September of 1919 that the formal dissolution of the Austro-Hungarian empire was declared at the Treaty of St. Germaine in Paris. Two days later a band of Italian nationalists, without the permission of the Italian government or the allies, took over the city from the thinly stretched allied forces in Fiume.

This opened the curtain on one of the most extraordinary episodes in the history of the twentieth century, an episode led by one of its most bizarre characters. Today Fiume is called Rijeka and is the Republic of Croatia's principal port. Through an eight-decade-long tortuous journey through a tortuous century, Rijeka began as Austro-Hungarian Fiume; then it became the Regency of Carnaro; then the Free State of Fiume before being annexed by Italy; then became a city in Yugoslavia; and finally, after the breakup of Yugoslavia, a city in Croatia. For not quite a year and a half, from September 1919 to the end of December 1920, Fiume became its own revolutionary city-state, with its own postage stamps, its own army, navy, and air force of sorts, its own constitution and its own foreign policy. Fiume embodied the personality of a man who was then Italy's greatest living poet, the war hero, orator, serial seducer of women, and intense Italian nationalist, Gabriele d'Annunzio. Although of middle-class origins, d'Annunzio was given the grand-sounding titles of Prince of Montenevoso and Duke of Gallese in the last years of his life. His "Italian Regency of Carnaro," named after the surrounding bay, was never officially recognized by the world's powers. However, Lenin saw in d'Annunzio a soulmate, a fellow revolutionary, and sent him a pot of caviar.

D'Annunzio was undoubtedly a revolutionary, but his appeal ranged from the extreme reactionary right to the far left. He despised the elites of his time, and in today's vocabulary he would be described as a populist—his power derived from the people, he believed, rather than from any established political party or doctrine. He had a gift for uniting separate, even hostile, factions under the spell of his oratory. Although d'Annunzio never became a Fascist—he considered Benito Mussolini a parvenu and advised him not to make an alliance with Hitler—as his biographer, Lucy Hughes-Hallett, put it, "Fascism was d'Annunzian."[8] Profoundly undemocratic, he believed that only an enlightened, Nietzschean superior being should rule. His tactics, mannerisms, and philosophies were copied by Mussolini and incorporated into his Fascist movement.

Even though historians doubt that d'Annunzio would ever have approved of what he spawned—the straight-armed salute, the torchlight parades, "the songs, the war cries, the glorification of virility and youth,"[9] the manipulation of popular opinion that Mussolini and Hitler would later adopt—were all part of d'Annunzio's modus operandi. The title *Duce* (leader) was bequeathed to d'Annunzio by his adoring followers well before Mussolini adopted the title as his own.[ii]

Largely ignored today, perhaps because he so influenced and inspired the early Fascists, the polymath d'Annunzio led several creative lives. He was not only among the best-known poets in an age when poetry still had the power to move the masses, but also among Europe's most famous playwrights at the turn of the twentieth century. He wrote scandalous novels that had all Europe talking. He was a renowned journalist, even writing articles for the Hearst newspapers in America. Although he didn't play a musical instrument, he was extremely knowledgeable about music and even collaborated with the French composer Claude Debussy, putting words to the composer's music. Puccini twice asked d'Annunzio to write librettos for an opera. The first deal fell through because d'Annunzio asked for too much money, the second because Puccini asked him to write more concisely. This was akin to asking a swallow to fly more slowly. D'Annunzio was not physically prepossessing, with wide hips, narrow shoulders, bad teeth, and a completely bald head in his later years. But his voice had a seductive quality to it that could fire up mobs in the street, inspire intense loyalty in men, and propel the most intimate relations with women. His legendary and elaborate seductions of some of the most famous and glamorous women in Europe were the scandal of the continent. His most famous love was

---

ii The word fascism comes from the Roman *fasces*, an ax surrounded by a bundle of sticks that symbolized authority in the Roman world. D'Annunzio, like Mussolini, saw in ancient Rome an inspiration to make Italy great again.

the actress Eleonora Duse, a well-known beauty of her day.

Yale's Paolo Valesio wrote that d'Annunzio's writings, "from adolescence to the first decade of the twentieth century, is more than sufficient in quality and quantity to establish him as one of the truly indispensable writers of international importance at the turn of the century,"[10] comparable to Gide, Yeats, and Rilke; "not only the most creative writer of the Italian twentieth century, but also the most intelligent writer of his times, and the most modern and cultured."[11] He loved the modern: fast motor boats, faster cars, and the newly invented age of flight. In his writing, he drew inspiration from the classical ages of the past, the Roman Empire, the exploits of Venice at the height of its power. His poetry ranged from the lyrical,

> Rain on the pines
> with their scales and bristles
> rain on the myrtle
> which are sacred to Venus

to the heroic:

> Where are the horses of the Sun
> with their manes of fury and flame,
> tails streaming out
> and bound about
> with bands of purple, their hooves
> resplendent as they flash
> on the parched ears of corn?[12]

D'Annunzio's prose and poetry might sound overripe to the Anglo-Saxon ear. "It remained for us a queer high-flavored fruit from overseas, grown under another sun than ours," wrote Henry James in 1902. Acknowledging d'Annunzio's "lyric genius ... rare imagination," and an "artistic intelligence of extraordinary range," James felt d'Annunzio's verse "brought no repose ... only agitation,"[13] a verdict with which d'Annunzio would have agreed. Agitation was his stock and trade. Some called him a "perverter," while others "hailed him as one bringing a current of fresh air and the impulse of a new vitality into the somewhat prim, lifeless work hitherto produced ... The faultlessness of his style and wealth of his language have been approached by none of his contemporaries whom his genius has somewhat paralyzed."[14]

However, there was a darker side to his brilliance. He was not averse to plagiarism when it suited him. He engineered reports of his death early in his literary career in order to pump up sales. His bizarre decadence gained him notoriety, as did his morbid romantic nationalism, doting as it did on war, bloodshed, and death. Like many of his contemporaries, including politicians such as Theodore Roosevelt and poets such as Rupert Brooke, he considered war a manly pursuit and believed that an armed conflagration would have a beneficial, cleansing effect, sweeping out the old and corrupt from a society corrupted by peace. Although he served briefly as a member of the Italian parliament, he believed that "representative democracy was bourgeois and lacked a romantic, dramatic arc," claiming that "sex and violence, even if they hurt people, were ultimately good because they were beautiful and sensational—the more baroque the better."[15] Influenced by Friedrich Nietzsche, he believed power should belong in the hands of an enlightened and cultured elite, which, of course, meant himself. D'Annunzio was a consummate narcissist. It was both a weakness and a strength. Analyzing narcissism in the context of American twenty-first-century politics, Harvard's Elizabeth Lunbeck has written that narcissists who are able to channel their narcissism can elicit in their followers "their willing submission and unwavering loyalty." What does such a personality offer in return? "Participation in his greatness," Lunbeck asserts. "The deal thus struck, many of the nation's most disenfranchised and aggrieved have sworn allegiance to this larger than life figure who, they feel, understands them and their struggle."[16]

The demagogic side of d'Annunzio was instrumental in stirring up popular feeling in Italy in favor of going to war alongside their fellow Latins, the French. He did not care about the English. But he hated the Germans, as well as Italy's traditional enemy, Austria. But while no one doubted German military prowess, many doubted Italy's. Italians in World War I had never fought together under a single flag before, and d'Annunzio felt that a display of valor in the war would make Italy more respected. Italy's government had already secretly agreed to join the allies, on the promise of territorial concessions at Austria's expense, but d'Annunzio was invaluable stirring up jingoistic, pro-war sentiments among the Italian people. When Italy joined the war in 1915, d'Annunzio leapt at the chance for glory. Not for him the brutal and degrading realities of trench warfare, however, nor the freezing high-altitude combat in the Alps that claimed more deaths from cold than gunshots. He would visit the battle zones at some risk to his life, but that was not the war he chose, and his fame was such that he could choose. And what he wanted, having been an early advocate of flight, was to organize bombing runs over Austrian armies in the flimsy aircraft of the day. Flying over Austrian Trieste, and even Vienna in broad daylight, he dropped a few bombs—more like grenades—over the side of the open cockpit as well as propaganda sporting green, white and red ribbons, the colors of Italy. That he never bothered to have his propaganda translated into German was beside the point. His goal was to glorify Italy, and even more, himself. He never actually piloted the planes. Daring pilots flew him over distances that no Italian had ever flown before. But he was always the center of attention. The government appreciated the propaganda value of letting the famous poet organize his own exploits. He lifted the morale of a nation at war.

Ernest Hemingway, an admirer along with Ezra Pound of d'Annunzio's poetry, called him "divinely brave."[17,iii] A plane crash

---

iii   Hemingway had a different opinion of d'Annunzio as a man. In a short poem, Hemingway wrote:

Half a million dead Wops;
And he got a kick out of it;
The son of a bitch.[18]

cost d'Annunzio an eye, but he refused to give up flying and was put in command of a squadron of bombers. He took to carrying a Roman terra-cotta phallus into battle along with the emeralds of a former mistress for luck. He returned from one flight with twenty-seven bullet holes in his plane, including one through his wrist, which only added to his ecstasy as well as his reputation.

In addition to his flights, d'Annunzio accompanied the Italian navy in fast torpedo boats that dashed across the Adriatic to harass Austrian warships in their harbors. In an incident later known as the *Beffa di Buccari* (the practical joke of Buccari), several torpedoes were launched in the heavily guarded Bay of Buccari with no damage to the Austrians except to their pride. No torpedo even exploded. The Italians had mistaken a large Hungarian Fiume-to-Venice ferry for a warship. Along with the spent torpedoes, d'Annunzio left behind bottles in the sea with scoffing messages.

Following these theatrical exploits, d'Annunzio would return to the comforts of Venice's Royal Danieli Hotel, or to his rented red house, the *Casetta Rossa*, on the Grand Canal, and dine at expensive restaurants with adoring mistresses. After the plane crash, he lay for several weeks at the *Casetta Rossa* with a bandage over his eyes. The doctors said he might lose his good eye if he did not remain completely still. But he continued to write. Narrow strips of paper were cut for him so that he could feel the edges and know where to put his pen. When his convalescence was over, he went right back to flying dangerous missions. He received numerous medals for bravery at a time when Mussolini was just being promoted to corporal in the Italian army. D'Annunzio would later write that few things in life were better than "to fight and to dare ... Danger works lyrically for me. My poetry is sustained by my courage ... I have never felt so full of music as during pauses of battle."[19]

D'Annunzio finished the war with an enhanced reputation, no longer just for his literary works, but for heroism and an intense Italian nationalism. Cheering crowds gathered wherever he went. He was arguably the most famous man in Italy. He had none of the disillusionment with war that affected the post-war generation of writers in England, America, and France. He surely would not have agreed with Wilfred Owen that Horace's *Dulce et decorum est pro patria mori* was an "old lie."[20] D'Annunzio gloried in war, in bloodshed, and in ever more corpses of the young.

A supreme egoist, he is virtually unique in combining art and poetry with warfare and radical politics. It was as if Lord Byron, the Marquis de Sade, and Casanova were rolled into one very political and dangerous, yet talented, personality. Such was his popularity and fame that there was a time in the immediate post-war year that he could have successfully organized a march on Rome and seized power, as Mussolini was to do in 1922.[iv]

D'Annunzio was quick to fan the flames of national outrage over Wilson's refusal to grant Italy the port of Fiume. At speeches and mass rallies he encouraged the politics of grievance on which he, and later Mussolini, capitalized. D'Annunzio denounced the work of the allies, and, evoking the bloodshed already spilt, said that blood must flow again if Italy was to be cleansed from the shame and filth of what had transpired in Paris. As Robert Greene writes in *The Art of Seduction*, d'Annunzio played upon the emotions of the crowd "… arguing that modern Italy should reclaim the greatness of the Roman Empire." D'Annunzio would "craft slogans for the audience to repeat, or would ask emotionally loaded questions for them to answer. He flattered the crowd, made them feel they were part of some drama."[21]

With these inflammatory speeches, d'Annunzio's moment of transition from poet to political leader had arrived. His widely printed *Letter to the Dalmatians*, published in the summer of 1919, made the case for annexing the entire Adriatic littoral, rejecting the "enfeebling transatlantic purgative offered by Dr. Wilson" and the "transalpine

---

iv   Mussolini did not actually join the march on Rome that brought him to power. He sent his followers, but stayed behind in Milan to be close to the Swiss border should the march fail.

surgery of Dr. Clemenceau."[22] The extreme nationalism that was to dominate Europe between the two world wars had begun.

D'Annunzio was indecisive at first about taking action on Fiume. But he succumbed when a delegation of Sardinian Grenadiers, who had been expelled from Fiume by the Italian government, came to him and begged him to take the city by force on behalf of Italy. The Grenadiers were based north of Fiume in the army camp of Ronchi. They had signed an oath to further Fiume's annexation by Italy, thus passing into legend as the Oath Swearers of Ronchi. "You cannot imagine the convulsion of patriots' enthusiasm that seized the hearts of the people of Fiume," their missal to d'Annunzio declared. "And you do nothing for Fiume? You who have all Italy in your hands, great, noble, generous Italy. Will you not break the lethargy into which she has fallen for so long?"[23] D'Annunzio rose to the challenge. He left his red house in Venice, assembled a few hundred men from the army camp and began the greatest adventure of his life.

After sending a telegram to his acolyte, Benito Mussolini, announcing that the "dice have been thrown,"[24] d'Annunzio climbed into a red Type 4 Fiat filled with roses—much as he once filled his lovers' beds with roses—and headed for Fiume, picking up followers along the way. There were so many roses that the Fiat was mistaken for a hearse. Most of his followers were war veterans, notably the Sardinian Grenadiers longing to return to Fiume, and the dagger-wielding *Arditi* (from the Italian *ardire*, to dare), the shock troops of the Italian army. Regular soldiers of the Italian army were under orders to stop d'Annunzio, even to shoot him if necessary. Recalling Napoleon Bonaparte on his return from Elba, when confronted by an Italian force blocking his way, d'Annunzio opened his coat to reveal his many war medals and said, "If you must kill me, fire first on this."[25] He was as successful as Napoleon had been in rallying to him those sent to oppose him. The Italian general in charge burst into tears. His soldiers mutinied to join d'Annnunzio's march. The poet turned insurrectionist had crossed his Rubicon, and his march continued on to Fiume unopposed.

Fiume had advance word that d'Annunzio was on his way. When he reached the city itself, he was greeted with deliriously happy crowds of Italians, complete with women in evening dresses toting machine guns, rifles, clubs, and knives, ready for any eventuality. These were the same crowds that had lamented the departure of their Sardinian protectors the previous month. The night before, these women of Fiume mobilized to keep an Italian warship in the harbor from departing should d'Annunzio need help when he arrived. It was said that these patriotic women "sealed the sailors' ears with the wax of their kisses"[26] so they could not hear the signal to return to ship. The Italian residents of the city were rebellious and ready to be absorbed into Italy. Bells rang and sirens sounded, laurel leaves cascaded from rooftops. The city seemed a forest of banners. Songs and cheers echoed through the piazza. The *Arditi* entered singing their marching song of youth, springtime, and beauty: "Giovinezza,"[27] a song that would be adopted by Mussolini's Fascists in the years ahead.

It was September 12, 1919. The sacred entrance, as it would be called, had been completed. That evening d'Annunzio addressed the people of Fiume from the balcony of the Governor's Palace, a building completed twenty-three years before to house Fiume's Hungarian rulers. He unfurled the "sacred banner of Randaccio," named after a fallen war hero whom d'Annunzio had lionized. The adoring crowds went wild with enthusiasm, engulfing d'Annunzio's "legionnaires," as he called his soldiers, and civilians alike in a state of political ecstasy inspired by his oratory.

> In the mad and cowardly world, Fiume today is the symbol of liberty. In the mad and cowardly world there is a single pure element: Fiume. There is a single truth: and this is Fiume. There is a single love: and this is Fiume! Fiume is like a blazing searchlight that radiates in the midst of an ocean of abjection.[28]

It was a scene that would be repeated again and again during the year and a half of his rule over the city. The ritual of the political rally that Mussolini and Hitler perfected, the ritual that can be seen at political rallies today, was born in Fiume in 1919.

D'Annunzio had long believed that the entire Dalmatian coast should be Italian, no matter what the demographics. In his view everything that had once been part of the ancient Venetian Republic should belong to Italy, and a good bit of what had belonged to ancient Rome as well. D'Annunzio's hopes of giving Fiume to the Italian government, however, were dashed. Prime Minister Francesco Nitti, who had replaced Vittorio Orlando, had no intention of accepting Fiume on d'Annunzio's terms. Nitti did not want to offend Wilson when Italy badly needed American aid to recover from the war. American grain shipments were pouring into Italian ports where real hunger lurked. Nitti had written to d'Annunzio explaining how important America was for war-improverished Italy. The Italian lira had fallen to one quarter of what it had been in 1914, and the cost of living for the average worker had risen to unaffordable heights. But d'Annunzio was not about to give up Fiume.

Wilson was beside himself with fury. Ever suspicious, he wrongly suspected Nitti of having put d'Annunzio up to his Fiume coup. "It is all part of a desperate endeavor to get me to yield to claims which, if allowed, would destroy the peace of Europe," Wilson wired his embassy in Rome. "You cannot make the impression too definite and final that I will not yield."[29] He then warned the American fleet to be on the alert for any attempts to seize more Dalmatian territory. As for Nitti, he bitterly opposed d'Annunzio's unilateral actions, but had to play his cards carefully given d'Annunzio's immense popularity. The Italian government established at least the appearance of a quarantine around Fiume, enough to cause shortages but not enough to starve the inhabitants. Neither Italy nor the allies thought it worth turfing out d'Annunzio and his merry men by force. As Clemenceau had said, the Italian government could not count on the loyalty of its army, and there was risk of civil war in the Italy of 1919. The French, American, British, and the Italian troops loyal to the government in Rome left Fiume quietly, leaving the field to d'Annunzio. He settled in as the popular dictator of his own state, which he named The Italian Regency of Carnaro, with himself as regent. He called himself *Commandante*.

And so began one of the most flamboyant experiments in building a new society in the modern age, using what d'Annunzio was to call "the politics of poetry."[30] It seemed as if every misfit, every revolutionary, every far-out idealist, every anarchist, Marxist, socialist, nationalist, and utopian dreamer was represented in those who came to d'Annunzio's Fiume. He took over the Governor's Palace for both his offices and living quarters. He turned the rest of the palace over to his *Arditi* storm troopers as an army barrack. The palace soon took on the aspects of an unruly fraternity house. Fine furniture was trashed and curtains were tightly drawn to create a gloom. Alcohol and drugs flowed freely. Almost daily, d'Annunzio gave speeches and poetry readings to the multitudes from his balcony to the cries of "Duce, Duce, Duce." He called these balcony harangues and the responding cries of approval from below his "parliament in the open air," and claimed it was the first communication between the people and their ruler since ancient Greece. There were endless parades, fireworks, torchlight demonstrations.

It was a government of spectacle long before Mussolini followed suit with his bombast, and Hitler with his flood-lit rallies. According to d'Annunzio, the ideal city-state was in the making. It would be his "City of the Holocaust," as he was lighting a fire that would consume and purify the corrupt Western world. The term holocaust was not then associated with anti-Semitism or the destruction of the Jews. But the forces unleashed in Fiume would soon lead d'Annunzio's imitators in that direction.

D'Annunzio outfitted his *Arditi* in black uniforms, black fezzes, and daggers, all of which Mussolini's followers would later adopt. Political clubs, often filled with thugs, sprang up. Anarchists, Socialists, and bully boys, who were beginning to call themselves Fascists, arrived in town. So did Irish Sinn Féiners dedicated to overthrowing British rule, as well as Egyptians, Indians, and other nationalities seeking an end to colonialism. D'Annunzio believed in the anti-colonial struggle, except when it concerned Italian colonialism. The hotels filled with journalists flocking to report on this strange political aviary. Spies and secret policemen interested in the activities of all of the above arrived as well.

Drugs were readily available in d'Annunzio's ideal city-state. Cocaine was carried by the fashionable in little silver boxes. Sex was cheap and venereal disease rampant. Inspired by d'Annunzio's amorous reputation, "citizens of Fiume began to imitate him," according to one of his biographers. "The city became a giant bordello."[31] D'Annunzio was not averse to homosexuality among his troops if that would bond them. Groups such as the Union of Free Spirits Tending Towards Perfection met under a fig tree to discuss free love and the abolition of money. Priests began to discuss the possibility of their marrying, alarming the Vatican. "It was a period of madness and bacchanal ringing with sounds of weapons and those, more subdued, of love-making,"[32] wrote another visitor. The city was in the "grip of a post-war frenzy"[33] that exceeded anything the Jazz Age could produce elsewhere.

The years after World War I were filled with the desire to create a brand new world rather than just sink back into what had gone before, and d'Annunzio's Fiume amplified that desire. "The general animation and noisy vitality seemed to herald a new land and new system," wrote the poet Sir Osbert Sitwell, one of the many writers who explored Fiume during that extravagant fifteen months:

> We gazed and listened in amazement. Every man here seemed to wear a uniform designed by himself; some had beards and shaved their heads so as to resemble the Commander himself [who was egg-bald at that time of his life]. Others cultivated huge tufts of hair half a foot long, waving out from their foreheads, and wore, balanced on the back of the skull, a black fez. Cloaks, feathers, and flowing black ties were universal, and every man—and a few women—were seen to be carrying the Roman dagger.[34]

In December 1919, the *Times* of London wrote:

> Like an adventurer of the Renaissance, he [d'Annunzio] made himself the master of Fiume and acts accordingly. He thinks himself above the laws, and proclaims that he is led by divine inspiration, says he is a seer, dreams of living forever the life of a rebel and talks wildly of bringing his sword to aid rebels all over the world—in Ireland, Egypt, India and Arabia, all of this being strangely unintelligible to any sane man.[35]

Naturally the European colonial powers detested d'Annunzio for his sympathy for colonized peoples. Wilson detested him for defying the American president's will. As for d'Annunzio, he delighted in defaming Wilson, calling him a "foolish old man" who had crucified justice with "fourteen blunt nails."

Wherever government blockades caused shortages, d'Annunzio's piratical band would sally forth and raid the surrounding countryside. Several Italian navy ships disobeyed their commanders and came over to d'Annunzio's side, sailing their vessels into the Bay of Carnaro, called Kvarner Gulf today. In one incident the freighter *Persia* was about to sail from Italy to Vladivostok bearing arms to defeat the Bolsheviks in Russia. Leftist sailors diverted the cargo to Fiume, delivering to d'Annunzio a quarter of a million rifles and ammunition. Using fast motor boats, d'Annunzio's legionnaires raided the coastal towns and commandeered cargo ships at sea to bring supplies into the renegade port. "Fiume was provisioned by piracy,"[36] wrote one of d'Annunzio's biographers.

Fighter pilots, some of them famous aces from the war, flew to Fiume to join the cause. From the beginning, one of d'Annunzio's chief lieutenants was a pilot named Guido Keller. Hailing from an old aristocratic Swiss family that had long ago moved to Italy, it was Keller who stole the trucks to bring d'Annunzio's original band of deserters from Ronchi. It was Keller who persuaded the city fathers to formally cede power to d'Annunzio. Upon hearing the news, d'Annunzio said, "Who, me?"[37] Until then d'Annunzio had thought that the Italian state would take over the city. Keller became the leader of the Commandante's most piratical followers, organizing his gang of *Disperata* (Desperates) as bodyguards for d'Annunzio. The *Disperata* was made up of men too undisciplined to be accepted in anyone's army.

On one occasion, while Keller was flying out in the countryside to steal what he could for the cause, his plane developed engine trouble. He was forced to land in Serbian territory. Seeing a donkey that he liked the look of, Keller tied the donkey to the airplane's struts, made the necessary repairs, and flew back to Fiume to present the donkey to d'Annunzio. Keller's eccentricities endeared him to d'Annunzio. With his Neptune-like beard, Keller had been arrested before the war for striding naked along Italian beaches.

So many army deserters wanted to join d'Annunzio, he had to turn them away lest he have too many followers to feed. He gave out so many medals that one historian called it "ornamentalism."[38] D'Annunzio declared, "On the verge of old age I have been reborn as the Prince of Youth."[39] He was having the time of his life. Fiume already had a reputation for moral laxity and exuberance even before d'Annunzio arrived. Under the Hungarian legal system, divorce was allowed. It was not permitted in Italy until 1974. D'Annunzio had his stream of mistresses who would visit him in the Governor's Palace. He kept calling for Italians back home in Italy to rise up and join the struggle. He denounced Mussolini for not doing enough to make Italy great again.

As with the counterculture of the sixties in America, Eastern religions became the vogue in d'Annunzio's Fiume. A newspaper called *The Hard Head*, named after d'Annunzio's bald pate, became the official outlet for the Commandante's thoughts. D'Annunzio insisted he was creating a brand-new, ideal state, "a searchlight radiant in the midst of an ocean of abjection."[40] His followers saw in it something beautiful and pure, born afresh amidst the ashes of the Great War.

On New Year's Eve, d'Annunzio proclaimed his intentions for Fiume's future:

> Today a miraculous year ends; not the year of peace but the year of passion ... not the year of Versailles, but the year of Ronchi. Versailles means decrepitude, infirmity, obtuseness, pain, cheating ... Ronchi means youth, beauty, ... profound newness. Against a Europe that suffers, stammers, and stumbles against an America that has yet to rid herself of the goal of a sick mind that still yet survived an avenging disease [Wilson's stroke] ... against all, against everything we have the glory of giving the name to this year of torment and ferment ... There is no spot on this earth where the human spirit is freer and newer than on these shores ...[41]

The inventor of radio, Guglielmo Marconi, a personal friend of d'Annunzio, arrived in Fiume on his yacht to set up a radio station so that d'Annunzio's orations could be broadcast to the world. Artists as well as musicians, such as Arturo Toscanini, came with his La Scala orchestra "to breathe the most resonant air in the world," as d'Annunzio put it.[42] The Commandante staged a mock battle for Toscanini involving 4,000 troops, using live ammunition in an old stone quarry on the edge of town. Sitwell reported that "one hundred were seriously injured by the bombs. The members of the orchestra, which had been playing during the quieter intervals, fired by a sudden excess of enthusiasm, dropped their instruments and charged the mock trenches. Five of them were badly injured in the struggle."[43]

D'Annunzio's motto, which he used on his letterhead, was *Me ne frego*, literally "I rub myself," a vulgar way of saying, "I don't give a damn." As with so many other d'Annunzioisms, Mussolini would adopt this slogan too, as the motto of the Fascist Party. Mussolini was one of the many who flocked to Fiume to see d'Annunzio in action. He hoped d'Annunzio might write an inflammatory poem for his Milan newspaper. Mussolini's Fascist movement was just forming, and Mussolini saw in Fiume how "dead elements of Roman culture had come to life under the breath of d'Annunzio's creative spirit ... Mussolini began dreaming of a 'Roman Italy,' an Italy under the leadership of a man of Caesarean stature, that would 'place the limit of its empire on the ocean and of its fame in the stars,'" which was

Mussolini's translation of Virgil's *imperium oceano, famam qui terminet astris*.[44]

D'Annunzio "had been capable of inspiring people to surpass themselves and invent new lives," observes the writer William Pfaff, "but his romantic commitment to war and violence as forces that could set people free contributed to the swindle that the Italian people subsequently were offered by Mussolini when he told them that conquest and empire would make them great again."[45] The relationship between Mussolini and d'Annunzio began when Mussolini was an understudy to the established star. But d'Annunzio's star was about to fade and Mussolini's to rise. When Mussolini departed Fiume, he took with him much of what became the trappings and rituals of the Fascist corporative state he was about to lead. Like d'Annunzio, Mussolini was a modern man whose nostalgia for the greatness of the past did not blind him to the possibilities of the new machine age. "Italy," he would say, "is a race, a history, a pride, a passion, a greatness of the past and an even more radiant greatness in the future."[46]

Mussolini might not be the orator that d'Annunzio was, but he had a gift for manipulating a crowd. He learned from d'Annunzio's political theater and his elevated rhetoric. In a letter to d'Annunzio, Mussolini declared, "Our ideas coincide on these fundamental points: The Italian victory must not be mutilated [d'Annunzio's phrase], not even under the pretext of democracy or of a Wilsonianism interpreted the Croatian way ..."[47]

Another visitor to Fiume was the Irish writer Walter Starkie, who, like so many others, had heard d'Annunzio's oratory and was impressed and enraptured. Starkie found d'Annunzio physically unimpressive, "a dwarf of a man, goggle-eyed ... sinister in his grotesqueness ..." But when he began to speak Starkie began to sink under the fascination of his voice, "like water from a clear fountain. It was a slow precise voice accompanying the words right to the last vowel, as if he had wished to savor to the utmost their echoing music. The tones rose and fell in an unending stream, like the song of a minstrel, and they spread over the vast audience like olive oil on the surface of the sea."⁴⁸ It was a voice of seduction, a voice that could win over a reluctant woman on a soft summer night, or recite some of the most lyric poetry in the Italian language, or incite men to murder and mayhem in a public square, all in the same bewitching cadences.

In was an age of -isms. Futurism was an artistic movement originating in Milan in 1909. Futurists were all the rage and well represented in Fiume during d'Annunzio's reign. Futurists were obsessed by technology in the age of motor cars and airplanes. They believed that art should abandon Italy's past and embrace the future. Though linked to the Futurists by his embrace of the modern, d'Annunzio was too wrapped up with the glories of ancient Rome and the Venetian Republic to be one of them. As Sitwell put it, "D'Annunzio had succeeded in uniting for a time those who lived in the past of Italy with those who hated it."⁴⁹

A better fit for d'Annunzio was the Decadent Movement, which subscribed to world-weariness and skepticism of the prevailing morals, a belief that creativity trumped logic. It was art for art's sake, excess, and a taste for the morbid and macabre.

President Wilson announced to the press in Paris that Italy's desire to acquire Fiume was imperialistic. Many Italians, however, thought that attempting to unite the Italian populations of the eastern Adriatic under Italian sovereignty was a noble pursuit, much in the spirit of Garibaldi's reunification of Italy half a century earlier. For many, d'Annunzio's march on Fiume helped salve the wounds inflicted by Wilson, as well as the British and the French, in what many Italians thought of as a plot to diminish Italy's victory in the war.

But there was always something clownish in the Fiume epic. "There was always a sense of falseness about [d'Annunzio's] takeover, an impression of play-acting, where the heroic was sometimes attended by the tragic and too often the comic."⁵⁰ As for d'Annunzio, he fulminated against Italy's political leaders and the Italian people for not rising up to overthrow their government. He called Mussolini a "gross windbag"⁵¹ for doing so little to help. No doubt he pictured himself a potential dictator of Italy, but unlike Mussolini he lacked the organizational discipline to make that dream come true. D'Annunzio was a terrible administrator, and as his bacchanalian year progressed, the city fathers of Fiume began to tire of his antics and wished him gone. His addiction to cocaine likely began as a way to alleviate pain in his blinded eye. Syphilis too, began to take its toll at this time. By night his mistresses came and went from his rooms in the Governor's Palace, but his favorite, who remained faithful to him for the rest of his life and would join him in exile, was the concert pianist Luisa Baccara.

In November of 1919, with Italy radically and at times violently divided between left and right, Italians went to the polls and swung left. The Socialists made considerable gains. Nitti was returned to power to the discouragement of the Fascists, Futurists, and d'Annunzio. With his authority now confirmed, Nitti offered Fiume a deal. The city would again become a *corpus separatum*, a separate entity under Italy's protection. All attempts by Yugoslavs to seize the city would be resisted, and Italy would promise "not to welcome or agree to any solution which separated Fiume from the motherland."[52] D'Annunzio would have to leave the city and disband his fanatical followers. It would appear that d'Annunzio had won, and that Fiume was on the verge of becoming part of Italy. But, although that was his original goal, now that he had experienced the limelight, he didn't want to lose the stage upon which he could strut and shout. He agreed to abide by Nitti's offer only if approved by the reconstituted Fiume National Council. The vote was forty-eight to six to accept Nitti's *Modus Vivendi*.

The Council was filled with businessmen and industrialists whose enterprises had been virtually shut down by the government's blockade. Unemployment was growing. D'Annunzio's followers raved and ranted, held marches and demonstrations against the vote, and beat up anyone who spoke up against their leader. Thus encouraged, d'Annunzio refused to accept the Council's decisions and demanded a plebiscite, to which the Council acceded.

During the plebiscite, d'Annunzio went to his favorite restaurant, *Cerva d'Oro* (Golden Deer), and sipped his favorite cherry brandy, which he called "blood." The restaurant had been informally renamed *Ornitorinco* (Platypus) because Guido Keller had snitched a stuffed platypus from the natural history museum and placed it in the restaurant. The plebiscite went against d'Annunzio and in favor of Nitti's proposal by a ratio of four to one. D'Annunzio reacted calmly, but he had no intention of giving in.

Many thought that d'Annunzio intended to make himself ruler of all Italy. He might have even succeeded if he had been less indecisive. For all his talk about Nietzschean supermen and the ideals of Plato, and a republic run by an enlightened philosopher king, d'Annunzio lacked the all-consuming will to power needed to take over all of Italy. "Selfish egotism governed his every action," wrote one of his biographers.[53] D'Annunzio was determined to stay master of his city-state laboratory where the competing ideologies simmered over the flame of his personality. His goal of forcing Italy to annex Fiume had shifted in favor of his imagined utopia. His call for Italians to rise up and overthrow the government went unanswered.

Prime Minister Nitti and d'Annunzio had known each other for a quarter of a century. While d'Annunzio denounced Nitti in the strongest scatological terms, Nitti thought d'Annunzio a posturing fool. Nitti recognized d'Annunzio's popularity and his ability to stir the masses, so he never tightened his military blockade of Fiume enough to do real harm. Nonetheless, in a dramatic gesture that was more political than humanitarian, d'Annunzio had hundreds of children evacuated to Italy in February of 1920.

In the summer of 1920, in the sweltering *Fenice* (Phoenix) theater, against the wishes of the National Council, d'Annunzio unveiled his new constitution for Fiume, the Charter of Carnaro, co-authored by Alceste de Ambris, who had signed on to the Commandante's vision. Referring to the heat, d'Annunzio described it as the "furnace in which the new order would be smelted."[54]

Shouts of "Eia, Eia, Eia, Alala!" d'Annunzio's battle cry, rang to the rafters, and there was talk that if Italy didn't annex Fiume, Fiume would annex Italy.ᵛ

In d'Annunzio's ideal state, society would be organized into corporations representing various sectors of the economy—industry and agriculture, seafaring, teachers and students, lawyers, and doctors. There would be a mystical tenth corporation of superior individuals, the criteria for which suited d'Annunzio's image of himself. There would be equality of the sexes, classes, races, languages, and religions, a "thoroughgoing system of social security, medical insurance, and old-age care, in addition to a method of direct democracy." One critic called it "a kind of Napoleonic Code rewritten by Ezra Pound."[55] The charter took inspiration from ancient Greece, medieval Italian city states, and the Venetian Republic. Music was to be the "Religious and Social Institution of the Regency of Carnaro," d'Annunzio said[56]—the glue that would bind together the proletariat, the bourgeoisie, the military and the church. Since the businessmen of the National Council objected to all of the above, the charter seemed to them like a coup d'etat in the making. But in the end, nothing came of it, as the curtain was soon to come down upon d'Annunzio's hour on the world stage. Then there was a project to create a League of Oppressed Peoples, to be led by the Belgian-Polish poet Leon Koschnitzky, d'Annunzio's foreign minister. The goal was to rival Wilson's League of Nations, which to d'Annunzio was a den of imperialist oppressors. The list of possible members included Indians, Chinese, Koreans, Burmese, Catalans, Persians, as well as oppressed African-Americans, and Chinese-Americans.

He made his appeal, saying:

> All the rebels of all the races will be gathered under our sign, and the feeble will be armed. Force will be used against force. And the new crusade of all poor and impoverished nations, the new crusade of all poor and free men, against the usurping nations,

---

v   The cry was adopted from the ancient Athenians, and was yet another aspect of d'Annunzio that Mussolini adopted.

the accumulators of all wealth, against the predatory races and against the caste of usurers who yesterday exploited the war in order to exploit peace today—the new crusade will reestablish that true justice has been crucified by an icy maniac [Wilson] with fourteen dull nails and with a hammer borrowed from the German chancellor ... Our cause ... directed against the evil of the world ... extends from Ireland to Egypt, from Russia to the United States, from Rumania to India. It gathers the white races and the colored peoples, reconciles the Gospel with the Koran ...[57]

While the budding Fascist Party found inspiration in d'Annunzio's words, so could Marxists. There was a fierce anti-colonial strain in the League of Oppressed Peoples. It was discovered that d'Annunzio sent 250,000 rifles from the *Persia*, the arms ship that had joined his cause, to Egypt to foment rebellion. Attempts were made to gain the formal support of the Soviet Union and the Italian socialist movement. Both failed. The league's policy was aimed at breaking up the new state of Yugoslavia by inciting the Slovenes, Montenegrins, and Croats against the dominant Serbs. This too, failed. Yugoslavia remained intact for another seven decades before it fell apart along the same fault lines that d'Annunzio had tried to exploit. By the middle of 1920 it was clear that the Fiume enterprise was going nowhere, either in Italy or internationally. An angry Koschnitzky resigned and left Fiume in July.

From then on d'Annunzio ruled with the help of his legionnaires, his *Arditi*, and his Desperates, and he ruled by brute force. Minorities, especially Croats, Slovenes, and Serbs living in Fiume, were forced out, their houses and properties expropriated by Italians. D'Annunzio called Croats "beasts born from the vomit of the dying Austrian vulture."[58] Those who resisted were beaten up and sometimes killed. The ideals of his Charter of Carnaro were spawning the authoritarian brutality that would soon consume all of Italy. Rival factions of d'Annunzio loyalists began to fall out. Violence replaced revelry in the tragic comedy that was Fiume.

Meanwhile, the allied powers in Paris had washed their hands of the Fiume Question, and had left the entire matter up to the Italians and the Yugoslavs to work out between themselves. Nitti's government fell in June of 1920. D'Annunzio celebrated by holding a mock funeral for the "putrid, blown-out windbag."[59] Nitti was replaced by sterner stuff in the person of Giovanni Giolitti, who had served four times as prime minister. Giolitti sat down with the Yugoslavs and hammered out the Treaty of Rapallo, signed in November of 1920. Under the terms of the treaty, Fiume was to become an independent state with a land bridge to Italian Istria. Italians living in Fiume and along the Dalmatian coast were to be granted Italian citizenship.

But once again d'Annunzio was not satisfied. For d'Annunzio a diplomatic deal was no substitute for a blood-soaked victory. Furthermore, although Fiume would not become part of Yugoslavia, neither would it become part of Italy. It would simply be a city-state without d'Annunzio, for the treaty made it clear that there would be no role for him. That was unacceptable to d'Annunzio and he refused to leave. He tried to interest Mussolini in an insurrection in Italy itself, but Mussolini turned him down. The Treaty of Rapallo spelled the end of d'Annunzio's plan for the ideal state, and his popularity began to deflate. Giolitti, unlike Nitti, was not afraid to move against him. D'Annunzio was given a deadline to leave town, which he predictably ignored.

The showdown came over the Christmas holiday, a three-day period during which Giolitti knew the newspapers would not publish. The Italian army moved in, and for three days there was desultory fighting in the streets of Fiume with both sides calling upon the other not to spill Italian blood. In the end the Italian battleship *Andrea Doria* steamed into the Bay of Carnaro and sent a shell into the Governor's Palace, stunning but not wounding D'Annunzio. That was enough for the Commandante, and he decided he was not going to die among the ruins of Fiume after all. It is said that he flipped a coin to decide whether to die fighting or capitulate, but no one other than he saw whether it landed heads or tails. In any event, he decided to capitulate. His utopian state of music and poetry had become a sordid and violent orgy, a drunken joke. As biographer Lucy Hughes-Hallett put it, D'Annunzio's Fiume was a "Never-Never land, an unregulated space out of the continuum of cause and effect, where lost boys could enjoy dangerous adventures untrammeled by good sense."[60]

He lingered on, officiating over the funerals of the thirty-three men killed in the three days of fighting but then left quietly for Venice. There would be no trial for treason, no punishment for his warring against his country. He was allowed to retire quietly in a villa above Lake Garda, out of the fray, while the rest of Italy fell to fighting between the left and right until King Emmanuel decided to hand power to Mussolini in 1922. The understudy had at last replaced the leading man, and a perverted version of d'Annunzioism would reign over Italy for the next twenty-three years.

Violence was not finished with Fiume, however. Fascists tried to seize control of the city, causing more shell-fire damage to the Governor's Palace. Mussolini finally absorbed the city into the Italian state in 1924. Ever solicitous toward d'Annunzio, Mussolini used the Commandante for propaganda from time to time, making it seem that his Fascist movement had grown out of the spirit of Fiume. But the old poet was now a spent force to be brought out only as a relic. Although both Mussolini and he were fervent nationalists, d'Annunzio could never stomach Italy's alliance with Hitler, which he warned against.

With Mussolini's help, d'Annunzio built a fantastical house above Lake Garda and named it *Vittoriale*. Mussolini supplied d'Annunzio with the same type of torpedo boat in which he had once harassed the Austrians. From time to time he would race it up and down the lake. Mussolini also had the prow of a warship, the *Puglia*, jutting out of the hillside near d'Annunzio's house. D'Annunzio would hold functions and greet people on the *Puglia*'s deck as if he were a receiving admiral. It had cannons that could fire blanks across the lake. D'Annunzio asked that a nearby hill be leveled to make a landing field for an airplane, but at that Mussolini drew the line.

Hard living, cocaine, and syphilis turned d'Annunzio toward decrepitude in his final years. He died most likely of a heart attack or a cerebral hemorrhage in the study of his home on the first day of March 1938, eleven days before his seventy-fifth birthday. His caretaker and last female companion was a young Austrian woman from the Sud Tyrol, recently made part of Italy, probably paid by the Nazis to keep an eye on the old reprobate. She left for Berlin immediately after his death, and was given a job in the German foreign office. When Mussolini's headquarters was informed of d'Annunzio's death, someone in the office was heard to say, "At last."[61]

In assessing d'Annunzio's philosophies, his biographer, Michael Ledeen, cautions that, "it is unthinkable that d'Annunzio would have presided over the creation of a regime as reactionary and oppressive as that of Fascist Italy; the Commandante's personality simply did not lend itself to the creation of a totalitarian state."[62] D'Annunzio's Fiume had been a Petri dish of competing political cultures on both the left and the right—from the anti-imperialism of his would-be rival to the League of Nations, to the thuggish violence of his legionnaires. However, it is hard not to draw a straight line from the behavior of his followers during their last days in Fiume to Mussolini's *Squadristi* and Hitler's Brownshirts, beating up political opponents. As Ledeen concedes, "the ritual of Fascism came in large measure from Fiume, and in this sense the Commandante undoubtedly served as a model for the future Duce,"[63] and in many respects for Hitler as well.

In his 1928 autobiography, in his chapter called "The Garden of Fascism," Mussolini wrote, "I, too, had been living this [the Fiume] drama day by day. D'Annunzio and I had been close together since the first days of the campaign ... had been accustomed to receive his brotherly letters." He never mentioned that many of these letters were scolding reproofs. Instead Mussolini chose to record that d'Annunzio had written that he admired Mussolini's "consistent and well-diverted blows."[64] There can be little doubt that "Fascism was the child of Fiume," as Osbert Sitwell put it.[65] But there is next to nothing in Mussolini's dictatorship that echoed the liberal and libertarian doctrines of the Carnaro Charter, that other child of Fiume that died at birth.

In today's Rijeka it is hard to find the echoes of the mad excitement that consumed the town a century ago. After d'Annunzio's ignoble departure, Italy and Yugoslavia compromised and Fiume became a free state, technically belonging to neither. The Italians annexed Fiume completely in 1924, only to lose it completely to Yugoslavia after World War II. The ships that crowded the harbor in d'Annunzio's time have, by and large, gone. Shipbuilding has moved to Asia. The torpedo factory, which supplied those instruments of war to many of the world's navies, is no more, its buildings abandoned or put to use for other purposes. Whereas Italians once made up the majority in the city itself, they are now roughly two percent. Rijeka is now a Croatian town with a population in decline.

The Governor's Palace, the scene of so many of d'Annunzio's speeches and theatrical demonstrations, remains but has been converted into a maritime museum and a venue for exhibitions and concerts. If you look closely on the second floor, you can see where one of d'Annunzio's legionnaires scratched *"Arditi"* on the marble balustrade. Of the Italian shell that burst in upon d'Annunzio in December 1920 during that bloody Christmas, there is no sign. Restoration work has taken care of that.

The Ornitorinco where d'Annunzio drank and caroused with his legionnaires is no more, replaced by a newspaper and sundries shop. Croatian children learn next to nothing about d'Annunzio in school. As for Ronchi, it is the site of nearby Trieste's airport today. Once named *Ronchi dei Legionari* Airport, in 2007 it was renamed after an Italian explorer.

In Venice, the *Casetta Rossa* remains on the Grand Canal, across from Peggy Guggenheim's museum and is little changed since d'Annunzio lived there. It is privately owned and not open to the public. The paint is peeling, and the garden gate, through which d'Annunzio exited to be sped to the airfield by fast motor boat, is broken. D'Annunzio's *Doll House*, as he called it, exudes the air of neglect and incipient ruin of much of Venice. Someone has sketched obscene graffiti on the wall, a gesture that would have no doubt have amused d'Annunzio.

It is on Lake Garda, at the *Vittoriale*, that you can best find the ghost of d'Annunzio's presence. School children are taken to see his last fantastic house which he bequeathed to the Italian people. It is crowded with the bric-a-brac that d'Annunzio collected for his final home. In his bathroom alone, there are between 900 and 1,000 objects, including several ivory and silver hair brushes, although he had not a hair on his head. The *Vittoriale* is filled from floor to ceiling with paintings and just plain "stuff," some of it antique shop quality, much of it junk. His glasses are still on the desk at which he was sitting when he died. Over the door of one room is written *genio et voluptati* (genius and voluptuousness). The room to which his mistresses were ushered is called "Abbesses in Transit." With d'Annunzio there was always the sacred and the profane. In the garden there is a statue of an agonized St. Francis staring up at the house. But follow his gaze closely and you see he is staring at the backside of Venus. The same Fiat in which d'Annunzio rode into Fiume is preserved. The plane in which he flew over Vienna hangs from the ceiling of his private movie theater. And the torpedo boat, in which he once sped across the Adriatic, is in a shed on the property.

It is to the prow of the *Puglia* that Mussolini had brought up from the sea that children flock. It juts absurdly from the hill just as it did in d'Annunzio's time. D'Annunzio would have appreciated the symbolic reference to the *Rostra* of ancient Rome. The Rostra were the rams, or beaks, of warships placed in the Roman Forum from which orators would address the people. D'Annunzio was also known to compare the rams of ancient warships with phalluses.

On a hillside above, d'Annunzio lies interred in a temple-like monument with his disciples, including Guido Keller, each in his own sarcophagus. One senses that d'Annunzio would not have chosen such a vulgar monument for his resting place. There are plaster casts of his dogs lounging about, adding to the amusement park atmosphere. Mussolini's entourage always wondered why he showed such favor to a potential rival who at one time had so overshadowed him, and might still present a danger. The dictator's philosophy was that with a rotten tooth you had two choices: either pull it out, or fill it with gold. Mussolini chose the latter.

In 2019 as Italian politics slid to the populist right, d'Annunzio had a comeback of sorts. A sitting statue of the poet reading a book was installed in Trieste, not a city associated with d'Annunzio, but the Italian rightists realized that Croatian Rijeka would never accept it. However, that has not stopped admirers from placing an Italian flag on the gates of Rijeka's Governor's Palace with the old Roman words of defiance, *Hic Manebimus Optime* ("Here we will remain most excellently"). D'Annunzio would have been delighted.

محمد بن عبد الكريم الخطابي

It is the natural duty to leave every people to manage its own affairs. Power and force fail before right. The Treaty [of Versailles] was drawn up by the chief men of great nations who had taken part in the war and experienced its terrible consequences ... In the end they couldn't fail to recognize the truth, and they gave to all nations, even the smallest, the right of self-government.
>   —Mohammed Azerkan
>   Foreign Minister of the Republic of the Rif (1921-1926)

CHAPTER THREE

Abd el-Krim

THERE IS NO RECORD of anyone from the Rif Mountains of northern Morocco having traveled to Paris in 1919 wanting to see Woodrow Wilson, as did Ho Chi Minh and so many others from lands under European colonization. There was no defense of Riffian interests made at the Paris Peace Conference as there had been for China and Italy and many other national claims. Nevertheless, Wilson's words had penetrated into the remoteness of the Rif, where few Europeans had any first-hand knowledge, giving succor to the first well organized and, at least temporarily, successful armed revolt for self-determination after World War I. Self-determination for Europe's colonies was not at the top of Wilson's agenda. He needed the imperial powers to support his League of Nations, always his first priority. Wilson was an anti-imperialist in the abstract, but seldom in the particulars, as many a disappointed suppliant would discover. None of Wilson's decisions affected the Spanish Protectorate of Morocco. Spain had remained neutral in the Great War, and had no say in a Peace Conference dominated by the victors: Britain, France, the United States, and to a lesser extent, Italy. Yet rebellion in the Rif against Spanish rule was partly inspired by Wilson's idealistic proclamations, and the leaders of that rebellion never ceased to hope that the big powers would recognize their independence and that of the newly declared Republic of the Rif.

The Rif War was a precursor to the revolts and wars of liberation after World War II, conflicts that eventually swept away all of Europe's colonial empires. Wilson's secretary of state, Robert Lansing, had seen the dangers of Wilson's stress on the right to self-determination. "Will it not breed discontent, disorder, and rebellion?" he wrote. "Will not the Mohammedans [sic] of Syria, Palestine, and possibly Morocco and Tripoli rely on it ... ?"[1] Wilson had lit an anti-colonial fire that was contained after World War I, but then burned out of control after World War II until, by century's end, Europe's overseas empires died. For five years from 1921 until its defeat in 1926, the self-proclaimed Republic of the Rif had its own government, its own laws, its own army, and its own flag. The Republic of the Rif ruled in Northern Morocco in defiance of its colonial master, Spain, and for a while in defiance of France as well. The republic organized its own administration, with a cabinet complete with ministries of war and foreign affairs patterned on the European model. Its army first defeated the Spanish in their Moroccan protectorate, and then badly mauled the French in French Morocco, before being overwhelmed by the superior manpower and industrial capacity of both France and Spain, using all their resources of modern war, including poison gas.

All but forgotten today, the rebellion in the Rif caught the imagination of the world in the 1920s. Its leaders were Mohamed ibn Abd al-Karim al-Khattabi, known to the Western World as Abd el-Krim, and his younger brother, Mhamed.[i] Among the most important guerrilla leaders of the twentieth century, their methods were studied by Che Guevara, Ho Chi Minh, and Mao. Abd el-Krim's stern image graced the cover of *Time* magazine in 1925, in which he and his associate were described as "brilliant in no ordinary sense of the word." *Time* praised "the efficiency of their administration, which shows itself in the able way the war against first Spain, and

---

i Mhamed is an archaic form of Mohammed. The brothers had essentially the same name.

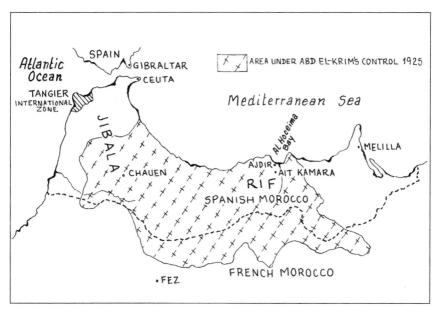

Spanish Morocco and parts of French Morocco that Abd el-Krim controlled at the height of his conquests.
Map drawn by Julia L. Greenway

A one riffan banknote. The currency was issued by the Republic of the Rif and circulated alongside Spanish and British issues.

then France, has been conducted ... [Abd el-Krim] fights for the independence of the Rif territory, but willy-nilly, he was forced to fight for Islam."[2]

Inspired by the revolt in the Rif, Sigmund Romberg and Oscar Hammerstein wrote a long-running Broadway musical called *The Desert Song* in 1926, ignoring that the Rif is mountainous, not desert. During the next three decades, Hollywood made no less than three movies based on the musical. Romberg and Hammerstein and all three movies fell into the same trap as did Abd el-Krim's French and Spanish foes. Thinking that no barbarous North African could possibly be a brilliantly organized leader, the movies and the musical had the Abd el-Krim character be a Frenchman in disguise. In 1977 an equally inaccurate film, *March or Die*, featured Sir Ian Holm as Abd el-Krim, but at least he was a Moroccan. Although there were a few European renegades fighting for the Rif, none had top leadership positions. Leadership and organization were in the hands of Abd el-Krim, his brother, and fellow Riffians. Their revolt gave encouragement to colonized people all over the world that they too, might one day throw off their colonial masters and take charge of their own destinies. Muslims in India, for example, attempted to send aid to the Rif throughout the war.

The Rif War did not erupt in a vacuum. The people of northern Morocco had been resisting Spanish control since the nineteenth century. Indeed, the Muslim "Moors" had been fighting the Christians both in Spain and then in Morocco for twelve hundred years. But the slaughter of World War I discredited the idea of European superiority. That, and Wilson's idealism, created conditions ripe for colonial uprisings and unrest throughout the colonized world. The French were having trouble in their new colony in Syria, bombarding Damascus in 1925 and 1926. In 1919 the Egyptians and the Afghans rose against the British, as did the Koreans against the Japanese. In 1920 the British faced an uprising in Iraq as well. The Italians were battling armed resistance to their rule in Libya under the leadership of Omar Mukhtar, who had been fighting the Italians since they arrived in 1911. Disillusioned by Wilson's failure to universalize his self-determination ideals, especially after the brutal Jallianwala Bagh massacre in the Indian city of Amritsar, where the British gunned down hundreds of unarmed demonstrators, the Indian nationalist movement "swung decisively toward the goal of terminating British rule in India," according to Harvard historian Erez Manela.[3]

The Rif War was the most successful of the post-war uprisings, even though it was ultimately defeated. It had to be defeated if the European empires were to sustain their "one convincing argument, the superiority of force,"[4] as the American journalist Vincent Sheean put it at the time. Abd el-Krim and the Rif garnered sympathy from many Americans and from those Europeans who were by then beginning to lose the will to rule over others.

In the scramble for African colonies that marked the late nineteenth and early twentieth centuries, Morocco was among the last to lose its independence. Spain had long been involved with the affairs of Morocco. In the Middle Ages the "Moors" of Morocco had elevated Spain over most of the rest of Europe in the arts and sciences. In 1492 Queen Isabella and King Ferdinand conquered and expelled the Moors from Spain as well as the Jews. Four years later the Spanish followed the retreating Moors into Morocco itself, founding a bastion for Christian Europe in Africa called Melilla. They then acquired Ceuta from the Portuguese, initiating Spain's expansion into Africa. Five centuries later Spain still owns its *presidios* of Ceuta and Melilla on Morocco's Mediterranean shore along with a handful of small islands and rocks, the last shards of Spain's broken imperial plate.

As the nineteenth century gave way to the twentieth, Spain was a minor European power that had lost its empire to the Americans. Cuba and Puerto Rico, as well as the Philippines and Guam, had been wrenched away. The humiliation over this loss spurred the need for Spain to regain its dignity and prestige. Their eyes turned towards Morocco. To gain promotions and martial glory, Spain needed a colony, a captive people on whom to impose its will. France and Spain agreed to divide Morocco into spheres of influence, with Spain taking the northern part and France the rest, except for a sliver of Spanish-controlled land bordering on the Spanish Sahara. In 1912 these were formalized into French and Spanish "protectorates," both nominally under the reign of the Sultan of Morocco, who was to become little more than a puppet of the French. But unlike the French, the Spanish had no formal agreement with the Sultan, so their protectorate became a colonial sub-let of the French Empire.

Tangier was the exception. Morocco's most cosmopolitan city, it was where foreign diplomats to the pre-colonial sultanate resided.[ii] Less than fifty miles from the British territory of Gibraltar, Britain wanted Tangier to become an international zone, only nominally under the Sultan's jurisdiction. This came to be in 1923–1924, leaving Tangier to be controlled by the consulates of nine nations: France, Spain, Britain, Portugal, Belgium, the Netherlands, Sweden, Italy and the United States.[iii] This arrangement lasted until Morocco got its independence in 1956. Being ruled by nine nations is to be ruled by none, so Tangier became a center of intrigue where Abd el-Krim's agents roamed freely, gathering information and supplies to smuggle into the Rif.

Spain's involvement in northern Morocco deepened with an armed incursion in 1909, three years before it became officially recognized as a Spanish protectorate. The Spanish, however, limited their activities to expanding their territories around their *presidios*, Ceuta and Melilla, leaving the wild interior of northern Morocco alone. The Berber tribesmen of the Rif, indigenous to the country before the Arab conquest in the seventh-century, were by and large left to manage their own affairs. "While travelers have penetrated to

---

ii In 1777 the Sultan of Morocco was the first foreign leader to recognize the independence of the United States.

iii The Soviet Union was offered participation in Tangier's administration but declined.

almost every point in Central Africa," wrote the *Times* of London correspondent, "this large and important region of Morocco has remained absolutely closed to all outside knowledge and discovery."[5] The Berbers of the Rif, often blue- or green-eyed with light hair, were a hardy mountain people, xenophobic and deeply religious, with little respect either for Spanish rule or for the Sultan of Morocco. But they had great respect for their Muslim religion. Before the coming of the Europeans, Morocco had been informally divided into two zones: the Blad el-Makhzen, the land where the government held sway, and the Blad es-Siba, the land of insurrection and dissent. The Rif was decidedly in the latter.

The Riffians, like so many other hill peoples, were divided into clans and tribes that continually fought against one another, uniting only when there was an outsider to be resisted. They were never effectively subjugated by outsiders in their mountain fastnesses. Blood feuds were frequent and could last for generations. At the same time, they were a resourceful and self-sufficient people, inured to hardship. In battle they were masters of their own terrain, using any bit of rock or tree to full advantage for cover. As classic guerrilla fighters, they attacked an enemy when and where it was weak, melting away into the hills when the enemy was strong, and constantly harassing the foe with sniping fire by marksmen who were second to none. The Berber tribesmen had a healthy contempt for central authority, reminiscent of the highland clans of Scotland in the seventeenth- and eighteenth- centuries, the American colonists fighting against British regulars in the American revolution, and the Afghans against the British, Russians, and then the Americans during most of the last two centuries. As with the Afghans, religion was a strong rallying cry. It behooved any leader seeking their loyalty to declare *jihad* and raise the banner of Islam against the infidel invader. It was Abd el-Krim's genius to play to his tribesmen's strengths and unite the tribes as they had never before been united. Although a devout Muslim, Abd el-Krim was not a fanatic in the Osama bin Laden or Islamic State mold. "Islam is the enemy of fanaticism," he once said.⁶ But he knew when to play the Muslim card to good effect when it would help his cause.

Abd el-Krim's origins are obscure. He was probably born around 1882 in or near Ajdir in northern Morocco near the Mediterranean Sea. Ajdir would later become the capital of his new-found republic. He was a member of the Beni Urriaguel tribe, the largest and fiercest tribe of the Rif. His father was a man of influence who made sure his sons got a good education. The very name of his family, Khattabi, means "eloquence." Abd el-Krim's father collaborated with the Spanish, which enabled his eldest son to attend a Spanish school in Melilla, and then a prestigious university in Fez. His younger brother, Mhamed, perhaps the more brilliant of the two, studied engineering in Madrid for three years. Abd el-Krim's family benefited from the sale of mining rights in the Rif, using the money to finance revolt.

It was not unusual for colonized people to cooperate with their European masters and then use their education and knowledge of Western ways to gain independence. Gandhi, Nehru, and Ho Chi Minh come to mind. In his early twenties Abd el-Krim became a teacher in Melilla and took a job with an Arab language edition of *El Telegram del Rif*, where he rose to become an editor. He also worked as a civil servant in the Bureau of Native Affairs, becoming an assessor working on legal matters concerning title deeds for iron deposits in the Rif. Mining rights in the Rif for copper, silver, iron, and lead were coveted by foreign mining companies, and the possibilities of mineral riches encouraged Abd el-Krim in his dreams of statehood.

Like his father, Abd el-Krim became a *caid*, a leader, and like his father, he collaborated to a certain degree with the Spanish. He hoped they could help modernize the Riffian people without trying to dominate them. But during his Melilla period, Abd el-Krim's collaboration with the Spanish began to fray. He developed an abiding hatred of the Spanish, as he observed firsthand the corrupt manner in which they exploited their protectorate. That, and the increasingly brutal attempt at pacification, turned Abd el-Krim against the colonial regime.

One of the hallmarks of European colonialism was the contempt of rulers for the ruled. The abiding myth of Spanish nationhood was the reconquest and expulsion of the Moors, and many Spaniards believed that the natives of Morocco were an inferior race, which led them to fatally underestimate the Riffians. Abd el-Krim felt the lash of Spanish contempt even as he benefited personally from Spanish rule. The Europeans will "never consider us as equals," he said, "they will always treat us like dogs."[7] And so, a nationalist was born.

Abd el-Krim began openly criticizing Spain and the Sultan of Morocco, whom he considered little more than a French puppet. He said he would sooner see Germans in Morocco than the French. Although Spain stayed neutral, this was a dangerous thing to say while the Great War was raging in Europe. Abd el-Krim also opined that the Spanish writ should not run beyond their *presidios* of Ceuta and Melilla. More provocatively, he wanted the Spanish to sign a treaty creating an independent state in the Rif. This was enough for the Spanish to imprison him in 1917. He escaped, breaking his leg, and was immediately recaptured only to serve a longer sentence. He walked with a limp the rest of his life. In 1919 Abd el-Krim slipped out of Melilla never to return.

Early in 1919, as Spanish pacification efforts began reaching out toward the Riffian interior, Abd el-Krim asked his brother to return from Madrid and join him and his father in Ajdir to organize his tribesmen in revolt. Thus began "the only sustained, disciplined, and centrally organized rebellion in the history of the Rif, led by two extraordinary brothers."[8]

In September of 1920, their father died—some say poisoned by someone in the pay of the Spanish or a rival tribe. The brothers continued on, and blessed with organizational skills, forceful personalities, and a new vision for an independent Rif free of foreigners, they raised an army. They weren't interested in dominating all of

Morocco at this stage. Nor were they Islamic visionaries peddling jihad for jihad's sake. Their vision was of an independent, modern state under Islamic law.

After World War I, the Spanish Army started moving out from their coastal enclaves in an effort to pacify the tribal interior. There was constant disorder in the Rif, as well as further west in the Jibala region, where there was always mischief to be expected from Ahmed er Raisuli, the most influential and ruthless Jibala leader of them all. Raisuli was known to send back the severed heads of emissaries in a basket of melons with their eyes burned out. Years before, Raisuli had gained an international reputation when he kidnapped a Greek-American, Ion Perdicaris, and held him for ransom. When President Theodore Roosevelt heard about it he was ready to go to war. His secretary of state, John Hay, sent a telegram to Morocco saying, "This government wants Perdicaris alive or Raisuli dead."[9] When read aloud, it electrified the otherwise dull 1904 Republican convention in Chicago, giving Roosevelt a boost towards re-election. American warships arrived off the Moroccan coast to emphasize the threat. Roosevelt eventually got Perdicaris back alive,[iv] but the Sultan had to pay the ransom. Raisuli's prestige was greatly enhanced in Morocco, as was Roosevelt's in America.[v] Raisuli was a master at playing adversaries off against each other, switching sides whenever it suited him. He inflicted serious damage on the Spanish when he was not on their side. It was inevitable that he would become a bitter rival of Abd el-Krim.

By the summer of 1921, Abd el-Krim had recruited a sizable force, with brother Mhamed serving as commander-in-chief of the army. Feelers were made inviting other Rif tribes to join the revolt. In the

---

iv It turned out that Perdicaris was no longer an American, having renounced his citizenship.

v Many years later Hollywood would romanticize the episode in *The Wind and the Lion* with Sean Connery playing Raisuli, and, changing the gender of his captive, casting Candice Bergen as Perdicaris.

meantime a Spanish force of some 20,000 Spanish and Moroccan *Regulares*—native soldiers in the pay of Spain—was establishing itself in the Rif west of Melilla. The force was led by Cuban-born General Manuel Silvestre, a dashing and compulsive officer with a reputation for recklessness. He had served in Morocco since 1911, and had a personal relationship with the Spanish king, Alfonso XIII, who encouraged his boldness. Silvestre established a string of blockhouses and small forts garrisoned by as few as twelve or as many as eight hundred men in Riffian territory. These forts were often inadequately maintained and built far from water sources, to the undoing of many a Spanish garrison when the war began.

The Spanish army was woefully inadequate. Many, if not most, of its soldiers were illiterate, badly paid, badly equipped, badly fed, and badly led. Officers were often corrupt and lazy. There was one officer for every four soldiers in the Spanish Army of Africa, a higher proportion than most armies in Europe. The High Commissioner, General Dámaso Berenguer, also Cuban-born, wrote to his superiors in Madrid complaining that many of his rifles and machine guns were defective; his artillery lacked shells; and many of his airplanes were grounded needing repairs. His doctors lacked medicine; his soldiers lacked food; and in winter he had only their ponchos, and instead of boots, wore only rope-soled espadrilles that disintegrated in the rain and snow. "This is the sad reality," Berenguer wrote, "which everyone feels and which cannot be missed by anyone who sees this army at close quarters."[10] Meanwhile, General Silvestre was raising havoc by burning Riffian crops, pulling down dwellings, and confiscating cattle without compensation, thus earning the hatred of the Riffians. The resentment was dry tinder for the fire Abd el-Krim was about to light.

Meanwhile in the west, the Spanish had captured the hill town of Chaouen in 1920, a site holy to Muslims where Christians were not allowed to enter. Berenguer was made the Count of Xauen (Spanish for Chaouen). Sebastian Balfour reports that the only people glad to see the Spanish were the town's Jews, descended from the Jews expelled from Spain in 1492. They showed the Spanish soldiers their collection of giant keys, the keys to their houses and synagogues back in Granada four centuries before. They spoke an archaic form of Spanish.

Abd el-Krim's task recruiting and unifying the disparate tribes of the Rif, and later the entire Spanish zone of Morocco, was daunting. No one had done it before, and it took great diplomatic skills to achieve. Traditionally, Moroccan tribesmen went to war, looted their enemy's territories, and then went home. It was Abd el-Krim's task to impose discipline and raise a professional army in which soldiers were paid salaries rather than a share of the loot. After a battle, Abd el-Krim's soldiers stayed together rather than drifting back home. Taxes were collected within the Riffian Republic, which caused some resentment. Occasionally, there were small but serious tribal revolts against Abd el-Krim and the Riffian authorities, but they were quickly put down, often brutally.

Abd el-Krim's goal was to transform tribal society into national unity. Murder, for example, became a crime against the state, punishable by death, rather than just a tribal matter to be settled by feuds or payments of blood money. Most of Abd el-Krim's officers were relatives or member of his tribe whom he could trust. There was also an appeal to religion: "If you are truly Muslims, hear us … If you join us we will be as one. We will defeat the Christians with your help or without it."[11] Success breeds success, and once Abd el-Krim started winning victories, winning the tribesmen over became easier.

Abd el-Krim was drawn to the Salafist movement, which at the time was a reformist movement, going back to Islam's roots. Salafists opposed what many young Muslim nationalists at the time saw as a corrupt, collaborationist, and superstitious Sufi tradition, not unlike how the sixteenth-century European Protestants felt about Catholicism. Today the Salafists are seen in the West as fanatics supporting al-Qaeda and the Islamic State, while the Sufis enjoy a more inclusive reputation. But that was not the case a century ago.

Abd el-Krim saw Salafism as a way to unify the country and break the power of dozens of divisive holy men who held sway over much of Morocco. "I wanted my people to know they had a nation as well as a religion," Abd el-Krim said to an Egyptian interviewer.[12] Abd el-Krim was not above emphasizing his secular, European values to Westerners, while stressing his Islamic values to Muslims. "We no longer live in the Middle Ages, or at the time of the crusaders," he would say to Europeans,[13] downplaying the religious nature of his fight, while calling for jihad to his followers. As a practical matter, Abd el-Krim could not forge a nation in Morocco at that time without an appeal to religion. *Sharia* law (Muslim law) would provide the societal glue that would bind his tribesmen to make it possible to rid the country of foreign rule, he believed.

The war began in the summer of 1921, as the Spanish were moving west out of Melilla to extend pacification deep into the Rif. Abd el-Krim sent a warning not to cross the Amekran River, a warning to which Silvestre replied that Abd el-Krim's "insolence merits new punishment."[14] General Silvestre had made his eagerness for war quite clear: "We need a victory so overwhelming that it will convince the Moors that they cannot afford the price of resistance to Spanish domination."[15] He sent a detachment across the Amekran River to set up an encampment on the hill of Abarran on the other side. On June 1, 1921, Abd el-Krim's tribesmen attacked, overrunning the Spanish outpost and massacring most of the garrison. Disturbing to Silvestre, the Moroccan soldiers in the pay of Spain mutinied and joined the tribesmen in the massacre. The few survivors fled back across the river.

Berenguer played down the Abarran defeat, saying it was a "painful episode, a misfortune of colonial war, but such a thing is a common occurrence in these wars and generally without consequences."[16] While that might have been true in the past, what Berenguer was about to face was something new: an increasingly well-organized resistance not seen before in the Rif. Abd el-Krim used Abarran very effectively as an inspiration to his tribesmen. "O Muslims, we wanted to make peace with the Spanish and with Spain, but Spain does not want it. She only wants to occupy our lands in order to take our property and our women, and make us abandon our religion," he said, hitting four of the hot spots that would motivate his followers. He issued a bold proclamation, saying, "The Spanish have already lost the game. Look at Abarran. There they have left their own dead mutilated and unburied, their souls vaguely wandering, tragically denied the delights of paradise."[17] The Riffians often mutilated the corpses of the Spanish in hideous ways in order to strike terror.

Abd el-Krim's words had a powerful appeal. The victory at Abarran provided a psychological lift that transformed the tribesmen into a far more formidable foe than before. The failure of Spanish intelligence to perceive this was another reason why the Spanish were caught by surprise at what was to follow. Berenguer told Silvestre not to advance further, but Silvestre replied, "I shall drink tea in Abd el-Krim's house whether he wills it or not."[18] Silvestre was under the impression that he had the king's blessing, and that trumped any orders from his superiors. So he pressed forward just a little bit more and began constructing a fort on the hill of Iqueriben, about three miles south of a larger Spanish garrison in a grassy, almost treeless valley called Anual[vi]—a name in military history that would soon rank with the Little Big Horn, with Silvestre about to play the role of George Armstrong Custer.

On July 17, 1921, Abd el-Krim's tribesmen emerged from rocks and ravines and attacked the Spanish along their entire line of fortifications. Twelve years of steadily advancing pacification efforts by the Spanish were about to come to an abrupt and violent halt. Heliograph messages, a system of reflecting mirrors used for communications, flashed the news to Melilla. The orders came back to hold fast at Iqueriben. When the Spanish position became desperate,

---

vi   Anual is pronounced Anwal.

Silvestre finally gave permission to surrender, but the garrison refused. Mustering the theatricality and heroism so close to the Spanish heart, the defenders replied, "This garrison swears to its general that it will surrender only to death."[19] And that is what they did. The nearest water supply was three miles away at Anual, so the men, in an agony of thirst, drank their own urine and died in a hail of Riffian bullets and the flash of knives. A relief column tried to reach the doomed garrison, but retired with heavy losses.

On July 21, the larger garrison of Anual, covering three slopes of the valley, came under violent attack. Silvestre and his staff, taken completely by surprise despite the fall of Iqueriben, rushed in from Melilla to try to halt the cascading disaster. The countryside was up in arms, and with ammunition running low and the garrison surrounded, Silvestre sent a final message saying that he was attempting a breakout and would retreat to nearby Ben Tieb. He never made it. An organized retreat under fire is a difficult maneuver in the best of circumstances, and at Anual the Spanish army simply broke and ran. The retreat became a rout, as more and more tribesmen poured down from the hills to join in the great killing.

For the next eighteen days, hundreds of Spaniards were shot down like running hares from hidden ambushes by Riffian marksmen. Anual was overrun and General Silvestre disappeared under a mass of tribesmen. His body was never found. Some say he committed suicide in shame of the debacle, but this is unlikely. It was more in Silvestre's character to go down, as had Custer, in a last stand, his body most likely hacked to pieces.

However, Abd el-Krim himself believed otherwise. More than thirty years later he described the attempted breakout's end to historian William Polk:

> Quietly we lay in ambush; then, as someone in your war of independence said, when we saw 'the whites of their eyes,' we were upon them. In a few hours, those who could had fled, four thousand were captives—we had hardly enough men to guard

them—and ten thousand lay dead before us.[vii] The proud Spanish general ... committed suicide. A week later we were able to take the offensive."[20]

As panic spread, some officers abandoned their men, commandeering cars and trucks to speed away. Historian Sebastian Balfour described the disaster:

> Eyewitnesses reported Dantesque scenes during the flight. Soldiers fought among each other to get horses and mules to carry them away. More officers tore off all insignia and clothing that could identify their rank. Ambulances and lorries were so full that they broke down or their axles snapped ... That day, two Spanish fighter planes flew over the area and reported seeing a trail of bodies, artillery pieces and abandoned lorries ...[21]

Spanish garrisons began to fall all the way back to the gates of Melilla. Civilians living and working in those posts fled; some were killed and mutilated, as were Spanish soldiers. There was no holding the tribesmen back now. The slaughter went on and on.

In some places the native troops, the *Regulares* in the Spanish army, cut the throats of their officers and joined the rebels, as they had done at Abarran. The British and French tended to deploy native troops from regions and countries other than from where they were asked to fight, but Spanish Morocco was too small for that. A train full of fleeing passengers trying to reach Melilla was derailed and the passengers slaughtered. On August 9th, the last fort outside of Melilla, Monte Arruit, fell to Abd el-Krim's forces. There had been no medical supplies, and 167 people within had already died in the intense heat of the Moroccan summer. No reinforcements ever came to their rescue. When the 3,000-man garrison under the command of General Philipe Navarro surrendered and marched out of the fort, most of them were set upon and killed. Abd el-Krim had not

---

vii A more accurate figure might be 9,000 Spanish dead left on the battlefield of Anual.

yet achieved the discipline his troops would later acquire. Navarro and his top officers were taken into captivity, because they might bring handsome ransoms.

Abd el-Krim's forces reached the outskirts of Melilla itself, and the city was at his mercy. But he withdrew. Some say he missed a golden opportunity. Had he taken Melilla, the Spanish might have had to sue for peace. Abd el-Krim maintained that he held off sacking Melilla because he feared international repercussions. His biographer, David Woolman, concludes that after what had already occurred, it would not have made that much difference internationally. "His failure to take Melilla was one of Abd el-Krim's very few major errors," Woolman writes.[22] But another explanation is that Abd el-Krim knew his rebels would never be effective occupying a city and holding it. That is not how guerrillas fought and won, at least not in the early stages. Also, a number of his tribesmen had already gone home with the loot they had acquired from the positions they had overrun. Had Abd el-Krim taken Melilla, his yet to be disciplined tribesmen would have slaughtered and plundered a European city—then, as now, Melilla was part of metropolitan Spain—causing a sensation in the international press. Abd el-Krim wanted international recognition, not universal condemnation. So his tribesmen simply slipped away back into the hills. What had once been the well-fortified "Silvestre Line" had been reduced to burned-out forts and blockhouses, and the mutilated bodies of Spanish soldiers lying inside and out on the hillside, many of them without eyes or genitals.

The Spanish tried to hide the extent of the unprecedented disaster from the Spanish public. Indeed, there was never an exact count of the dead and wounded. The Spanish did not even know exactly how many men they had in the field. Some say as many as 19,000 casualties were inflicted on the Spanish at Anual and its aftermath. Estimates vary, but the final report to the Spanish parliament put the figure at 13,000 dead and wounded. No one ever tried to tally the Riffian dead, but it is unlikely that the attacking force at Anual was more than 3,000. The mutilated Spanish dead caused both horror and burning thirst for revenge among the Spanish. Hideous atrocities committed by both sides became the norm.

In terms of the sheer number of Spanish soldiers left dead on the field at Anual, it would be hard to find a colonial disaster of greater magnitude in the history of European colonialism. The thousands of rifles, cannons, and cases of ammunition captured by the Riffians at Anual would keep Abd el-Krim supplied for many a month. In the official investigation of the Anual disaster, it was revealed that Spanish soldiers had been bartering their guns and bullets in the market place for food. Acts of cowardice and corruption were exposed. When military stores were opened, some were found to be empty, their contents sold on the black market. The report hit an already agonized Spain hard.

The repercussions of the Anual disaster would roil Spanish politics for years. A member of the Congress of Deputies rose to say, "We are at the most acute period of Spanish decadence. The campaign in Africa is a total, absolute failure of the Spanish Army ..."[23] King Alfonso XIII came under increasing criticism. Silvestre was known to have been one of his favorites. And a resentful military claimed they had not been given a free hand to get the job done. The Spanish doves, called *Abandonistas,* argued strenuously that Spain should cut its losses in Morocco and withdraw. It was an unprecedented hour of shame for Spain. Having lost its empire to an industrial giant such as the United States was one thing, but to be so defeated by a bunch of rag-tag Berber tribesmen? As Spain would discover in the following decade, a beaten and humiliated army can become a dangerous thing. The Spanish hawks, the *Africanistas,* argued for more force to quell the rebellion. The Spanish would continue to underestimate Abd el-Krim, and war in the Rif would last longer than World War I.

Spanish blockhouses were often poorly constructed by piling sandbags behind wooden walls with firing loops and a corrugated iron roof on top—one barrel for water and another for a toilet. Often soldiers wore summer uniforms through the cold of a northern Morocco winter, because winter uniforms were either not provided or the money to pay for them was embezzled by corrupt officers. One Spanish officer observed that many officers in the Army of Africa "spent their time whoring and gambling ... while the half-starved youths of Spain in shoddy, torn clothes wandered miserably through the Rif hills, not knowing where they were going or even why they were engaged in this fantastic adventure. Their one desire was to return to Spain and their homes."[24] Seldom had a tribal revolt inflicted such damage on an industrial country. And it was not just the army. All the pacification efforts, schools, modern agriculture, medical facilities—what there had been of Spanish soft power—had been swept away in less than two weeks by what had been considered backward tribesmen. General Berenguer came to Melilla saying, "All is lost, including honor."[25]

Heavily reinforced from mainland Spain, the Spanish Army regrouped in Melilla and moved back into the Rif again. Harassed by snipers everywhere, they did not reach Monte Arruit until November. There, they found unburied Spanish corpses littered about outside the abandoned fort as well as in the surrounding hills. Further west in the Jibala, the Rif disaster caused the Spanish army to abandon their attempt to capture or kill Raisuli. Every soldier was needed in the campaign in the Rif.

After Anual, however, the revolt began to spread beyond the Rif to other tribes across northern Morocco. Abd el-Krim's reputation soared. His role as a leader required diplomatic and political skills, and Abd el-Krim rose to the challenge. He had to keep disparate and formerly warring tribes united through constant negotiations. "Tribes whose animosity was a byword, whose hatred was proverbial, made peace [with each other] in order to obey, and to obey blindly, the first Riffian who has ever been able to unite them ..." wrote the correspondent of the *Times*.[26]

The Spanish brought armored cars and airplanes along with reinforcement from the mainland, but the Riffians learned to wait in ambush until the armored cars were right on top of them. Then they surrounded the vehicles, pouring gunfire into their gun ports. They poured gasoline in, too, setting the vehicles on fire, killing all within. The tribesmen, armed only with rifles and a few machine guns, became uncannily adept at shooting down low-flying airplanes.

There were exceptions to the rot infesting the Spanish Army in Morocco. In 1920 the Spanish formed their own foreign legion, copying the famed French Foreign Legion. The hope was that desperate men and outcasts from abroad might take some of the pressure of combat off the shoulders of the Spanish recruits. With fewer conscripts dying, there would be fewer political repercussions back home in Spain. They were called the *Tercio,* named after a military formation of the sixteenth century. The Spanish Foreign Legion was destined to do most of the fighting and dying, alongside the native *Regulares,* while the Spanish army inhabited blockhouses performing rear-guard duties. Their leader, a veteran from fighting natives in the Philippines, was Major José Millán Astray y Terreros. He would eventually leave in the Rif an arm, a leg, and most of the fingers of his remaining hand. Foreign nationals volunteered for service along with criminals and adventurers. There were Portuguese, Cubans, Germans, English, a black man from America, a Russian prince, a few Chinese, and a Japanese. In contrast to the French Foreign legion, more than eighty percent of the *Tercio* was recruited from Spain. Their pay was better than the army and the morale was higher. Recruits were told when they enlisted that they had "come to die, yes to die!"[27] Their battle cry was "Long Live Death!"[28] The Legionnaires were expendable.

A rising star in the Spanish Army, who had made his reputation leading *Regulares,* was an infantryman named Francisco Franco. He was commissioned at seventeen, and had come to Morocco in 1912 when he was only nineteen. He soon demonstrated his valor, and became a leading member of the *Africanistas* hawks. After the disaster at Anual, the Spanish colonial army began to reform itself. Along with the army's growing competence and efficiency came a thirst for vengeance against Abd el-Krim and the people of the Rif, as well as the politicians back home, whom the army thought had not given them sufficient support. This was to have serious repercussions for Spain in the following decade.

Fighting was sporadic during 1922, but Abd el-Krim's men sank a Spanish warship out in the Mediterranean using a captured cannon. As Abd el-Krim's star rose, more and more tribes across northern Morocco were drawn to his cause. In the Jibala, the Spanish managed to overrun Raisuli's stronghold, but Raisuli escaped into the mountains. The Spanish decided to negotiate with Raisuli, and sent out peace feelers to Abd el-Krim hoping to gain the release of Spanish prisoners. Whereas the opportunist Raisuli was willing to switch his support to Spain, Abd el-Krim held firm. In November the Spanish began advancing from the plain into the hill country of the Rif, but were turned back at Tizi Azza by Riffians firing from behind every boulder as the Spanish tried to force the passes into the mountains. After losing 2,000 men, the Spanish were forced to retire.

Then the Spanish began a blockade of the Rif in order to starve the rebels out. Spanish warships patrolled the Mediterranean coast to prevent supplies reaching the Rif by sea. But whenever the ships came too close to shore, they could count on artillery fire from the tribesmen using captured Spanish guns cleverly hidden in caves in the cliffs above the rocky coast. In December 1921, the Spanish sent the Red Cross into the Rif in another attempt to obtain the release of prisoners. Abd el-Krim demanded a sizable ransom and reparations for the damage done to the Rif. He also insisted that all his tribesmen held prisoner by the Spanish be immediately released and repatriated. The Spanish found these conditions unacceptable and refused. Meanwhile, Abd el-Krim sent messages to the nations of the world asking for international recognition of his Rif Republic. None obliged. He was learning the hard way that Wilson's ideals were but hollow words. Other colonized nations, however, drew inspiration from Abd el-Krim's struggle, and much of the world press portrayed him as a romantic hero fighting for independence. But despite their interest in mining rights, none of the nations of the world would help him.

Back in Spain, public pressure for a prisoner release escalated, forcing the Spanish to reconsider their refusal to pay ransoms. Four million pesetas were then paid to Abd el-Krim, infuriating the *Africanistas*, but the prisoners were released early in 1923. Most of them were in bad shape, bearing the marks of chains they had worn during captivity. Of the 570 Spanish taken prisoner, only 327 remained alive: one general, forty-four officers, 239 soldiers, and forty-three civilians, thirty-three of whom were women and children. Most of those who died had contracted typhus, which the Riffians were unable to prevent. Many of the guards had died of typhus as well, and the European prisoners were not used to the hardships of Riffian life. A Tangier newspaper reporting on the prisoner release quoted the former captives as saying they had been treated with "compassion" by Abd el-Krim's brother, but when he was away their condition became "almost unbearable." Upon reaching the steamship that was to take them from Alhucemas Bay to Melilla, one of the just released prisoners, Diego Esteves Muñoz, "saluted the [Spanish] flag and fell dead ... On arrival in Melilla over one hundred men and several of the officers had to be conveyed to the hospital," the paper reported, "several of them suffering from tuberculosis [suffered] at the hands of cruel and ferocious guardians."[29] In Spain the debate between hawks and doves, *Africanistas* and *Abandonistas*, raged on. Soldiers refusing to board Morocco-bound troop ships added to the unpopularity of the Rif War. Governments fell and were reconstituted, and the Army of Africa's bitterness against these governments grew. Franco was promoted to lieutenant colonel for his gallantry, and was appointed leader of the foreign legion, replacing the shattered Millán Astray.

Early in 1923, at the height of his power and prestige, Abd el-Krim formally declared the Republic of the Rif's independence from Spain. He gave himself the title of Emir. King Alfonso XIII made the mistake of asking the Vatican to declare a crusade against the Muslims of the Rif.

Abd el-Krim had the king's words translated and communicated throughout the Rif, thus reinforcing the idea that the Spanish were against Islam, not just Riffian independence. In June Abd el-Krim sent peace feelers to Melilla proposing a temporary truce. He hoped that after so many defeats, the Spanish would be willing to abandon the Rif and recognize the new state. The Spanish were willing to discuss it, and so delegates from both sides met offshore on a Spanish warship. Proposals were exchanged. The Spanish offered commercial, agricultural, and industrial development, which they said would be in Morocco's interest as well as Spain's. In addition, the Spanish offered a measure of autonomy, recognizing Abd el-Krim as the leader of the Rif, but not full independence. Then came the threat, "If you continue in error, Spain will adopt every means to put down this rebellion in a way that is lesser choice than her duty to the civilized powers that entrust her with this mission."[30] Protecting civilization, and granting it sparingly to barbarians, was very much the mindset of colonialists in the early twentieth century.

The Rif's foreign minister, Mohammed Azerkan, replied with dignity that belied Spanish assumptions about Riffians being savages. "Your letter resembles a final ultimatum, and as such its contents have caused much surprise. As minister of foreign affairs to the Riffian government, I feel bound to inform you that our terms are as follows," he wrote. The Riffian government, "established upon modern ideas and on the principles of civilization ... considers itself independent politically and economically—privileged to enjoy our freedom as we have enjoyed it for centuries and to live as other people live." He said the Rif had never recognized the Spanish protectorate. With a nod to Woodrow Wilson and his ideals of self-determination for even the smallest nation, he went on to write that the Great War "has taught mankind the penalty of ill-doing, of violation and of pride, and by it the world has learned that no man is to be despised."[31]

Azerkan maintained that it was in Spain's interest to recognize and cooperate with the new Republic of the Rif rather than "humiliating and attacking its legitimate human rights," All of this, he said, would be, in accordance with the code of civilization and the Treaty of Versailles.

> Yet politicians have said that treaties are only ink upon paper, and that power rests with the sword. But truth is truth; otherwise the world would remain always in trouble and perplexity. Peace will not come until every nation in the world is at liberty to defend it rights. It would be no disgrace to Spain if she were to live in peace with the Riffians after recognizing our government and its independence, and thus increasing the common interest of our two countries. On the contrary it would be a noble action and an honor to her ... The Riffian government will be truly sorry if the Colonial Party persists in its transgressions and in its tyranny ... Know that the Rif and all its people are ready to die, and believe me we will die in the cause of truth ... I must declare once and for all that the Rif will not change its attitudes, nor give up the principles upon which we act, that is to say, we will not reopen negotiations for peace except upon the conditions of the recognition by Spain of the independence of the Rif.[32]

In Wilsonian language, Azerkan laid out the principles of freedom and self-determination that Wilson had professed, but never delivered beyond the confines of Europe—and not in all cases even there. But the Spanish were not about to accept the Riffian's terms, and that was the end of Abd el-Krim's peace overture.

Spanish discontent with the Rif War boiled over again in August 1923, when Spanish troops embarking for Morocco mutinied in Malaga. One officer was killed and three were injured in incidents resembling the "fragging" of American officers in Vietnam during the demoralized final years of that war, when morale hit its nadir. In Barcelona, which then as now was demonstrating for Catalan independence, there were cheers for Morocco and jeers for Spain. That month a small group of tribesmen in Tetuan, the capital of Spanish Morocco, opened fire on the crowded main street with weapons they had concealed under their *djellabas,* the loose flowing robes of the countryside. Eight people were killed and twenty wounded. The attackers got clean away. It was borne home that the tribesmen could strike at any time, anywhere in a place of their choosing. These terrorist incidents had a demoralizing effect on Spanish morale. The Rif War was having as dispiriting an effect on the Spanish as Vietnam was to have on the U.S. so many years later.

War in the Rif cost the Spanish government the support of its people. A popular general, Miguel Primo de Rivera, staged a bloodless coup. He had been in the military since the age of fourteen, and had been severely wounded in Morocco in a previous campaign, where he served with heroism. He had also fought for Spain in Cuba and the Philippines. Known as a dove when it came to the war in the Rif, he criticized Spain's conduct in Morocco as "the most expensive, the most protracted, the most useless and the most unworthy" of wars.[33]

The *Abandonistas* took heart. The Spanish press was calling Morocco the graveyard of Spanish youth, a bottomless pit into which Spain's wealth drained. But Spanish nationalists also took heart hoping Primo de Rivera could end the independence movement in Catalonia. He promised to do so, and treated the Catalan separatists with severity while promising autonomy sometime in the future. He also promised to extricate Spain from Morocco, seeking a peace with honor. The Spanish had grown sick of the parliamentary system with its interminable squabbles, and were relieved when the king offered Primo de Rivera full control of the government. Thus did the Rif War end democracy and bring dictatorship to Spain.

Primo de Rivera was an aristocrat as well as a general, the second Marquis of Estella. He was amiable and honest, and he promised a "quick, dignified solution" to the war.[34] In November 1923, he went to Morocco to personally take charge of the war. But by the following summer, he had decided that his troops were too scattered and vulnerable, so he decided to abandon the tribal interior and draw back to more defensible lines closer to the coast. That decision was very unpopular with the *Africanistas,* but it played well with the *Abandonistas.*

In an interview with the American war correspondent Webb Miller working for United Press, Primo de Rivera confessed that "Abd el-Krim has defeated us. He has immense advantages of terrain and a fanatical following. Our troops are sick of war, and they have been for years. They don't see why they should fight and die for a strip of useless territory. I am withdrawing to this line," he said, marking his defensive positions on a map. "I will hold only the tip of this territory," he said. "I personally am in favor of withdrawing entirely from Africa and letting Abd el-Krim have it. We have spent untold millions of pesetas in this enterprise and never made a centime from it. We had had tens of thousands of men killed for territory that is not worth having."[35] But he acknowledged that Spain could not withdraw entirely from northern Morocco.

The reaction from the *Africanistas* came fast and furious. General Franco made an impassioned speech saying Spain should never withdraw from territory that had taken so many Spanish lives to hold. Primo de Rivera could not afford to alienate the army too much, especially not Franco's foreign legion, so he compromised. He would withdraw to more secure lines in the Jibala, but not pull back from the territory the army held near Melilla in the Rif.

One of the Jibala towns to be abandoned was the dangerously exposed mountain town of Chaouen, now called Chefchaouen, which the Spanish had captured only four years before. It was a place held holy by Muslims, a town where Christians had been forbidden to enter. A strategic withdrawal began with troops ordered to fall back towards the coast to fortified positions on what came to be known as the "Primo Line." Once completed, the plan was for the Spanish army to regroup, retrain, and wait until they were ready to move out again to renew the pacification efforts that had so far failed. The fact that this withdrawal plan was made public horrified the French in French Morocco to the south. Marshal Hubert Lyautey's reaction was, "My God, an army retreats when it must, but it does not announce the fact to an enemy in advance."[36] Primo de Rivera planned to hold out olive branches to Raisuli and Abd el-Krim, and if that failed, to co-opt Raisuli against Abd el-Krim. He failed with Abd el-Krim, but not with the ever-ready turncoat Raisuli. Thus began the bitter rivalry between Abd el-Krim of the Rif and Raisuli of the Jibala. At this time, however, Raisuli was swollen with "dropsy," which we now call edema, and kidney failure. He had to be carried from place to place on a litter.

The Spanish withdrawal from Chaouen to more secure lines began in the pouring rain in September 1924, with the Spanish army taking most of the town's Jews and Muslim collaborators with them. As Vincent Sheean, the American journalist who visited the town after the Spanish retreat, explained, the Jews conducted all of the town's commerce and held most of the town's wealth. The Spanish thought "this wealth was better off on the Spanish side rather than in the hands of the Riffi."[37] As expected the retreat proved to be difficult, but Primo de Rivera did not anticipate the disaster it became. The Jibala tribesmen were beginning to come over to the Riffian cause and away from the increasingly isolated Raisuli. Constant ambushes slowed the retreat, and soldiers were sniped at all along the way. Many Spaniards feared another Anual was in the making and Primo de Rivera felt it necessary to deplore the army's pessimism. "It's regrettable that the troops should give way at this moment to pessimism, which is destroying the morale of the army."[38] Court-martials, even executions, were threatened. Franco, always the rock-hard *Africanista,* was ready to have the dictator and his staff arrested, but he backed down. Although King Alfonso supported the Primo de Rivera coup, his heart remained with the *Africanistas.* "I cannot hide the fact that the desires of my colonial troops coincide with my own," he said.[39]

Abd el-Krim had installed a surprisingly modern telephone system, with telephone poles and wires strung out over mountains and valleys. This enabled him to communicate with his forces in the Jibala far from his home base in Ajdir. When Spanish bombers took off from Melilla to bomb further west, Abd el-Krim's men could warn his forces by telephone that the bombers were on the way. Thus Abd el-Krim could keep in close touch with his men while the Spanish were evacuating Chaouen. Seven thousand Riffians and Jibalis converged on the road to Tetuan to harass the Spanish retreat. The Spanish had to fight for every inch, under constant attack as they dragged their cannons and equipment through the rain and mud. They were under fire all the way from an enemy they seldom saw, so effective were the Riffians and Jibalis at concealment in the rocky terrain. "We made war against shadows, and we lost thirty men to their one," said a Spanish survivor.[40]

Spectator magazine described the hazards. The road in and out of the town "plunges for thirty miles into the mountains at right angles ... [the] fact that the Spaniards have light tanks and some hundreds of aeroplanes and are able to protect their lorries with bullet-proof armor, by no means compensates for the length and riskiness of the road ... The Riffi as fighting men are very much like the Boers (of South Africa). They know every inch of their country and are experts at invisible warfare."[41] One Spanish armored car was disabled during the retreat, but the fourteen soldiers inside held out without food and water for three days. When the last four left alive finally surrendered, the Riffians stood at attention in admiration of their bravery and took them prisoner. But on the whole, few prisoners were taken. It was a no-quarter war. Whenever the weather cleared, Spanish bombers came to the aid of the battered columns, but they were not much help. The Riffians harried the Spanish all long their route with constant ambushes and sniping from concealment.

The surprising mobility of the Riffians won the day. Each man carried his own food and ammunition, and unlike the Spanish, they were moving fast on foot, free from dependence on roads, cars and trucks. The exhausted Spanish took almost a month to make the forty-mile retreat to Tetuan. The army never revealed its losses, but the *Times* correspondent, Walter Harris, put the figure at

17,000 dead and wounded. Primo de Rivera said that "a new trail of Spanish blood" marks the "track of civilization," [42] and he promised the army its revenge. Bringing civilization to benighted savages, *objeto civilizadora*, to the Spanish, *civilisatrice* to the French, was the omnipresent justification for colonizers of that era. As Sebastian Balfour would comment, bringing civilization became the "rationalization for uncivilized behavior"[43] in Morocco.

Abd el-Krim's brother Mhamed entered Chaouen with his army on November 17. For the Rif it was a considerable victory even though the Spanish had abandoned the town without a fight. Liberating Chaouen from Spanish control was a major blow to Spanish power in the eyes of the Riffians because of its religious significance. It boosted morale among the Jibala tribesmen who might have been wary of the brothers. When the rebels entered the town, Mhamed was wise enough to remove his shoes and walked barefoot with his head bowed as a gesture to Muslim sensibilities. The Spanish had left their hospital intact, and a Danish doctor from Tangier volunteered to run it for the Riffians.

The Spanish had suffered yet another military disaster comparable to Anual. Vincent Sheean visited the area after the Spanish retreat and wrote, "Here the bodies lay sometimes five and six deep, blackened and half devoured, or sometimes isolated and picked clean, with bones whitening in the brilliant African sunlight."[44] By now most of the tribes of northern Morocco were coming over to Abd el-Krim's cause. The Rif rebellion was reaching its full tide as 1924 turned 1925. The Riffians had never been beaten and were able to hold the ground they chose to hold. The initiative was theirs. The brothers had reason to hope that the *Abandonistas* would soon prevail in the Spanish debate about the war. They believed that independence and international recognition would soon follow.

Delegates from the Rif visited western countries to promote the Riffian cause. Abd el-Krim himself remained remote, a godlike figure to his people. He was a man of mystery, seldom seen. Fear of assassination was always present in the Rif. Yet, unlike Raisuli, there was nothing of the oriental despot in Abd el-Krim. He lived and spoke modestly. His brother, Mhamed, was a very popular head of the army, and one of the best educated men in the Rif. The brothers were in full control.

Many of their relatives and fellow members of the Beni Urriaguel tribe ran the government. They were the best fighters, but inevitably resentments set in.

The tribes of northern Morocco had never before fought under one banner, and keeping coalitions together was never easy. Examples were made of dissenters, some of them being blinded or burned alive. As the war dragged on, brutality increased. Mostly farmers, Abd el-Krim's soldiers were rotated in and out of the army so as to tend their crops. Foreigners in the Rif army were rare: a couple of Scandinavian doctors, a Serbian artilleryman, a German telephone technician, a sprinkling of deserters from the French and Spanish foreign legions.

The most remarkable was Joseph Klems, who had been a German intelligence officer in Morocco before World War I. He fell out with his German masters and joined the French Foreign Legion. When the French discovered he was embezzling funds he deserted and became a Muslim, marrying more than one Berber girl, and joining Abd el-Krim in 1924. Abd el-Krim called Klems "my grand artillerist."[45] Klems was known for leaving a card with the words *Hadj Aleman* (German holy pilgrim) pinned to the corpses of the men he killed. Vincent Sheean met Klems in the Jibala, and found him to be a stereotypical German, "kind heart, sentimental, romantic, but capable of unlimited ferocity in organized combat."[46]

Klems managed to buy three airplanes from French Algeria, and there was wild talk among the Riffians about bombing Melilla and maybe even Spain itself. But no Riffian plane ever flew. It was rumored that Abd el-Krim had a Swiss mechanic executed for not putting the planes in service. Klems also obtained three cars for Abd el-Krim: a Ford, a Renault, and a Turcat-Méry. The Riffians mastered the art of making grenades from unexploded Spanish bombs, of which there were many. They also had several hundred machine guns and artillery pieces captured from the Spanish as well as ammunition. Many in the Riffian army were deserters from the Spanish *Regulares* and were well-trained soldiers. Klems and his handful of Germans set the tone for Riffian army drills, right down to German-style goose stepping on parade. But the *hakas*, as the Riffian military units were called, did not fight as European armies fought. They fought as guerrillas, the way they had always fought, and were much the more effective for it.

Abd el-Krim was a master at keeping the Spanish guessing. He led them to believe that he might be receptive to a peace overture, but the only deal he was ready to make was complete independence for the Rif and a Spanish withdrawal from their protectorate. By 1923 the French had become sufficiently worried about Spanish Morocco that they began sounding out Abd el-Krim about his intentions. The French were contemptuous of the Spanish army and its defeats at the hands of Abd el-Krim. The Spanish, having pulled back from the interior, now regrouped behind the "Primo Line," a line of forts and blockhouses, each a quarter of a mile apart with mine fields and powerful search lights. The Spanish Navy was tasked with blockading the coast.

In his capital of Ajdir, Abd el-Krim had many foreign newspapers brought to him so that he could keep up with international affairs. He remained adamant that his cause was Riffian nationalism and self-determination, not a pan-Islamic movement. He wanted to establish that North Africans were fully capable of governing themselves. His only enemy, he maintained, was Spain, but if Spain would leave Morocco there would be peace. Abd el-Krim would allow Spain to keep their *presidios*, Ceuta and Melilla, but not the rest of their protectorate. Although he despised colonialism, Abd el-Krim was not anti-European. He believed that Europe provided the best example of how to organize a government. All the while, Abd el-Krim's representatives abroad kept trying to promote the cause of independence for the Rif along the lines of Woodrow Wilson's ideals and self-determination. In 1924 Abd el-Krim wrote to British Prime Minister Ramsay MacDonald, saying "The future of our country is unlimited. We have confidence in our industrial capacity and in our ability to distinguish ourselves in peace as well as war, and we ask the outside world, in the name of justice, to give us that opportunity ..."[47] But Great Britain was not about to back a native rebellion against a colonial power. The British were experiencing enough problems in their own troubled colonies.

There were, however, Riffian sympathizers in England. Robert Gordon-Canning headed a Rif Committee in solidarity with the Republic of the Rif. The committee had support from German mining interests that had an eye on the mining riches of the Rif. Another was A.P. "Percy" Gardiner, a gun-runner who smuggled arms into the Rif, and who set himself up in London as Agent General for the Rif Government and later as Minister Plenipotentiary for the Government of the Rif. He signed a contract with the Rif which would have allowed him to set up a state bank, arrange commercial concessions with foreign government, build schools, railroads, even an opera house in the Rif should the Rif gain its independence. He was paid to have Riffian bank notes printed in London for the State Bank of the Rif, one riffan to be equal to ten English pennies. Gardiner tried to obtain international recognition for the Rif, urging the British government and others to set up a consular service in Ajdir. He was rebuffed. His relationship with the Rif ended badly, with the Riffians suing Gardiner for breach of contract in 1924.

Sheean was one of the few foreign correspondents to interview Abd el-Krim. The meeting took place a few miles south of Ajdir in a gentle valley, half hidden from Spanish airplanes, called Ait Kamara. The site of the interview was Abd el-Krim's country house at the end of a road built by Spanish prisoners of war, a road traversed by Abd el-Krim in one of his three automobiles. It was January 1925, at a time when Abd el-Krim had never been beaten in the field and was at the height of his power. "For the first time in recorded history, all, or virtually all, of northern Morocco was ruled by one government, one man," Sheean observed.⁴⁸ Abd el-Krim's rival in the Jibala, Raisuli, would soon be captured by Abd el-Krim's forces later that same month, consolidating Abd el-Krim's power. Raisuli died three months later, old and swollen in captivity. He outlived Theodore Roosevelt by six years.

By the time Sheean met him, Abd el-Krim had declared himself Emir. "He had been democratic, genial and friendly throughout the first years of his successful war against Spain," Sheean wrote, but "lately since an attempt to assassinate him ... he had lived in the greatest possible seclusion so that even at Ajdir, I was told, nobody had caught a glimpse of him for months."⁴⁹ Now that Ajdir was subjected to air raids, Abd el-Krim was spending most of his time in Ait Kamara. The village was where Spanish prisoners of war were held, and on his journey there Sheehan reported seeing prisoners working lazily on the roads while Riffian guards "watched them leaning on their rifles."⁵⁰

Sheean was ushered into a bare room with a table and three chairs, the first chairs he had seen in the Rif where most people sat on the floor. The man whom Sheean had risked his life to interview, Abd el-Krim, was sitting behind a table covered with papers. He looked at Sheean "with a slow, appraising glance, [his] brown eyes set penetratingly at last upon the Christian visitor." He was short, dark, and "inclined to stoutness."⁵¹ Abd el-Krim was dressed in a simple homespun *djellaba* and "spotless white linen. He extended his hand; I touched it with mine and raised my fingers to my lips, Riffi fashion."⁵²

Abd el-Krim spoke directly without evasion. "All talk about pan-Islamism has the sole object of frightening the French and the English into an attitude of opposition to the Rif government in its struggle with Spain,"⁵³ he said, but he repeated his demand that Spanish troops would have to withdraw to Ceuta and Melilla. "Nothing less than the complete surrender of the protectorate will satisfy us. We demand this in the name of the whole Moroccan nation, as the Spanish Protectorate has brought and brings nothing but misery and desolation on our people. The protectorate protects nothing, not even the Spanish soldier."⁵⁴ Abd el-Krim's ambitions had spread beyond just the Rif at this point in his struggle. He told Sheean that he would consider internationalizing some of the coastal areas, as Tangier had been internationalized, but not under Spanish rule. "Spain is entitled to the *presidios* of Ceuta and Melilla, which are virtually Spanish now after all these centuries, but to nothing else."⁵⁵

"I had plenty of time to study that remarkable face," Sheean would later recall. "Shrewdness I saw, great shrewdness, and a biting intelligence, allied to a certain healthy cautiousness ... no barbarian and no fool. But neither, I felt, was he a genius, a genius of the pure tradition; he was not the flame-like and prophet-like creature one might have expected. He was a superior brain attacking a difficult national problem, no more."⁵⁶ Sheean's opinion of him would improve when next they met, when Abd el-Krim was facing defeat.

If peace and independence could be achieved, Abd el-Krim's preference was for an absolute monarchy at first, "demonstrated to be the best for our people." Later it could become a constitutional monarchy "on broader, more liberal lines ..."⁵⁷ but not yet; not for at least a generation. He explained to Sheean that the name Republic of the Rif did not mean a republic in the Western sense. In the Rif, republic meant a group. As for the Sultan of Morocco, Abd el-Krim made it clear that he had no intention of recognizing his authority. The sultan's dominion over Morocco was a fable to which all the powers had agreed to accept in deference to France, but everyone recognized that the sultan was really a prisoner of the French.

As for France, Abd el-Krim said, "Our attitude towards France is friendly in the extreme. We have never desired anything but peaceful relations with France and we have no intention of attacking French Morocco. To me, war with France is inconceivable unless we are attacked."⁵⁸ But Abd el-Krim said a proper delineation of the frontier was necessary, and he suggested that a frontier commission should be established to draw a practical boundary. The border between the French and Spanish zones of influence had been drawn in 1904, he said, and "we do not recognize that treaty and cannot recognize that boundary which passes through the middle of tribes and sometimes the middle of villages. I can guarantee," Abd el-Krim said, "that were a practical and natural frontier established, regulated by rivers and mountains, we should never again have any trouble with France."[59] The colonial frontiers of Africa and Asia seldom took into account tribal territories, and the boundary between French and Spanish Morocco not only divided families and tribes, it cut the Rif off from agricultural areas essential for its survival. The French, of course, were well aware of Abd el-Krim's concerns, as well as the potential danger he represented. They had begun building blockhouses and fortifications along the border, some of them actually on the Spanish side under an agreement with Spain. This encroachment began to trouble Abd el-Krim and his followers.

As Sheean left Abd el-Krim, riding back to Ajdir "through an enchanting spring landscape, over slopes tinted by the bluish rose of the almond tree in flower,"[60] Sheean reflected on the man he had just interviewed, "a shrewd child of the twentieth century, a man keen and capable, world-wise. No genius here, but something better; the capacity to appreciate and direct collective forces,"[61] something new for the Rif and Morocco. What impressed Sheean most was the complete devotion the Riffians had for Abd el-Krim, treating him as if he were a descendant of the Prophet, which he was not.

Later, Sheean met Abd el-Krim's brother Mhamed, commander of the armed forces, whom he found more impressive than the older brother. "From the moment I came into his presence I felt the influence of an extraordinary personality …" Dignified, even noble, "here was at last the Great Man."[62] They spoke in Spanish, which Sheean thought the younger brother spoke better than Primo de Rivera with his Andalusian dialect. Yet, for all the attributes of leadership qualities that Sheean sensed in the younger brother, "he alone could never have aroused and directed the national energies dormant in the Berber tribes …" For it was the elder brother who, in Sheean's view, had the "one essential quality of single-mindedness and vision which inspires the legend ... And without the inspiring legend obviously nothing could be done about making separate and anarchic Berber tribes into an organized nation. The legend was a vital necessity; the elder el-Krim supplied it, but the younger el-Krim supplied the reality to maintain it."[63] In this the brothers were like other revolutionary leaders who would follow in the twentieth century: Fidel Castro and Ho Chi Minh supplied the legend, while Che Guevara, Le Duan, and Vo Nguyen Giap often supplied the reality.

Abd el-Krim and his brother were soon to confront a man of far greater stature and competence than any of their Spanish adversaries: Marshal Hubert Lyautey, Resident-General of French Morocco, perhaps the most capable colonial administrator France had ever produced. Lyautey had convinced his masters in Paris that imposing French systems and customs on Morocco, as they had done in Algeria, was a mistake. Lyautey argued for the British style of colonialism whereby Europeans ruled through traditional leaders, observing their customs, rather than imposing French ways of governing. For this, in Morocco, he needed the sultan if only as a figurehead chief of state. Lyautey went about promoting the prestige of the sultan. While Lyautey could be hard once he had imposed his control over the Moroccan tribes in the French zone, he stressed tact rather than force, persuading many Moroccans that bringing modernity was in their interest. His motto was "govern through the Mandarins, not against them. Do not offend a single tradition; do not change a single habit."[64]

As the British had done in India, Lyautey gained many collaborators among the Moroccan elite. "He tried to preserve what was best in their civilization [while trying to] inculcate a fresh approach and a more modern outlook."[65] Lyautey was able to persuade Moroccan notables that the French could improve their lives rather than just exploiting them as the Spanish did in their zone. As Sheean put it, "France's success, so brilliantly contrasted with the debacle in

Spanish Morocco, is a success of administration and construction ... popular education, good roads, clean streets, telephones, telegraphs, ports, bridges, culverts, and a medical and veterinary service."⁶⁶ Lyautey was wise enough to realize that while the French might never be loved, they would be respected. The carrot would prevail over the stick.

Lyautey believed in the "oil spot" (*tache d'huile*) theory of pacification. You establish a small zone where the population can be protected militarily, then you introduce civil action, economic developments, schools and projects to improve people's lives in order to win them over. In theory these "oil spots" would expand outward, linking up with each other to win over more people and territory. It is a theory that has influenced counter-insurgency efforts ever since. The British used it in Malaya in the 1950s. The Americans tried it in Vietnam, Iraq, and Afghanistan without lasting success. According to historian Max Boot, Lyautey's "most valuable contribution was to stress the need for 'flexibility, elasticity, adaptation to time, place, and circumstance,'" rather than a one-size-fits-all approach to pacification.⁶⁷ By modern standards, Lyautey was condescending and manipulative, employing classic divide-and-rule colonial methods. But for his time he was an enlightened administrator. He took the term "protectorate" seriously, stressing the need to actually protect people and their culture rather than exploiting them. Realizing that French settlers would create problems for his administration, he resisted European migration that the French had encouraged in neighboring Algeria.

Unlike some of his officers who wanted to provoke a war against Abd el-Krim, Lyautey was not eager for war with the Rif. Similarly, Abd el-Krim wanted to avoid a conflict with the French. However, the French viewed Primo de Rivera's retreat with horror. If Abd el-Krim were allowed to establish a successful native state in Spanish Morocco, what would that mean for the future of colonialism? Algeria, Tunisia, even French Indochina, would surely follow in rebellion. It was clear to the French that Abd el-Krim must not be allowed to succeed. In 1924 Lyautey warned the French government that "a Muslim State, arriving out of North African nationalism is establishing itself" next door to French Morocco.[68]

He warned that such a state, "modernized and supported by the most war-like tribes, with a morale exalted by success against Spain," was presenting "the most serious kind of menace."[69] Primo de Rivera agreed, backing away from his earlier *Abandonista* position. He told British journalist Ward Price that "the idea of a small, savage, independent state on the southern shore of the Mediterranean so near Europe is out of the question."[70]

As for Abd el-Krim, he said, "I recognize that the French have given Morocco order, security, and economic prosperity, but I shall bring the same benefits with the further advantage that I am a Muslim, and so it will be from a leader of their own faith, and not from an infidel, that Moroccans shall receive these blessings."[71] He reiterated that he would only fight the French if attacked, but his words were not what the French wanted to hear if colonialism were to continue. Abd el-Krim was not a religious fanatic. He wanted a modern state along the lines of France and Spain, not a medieval theocracy. But he wanted it to be a state in which Sharia law prevailed. He also realized that Islam and jihad against foreigners were his most powerful arguments uniting warring tribes into a nation. The Spanish had encouraged blood feuds and tribal differences as a way to divide and rule. No European colonial power could accept that a colonized people could govern themselves.

So the French continued to construct forts and outposts, pressing into Riffian territory, often with troops from Senegal and Algeria, lest their Moroccans prove unreliable, as had some of the Moroccans in the Spanish army. The forts were a deliberate provocation as they blocked the Riffians from their agricultural lowlands. The French refused Abd el-Krim's request for a border commission. An agreement to do so would have implied recognition of the Riffian state, which the French could not permit. Lyautey may not have wanted war, but he had made it unavoidable. In the meantime, Abd el-Krim was preparing a genealogy that would make him a descendant of the Prophet. His followers were beginning to call him sultan, and the French and Spanish feared that Abd el-Krim was preparing to declare himself sultan over all Morocco.

When the French began moving north into the Rif country across the Wergha River, Abd el-Krim prepared to attack. It was a classic fear-driven situation on both sides. The French moved north because they feared an attack from the Rif, and the Riffians moved south because they feared a French invasion. Abd el-Krim knew the French would be a far more formidable enemy than the Spanish, but the French provocation proved too much, and he overcame his caution. Perhaps his victories over the Spanish had overinflated his confidence. He knew he could not defeat such an adversary. But he may have thought he could wound them enough to leave him and the Rif alone. Abd el-Krim's brother, Mhamed, told Robert Furneaux many years later that Abd el-Krim was honor bound to keep the French south of the Wergha, because the local tribes within his alliance had called for assistance. And under the rules of tribal alliances, to have refused might have jeopardized his other tribal alliances on which he depended. "Our honor was at stake."[72] Whatever his reasoning, it was a fatal miscalculation. As for the French, they had attributed Abd el-Krim's successes to Spanish incompetence, rather than to his acumen. Lyautey could not believe that Abd el-Krim would, or could, mount a successful attack against the French.

On April 12, 1925, the Riffians and their tribal allies struck the French line of fortifications, and to the astonishment of Marshal Lyautey, they broke through. Fortresses that the French had thought impregnable fell as the Riffians poured south. By June forty-three of the sixty-four French outposts had been overrun with most of their defenders massacred. Some local tribes that had been indifferent to Abd el-Krim joined him now that there was French blood being spilled. Before the French could recuperate, the Riffians were advancing on Fez, a former capital, the seat of Muslim learning, and perhaps the most significant city in all Morocco. Lyautey was caught flat-footed. He had been warning of a Riffian attack, but when it came he never believed it could break through his defensive line. By provoking Abd el-Krim, the French had set a trap, and now the mouse had taken the cheese and was about to run off with the trap as well.

There was a moment when Abd el-Krim could have taken Fez, but he hesitated, perhaps because the religious authorities in Fez had refused his request to back him, or perhaps for the same reasons he did not take Melilla in 1921. Trying to take and hold a city, while the French bombed and shelled it as Syrian rebels in Damascus were to do that November, was not playing to a guerrilla army's strength. Then again, not all of the tribes in French Morocco had come over to Abd el-Krim as he had hoped. But in those early days of the incursion, Abd el-Krim had seemed unbeatable, as he had been in Spanish Morocco. As before, the Riffians piled the dead and mutilated corpses of French soldiers in front of those still-defended fortresses to shock and frighten the defenders. The French deployed tanks, artillery, and airpower against the Riffians, but the tribesmen seldom presented massed targets. Superior weaponry was less effective than the French anticipated.

Gradually the French stabilized their position, pushing the Riffians back over the Wergha River, but they realized that subduing Abd el-Krim was going to be much harder than any other uprising they had encountered. The French began making plans with the heretofore despised Spanish military for a combined attack against Abd el-Krim. They met in Madrid to forge a joint strategy. Abd el-Krim was now about to face a two-front war against two European industrial powers. But first, peace feelers were sent to Abd el-Krim to see if there could not be a political solution. The French and the Spanish agreed to give the Rif a certain measure of local autonomy, under the sultan's nominal sovereignty, but not the complete freedom and independence that Abd el-Krim demanded. Abd el-Krim sent a message to the British through the Tangier-based journalist, Walter Harris, saying that he trusted the British and would accept any terms to which they agreed. But again, the British had no intention to become involved. Had Abd el-Krim at that moment compromised with the Spanish and French while he was holding high cards, the history of Morocco might have been very different. But to do so would have diminished the legend that he had established, and the legend was the source of his power and authority. Abd el-Krim, up to that point, had not been defeated in battle. The Spanish had abandoned much of their protectorate to his forces and were huddling behind their defensive lines, and in the summer of 1925 the French were still on their back foot struggling to defend against sneak attacks south of the Wergha. Unlike Raisuli, Abd el-Krim was not a man willing to switch sides.

Although less effective in Morocco than hoped, airpower was proving to be an invaluable weapon in colonial warfare. The Italians had conducted the world's first bombing raid against Libyan tribesmen just before World War I. The British had bombed Kabul in 1919 in the last of their Afghan wars. The French had developed an airplane especially designed for colonial warfare, with a traversing machine gun to mow down tribesmen. The British relied on airpower to control Iraq, where the wide-open landscapes and better weather suited this comparatively new weapon of war. Airplane design leapt forward in the years between the two world wars. For a while there was even an American contingent fighting against Abd el-Krim. In the spring of 1925, just when the French were faltering, an American adventurer, Charles Sweeney, who had once served in the French Foreign Legion, appealed to American pilots to form a new Lafayette Escadrille—the famed American squadron that had flown for France during the Great War. The new outfit was called the *Escadrille de la Garde Chérifienne* (Squadron of the Sherifian Guard) to make it appear they were under the command of the sultan.

The French hoped to score a propaganda coup to counter pro-Riffian sentiments in the United States, but that backfired. Between September and November 1925, the Americans flew 470 bombing missions against the Rif, even bombing the newly recaptured holy city of Chaouen. "It had not been bombarded previously because of its prestige and the sacredness as a holy shrine," one of the Escadrille's pilots, Paul Rockwell, recalled many years later. The air attack was expected to intimidate the Jibalis, "and be effective in detaching them from the cause of Abd el-Krim ..." Rockwell wrote:

> The city looked lovely from the air, hugging its high mountains and surrounded with many gardens and green cultivations ... I looked down upon the numerous sanctuaries, the six mosques, the medieval dungeon, the big square with its fourteen fountains playing, and I fervently hoped none of them had been damaged. I regret to attack a town that had always maintained its independence except for a few years (1920–1924) of Spanish occupation.[73]

Rockwell was not the only Westerner to have regrets. The war correspondent, Harris, would write, "In my opinion the most cruel, the most wanton, and the most unjustifiable act of the whole war was the bombing of the open town of (Chaouen) in 1925—when every male inhabitant capable of bearing arms was known to be absent—by a squadron of volunteer American airmen with the French Flying Corps. A number of absolutely defenseless women and children were massacred and many others were maimed and blinded."[74] The U.S. State Department was furious, and threatened to revoke the pilots' citizenship. The American consulate in Tangier had warned the airmen that it was illegal to fight for a foreign power in a war in which the United States was not involved. It was one thing to fight for France against the Germans in World War I, but quite another to help France suppress a freedom fighter such as Abd el-Krim whose cause was gaining support in the United States. Newspaper articles, telegrams and letters flooded in. "We were told ... that we were a disgrace," Rockwell recorded half a century later. "We learned that we were baby-killers and that our principal occupation was burning the crops of peaceful farmers."[75] The publicity was so unfavorable that the Escadrille was shut down after only six weeks.

Poison gas was the scourge of World War I, and the so-called civilized nations were willing to ban its use against each other. But the ban did not extend to their colonies. The Italians used poison gas in Libya and the British used it against the Bolsheviks in Russia in the summer of 1919. The British Manual of Military Law of 1914 states that such bans did "not apply in war with uncivilized states and tribes."[76] Winston Churchill, Britain's secretary of war, said, "I don't understand this squeamishness about the use of gas. I am strongly in favor of using poison gas against uncivilized tribes."[77] While France refrained from using it in Morocco, Spain was one of the first nations to use poison gas against a civilian population in their war against the Rif. Dámaso Berenguer, high commissioner of Spanish Morocco, wired the war ministry after the Riffian atrocities at Anual, saying, "I have always been opposed to the use of asphyxiating gases against those natives, but after what they have done, and their treacherous and dishonest conduct, I have to employ them with real effectiveness ..."[78] Berenguer was not alone in his anger over Riffian atrocities. King Alfonso wired back, saying, "It's a pity we could not have sent you a squadron of bombers with gas to devastate the Rif countryside and quickly make them feel our strength in their land."[79] In due course, Spain had plenty of bombers ready to deliver gas attacks flying out of Melilla. Revenge infused the Spanish army, and it wasn't long before it began to indulge in its own atrocities against the Berbers. The Spanish military denounced Abd el-Krim's tactics as cowardly, as conventional armies are wont to do whenever faced with guerrilla warfare.

Spain tried to keep its use of chemical weapons a secret to protect its reputation. As historian Sebastian Balfour explained, the Spanish Foreign Legion shock troops could not contain the Riffians on their own. "Nor was the massive mobilization of military recruits from Spain a practical solution. Most of them were barely trained and lacked motivation ... they were not the stuff of a successful colonial army. Thus the notion that expensive technologically advanced chemical weapons could replace the foot-slogging soldier as the main weapon against an enemy began to seize the imagination of colonial officers and politicians alike."[80] After all, the Riffians were just savages as far as Spain was concerned. Primo de Rivera was keen to use gas in the areas from which he had pulled back, and these areas were gassed extensively. The Spanish obtained gas-making technology from Germany, the country which had first used gas in World War I. The allies had banned Germany from making poison gas, but not the transfer of its technology.

The initial success of the Riffians in French Morocco had repercussions in Paris, and Marshal Lyautey got the blame. He was removed as commander in chief of French forces in Morocco, but remained resident general. The hero of World War I, Marshal Philippe Petain, was sent to Morocco to review the situation, and was soon put in charge of military operations. "The brutal fact is," Petain reported back to Paris, "that we are unexpectedly attacked by the most powerful and best-armed enemy we have ever had to encounter in the course of our colonial campaigns."[81] Petain gave credit where credit was due, describing the Riffian fighters as "keen, vigorous, skilled in the use of arms, exalted by their successes in previous years, knowing thoroughly the rough country in which they fight, requiring so little that they are able to do without [motorized] convoys which so weigh down our columns, and in possession of machine guns, cannon, and an abundant supply of ammunition."[82] The French would not encounter another such organized colonial uprising until they faced the Viet Minh in Vietnam after World War II.

Thoroughly alarmed, the French sent an additional 100,000 troops to Morocco to stem the Riffian tide. Abd el-Krim's forces, with some new tribesmen joining the rebel cause, avoided mass attacks. They kept their forces mobile, fading away when confronted with overwhelming force, only to advance again where the French were weak. Some of the less experienced tribesmen tried to hold the forts they had captured, presenting themselves as easy targets for French artillery and airpower but not Abd el-Krim's veterans. The Riffians used mules to transport ammunition and a rudimentary medical service to treat the wounded. They used traditional medicines, such as spider webs or hot cinders applied to wounds.

By the late summer and early fall, the overwhelming force the French were bringing to bear was beginning to tell. Meanwhile, the Riffians continued to pressure the Spanish, who remained on the defensive behind the Primo Line throughout the summer. The plans for joint Franco-Spanish action were revived, calling for a Spanish amphibious landing on the broad beaches of Alhucemas Bay on the Riffian shore of the Mediterranean near Abd el-Krim's capital of Ajdir. From there the plan was to strike landward into the mountains of the Beni Urriaguel, the beating heart of the Riffian rebellion. The plan was to reduce the pressure on the French. At first the French were skeptical, knowing full well the incompetence of the Spanish military. But with Primo de Rivera in charge, the French agreed to the plan, even providing a few ships and troops to support the landing.

By the end of August 1925, everything was ready: ships, planes, even an observation blimp. Primo de Rivera issued a last ultimatum to the Riffians. They were about to be faced with an invasion of great force, and had three days in which to surrender. Abd el-Krim was to be seized, the Spanish said, and turned over to them. Leaflets were dropped by air over the Rif. Of course, few Riffians could read, but not one of them is known to have complied with the ultimatum. Instead of surrendering, Abd el-Krim ordered a diversionary attack on a Spanish fort near the capital, Tetuan, in a place called Cudia Taharas, as a diversion. By the 12th of September a Spanish garrison of 200 had been reduced to thirty-four, of whom twenty-two had been wounded. Not a single Spanish officer was left alive or unwounded. Yet the Spanish garrison held on. Ice was dropped from the air to provide drinking water.[viii] The diversion caused

---

viii The Spanish developed the idea of supplying besieged outposts with water by dropping ice from the air because water bags or barrels would break open upon impact.

the Spanish to send 4,000 Legionnaires to Tetuan to relieve the fort. By then the amphibious landing was already underway, with sixty-three troop transports containing Spanish and a few French, as well as cargo vessels carrying ammunition, supplies, and poison gas canisters. The flotilla was escorted by thirty-six Spanish naval vessels to bombard the coast and assist the landing. Such an operation would not be seen again until World War II. And for once the Spanish carried it off well. There were mishaps. Landings were made at the wrong beaches, but on the whole the landing was a success.

Primo de Rivera was there in person and in command. "I promised Marshal Petain I would disembark, and I will disembark whatever it costs," he said.[83] The Spanish Foreign Legion led the assault, Colonel Francisco Franco in command. Abd el-Krim had been warned in advance that an invasion fleet was on its way, but he did not have enough troops to successfully oppose the landing. But, firing his artillery only at night so that Spanish spotters would have difficulty finding them, he held up the Spanish advance inland from their beachhead. It took them fifteen days to advance a mile and a half.

Vincent Sheean met Abd el-Krim again during the Franco-Spanish invasions when Abd el-Krim was encamped on a headland overlooking the broad expanse of Alhucemas Bay. The Spanish were shelling the headland, and Spanish planes were bombing and strafing. Abd el-Krim presented a heroic figure in Sheean's eyes, standing at the mouth of a cave and without interrupting his conversation, he took up a rifle and started firing at Spanish planes. "He continued the sentence he had already begun," Sheean reported, "and punctuated it thus, 'La independencia Bang! ... absoluta Bang! ... del Rif Bang!'" For Sheean, "the sight of such intrepidity against such odds might have served as a figure for the whole war: one man, and lame at that, firing with a rifle at a squadron of aeroplanes."[84] By early October the Spanish had taken Ajdir, burning most of it to the ground. Abd el-Krim and his cabinet had escaped, but the Alhucemas operation was undoubtedly a success, one of the few in the entire war. Colonel Franco distinguished himself. As Marshal Lyautey had said, "Spain has only one man in Africa—Franco."[85] Promoted to brigadier general at thirty-three, Franco became the youngest general in Europe.

In coordination with the Spanish landing, the French advanced northward across the Wergha River, heading for the Rif where they joined with the Spanish coming south. The Riffians kept fighting. They still controlled most of Spanish Morocco, and Abd el-Krim hoped that something could be salvaged. But essentially his dream had come to an end. His countrymen had endured nearly five years of heavy fighting. Their villages had been bombed, their crops destroyed, typhus stalked the land, and winter was on its way. Remarkably, the tribes had remained united under Abd el-Krim.

An ailing Lyautey asked to be relieved of his remaining duties. He returned to France in semi-disgrace. Tears were seen in his eyes as he departed Morocco. The old marshal had always been unpopular with many in France for not allowing the full exploitation of French Morocco. His most serious fault, as with all the French and Spanish military officers in Morocco, was underestimating the capabilities of Abd el-Krim and his brother.

In order to forge a joint strategy, Petain and Primo de Rivera met in Madrid in February 1926, while Abd el-Krim kept up his harassment of both the French and Spanish armies. Tetuan was shelled from the surrounding hills. Worldwide public opinion remained on the side of the Riffians. Many in France and in Spain demanded that Abd el-Krim be treated fairly. So, when Abd el-Krim, in the spring of 1926, with defeat staring him in the face, wanted to reopen negotiations, neither the French nor the Spanish government could reasonably refuse. The Spanish Army, however, was incensed at the thought of bargaining with Abd el-Krim now that they had the battlefield advantage. The army wanted him captured and hanged. The bitter end game to the Rif War had arrived, and Abd el-Krim knew how vulnerable he was.

Riffian manpower reserves were reaching bottom early in 1926. Morale was plummeting, and the Rif was running out of food. With the war going badly, Abd el-Krim's absolute authority began to fray.

There had been assassination attempts before, but now the danger increased. He seldom spent two nights in a row in the same place. Abd el-Krim had little choice but to sue for peace. A meeting with the French and Spanish was arranged near the border with Algeria in a town called Ujda. A temporary truce was declared. Abd el-Krim did not attend, but the delegates under his authority agreed to the Franco-Spanish demand that the Republic of the Rif recognize the religious authority of the sultan, something Abd el-Krim would never have agreed to before Alhucemas. The Riffians also agreed to disarm, but they insisted that they would surrender their weapons only to Abd el-Krim, not to the French or the Spanish. Once that was done, Abd el-Krim agreed to be deported from Morocco. Spanish and French prisoners of war were to be released. About half the prisoners had already died of neglect and disease. Neither the Riffians nor the Spanish treated their prisoners well, but the Riffians had the excuse that they themselves were short of food and medicine.

When the prisoners were finally released, many resembled concentration camp inmates of a generation later. When the Rif delegation wanted to consult with their leader back in the Rif mountains, the French took them to a small port in Algeria and brought them by launch along the coast to a place where they could travel inland in safety. The sticking point came when the Riffians demanded more autonomy than the French and Spanish were willing to concede. The French then made an ultimatum. Surrender now or we will relentlessly resume the war. The Rif delegation refused, and the war began again.

The combined French and Spanish forces now moved into the mountains where Abd el-Krim was holed up with about 12,000 loyal tribesmen, mostly of his own Beni Urriaguel tribe. Abd el-Krim was now outnumbered forty-to-one. The final pitched battle of the war took place in May 1926. The Riffians were defeated and the power of the Beni Urriaguel broken. Isolated and uncoordinated pockets of resistance would continue on, but the Rif rebellion was essentially over. Abd el-Krim realized that he had to surrender to the

French, as the Spanish would surely hang him. So, he sent a letter to the nearby French garrison commander. "I have decided at this moment to come to you. I ask for the protection of France for myself and my family."[86] Abd el-Krim made his way to the French garrison where he was treated with courtesy and consideration. The French said they knew "how to welcome a conquered enemy who has given proof of military qualities."[87] There were no less than twenty-seven people in Abd el-Krim's surrender party, including his brother, his mother, two wives, their three young sons, and a daughter, as well as a smattering of cabinet ministers and loyal supporters. It took 270 mules to transport the party and their luggage out of the mountains. The French decided that the family, and those whom they considered the most dangerous of their supporters, would be exiled to the island of Réunion in the Indian Ocean off Africa. Lesser figures in the revolt could remain in Morocco. The Spanish were furious, but the French refused to hand Abd el-Krim over to them. The Spanish felt cheated, and a grim determination that they would never be humiliated again set in among the *Africanistas* in the army. The consequences of that would soon emerge in the following decade in Spain itself.

Abd el-Krim's family were treated well in Taza, then Fez, and finally in Casablanca, where they were put onboard a warship and taken to their Indian Ocean exile. Once there, they lived comfortably, with a handsome annual stipend, courtesy of the French government. The Jibalis were the last to surrender, but like stars when clouds roll in, little pockets of resistance went out one by one. Sporadic fighting continued until the summer of 1927, when the war was finally declared over. Primo de Rivera insisted on no reprisals, and some in Abd el-Krim's government were offered jobs in the Spanish administration. In July King Alfonso XIII and Primo de Rivera made a triumphal tour of Spanish Morocco. The dream of self-determination even for the smallest of nations was over.

"Moroccan nationalism came to birth under the boughs of a mulberry tree in the evening of the first of August 1926, when the country still resounded with the echoes of Abd el-Krim's war."[88] A dozen or so young men, meeting in a private garden in Rabat, discussed Moroccan history, the loss of independence to the French and Spanish, and what could be done about it. Other countries were gaining at least a measure of independence—Egypt, Syria, Transjordan—and they plotted the day when all of Morocco would be free. This discussion was prompted by Abd el-Krim's struggle against overwhelming odds, which fired the imagination of young idealists. "In the eyes of the Moroccans [Abd el-Krim] was champion of both Islam and nationalist independence, the two ideals nearest to their hearts."[89]

Ironically, Abd el-Krim's legacy was to affect Spain more than Morocco. The Spanish simply re-established their authority over Spanish Morocco, but in Spain constitutional government had been destroyed when humiliation over the army's defeats brought Primo de Rivera to power. Spain was soon to turn against him, and in 1930 he fled Spain, seeking exile in Paris where he died shortly thereafter. King Alfonso was irreparably sullied by the Rif War. He left the throne the following year, and Spain became a republic in 1931. Alfonso died in Rome ten years later. Constitutional government had been restored, but not for long.

One of Abd el-Krim's enduring legacies was the resurrection of the Spanish Army of Africa as an efficient fighting force with political intentions during and after the Rif War. Bitter and resentful of the civilian authorities at home whom they thought had betrayed them, the Army of Africa would soon become a danger to Spain itself. France would find itself in a similar situation with its army in Algeria in revolt in the 1950s, during another colonial war gone bad, but the worst was avoided and democracy in France prevailed. Not so in Spain.

By the 1930s Spain had become bitterly divided between left and right with neither willing to compromise. Democracy dies when those with whom you do not agree are defined as enemies who must be destroyed. In Spain governments rose and fell. Public order began to disintegrate. In 1936 the army, claiming to speak for the established bourgeois order and the Catholic Church, staged a coup against the elected left wing government to save Eternal Spain from the Reds, or so they said. Not surprisingly, the *Africanistas*, especially those who had served in Morocco, were prominent among the plotters. The coup was only partially successful, and when it looked like it might fail, the plotters looked towards Morocco and the Army of Africa.

The Republican government controlled the sea lanes between Morocco and Spain but not the skies. Franco was flown to Melilla from the Canary Islands, where a wary republic had sidelined him. Then, in the world's first significant military airlift, Hitler and Mussolini provided the planes to fly Franco and the Army of Africa over the Mediterranean to Spain in order to save the coup. Fourteen thousand men, fifty-two artillery pieces, and 238 tons of material crossed the narrow strait in two weeks. These planes provided air cover for a sea convoy later. The Spanish Civil War had begun.

As they had in Africa, the Moroccan *Regulares* and the Foreign Legion provided the shock troops for the Nationalist forces, as the rebels came to be known. General Francisco Franco soon became the leader of the Nationalist cause. The Army of Africa soon brought the brutality for which they were known to Spain in their fight against the Loyalists of the Spanish Republic. At the height of the war, there were as many as 50,000 Moroccans fighting on the Nationalist side, four hundred years after the Moors had been expelled from Spain.

With Hitler's Germany and Mussolini's Italy aiding the Nationalists and the Soviet Union trying to bolster the Loyalists, the Spanish Civil War would become the curtain raiser for World War II, which began only half a year after the Nationalist victory in 1939. England, France, and the United States refused to help the Spanish Republic. Franco became the new, Fascist-leaning Spain's chief of state. But he scrupulously kept his war-torn country neutral in the greater war that was raging. His only concession to the Axis cause was to send a division of troops to fight alongside the Germans in Russia.

World War II came to Morocco in 1943 with Operation Torch, the Anglo-American invasion of North Africa. French Morocco was controlled by the pro-Nazi Vichy government, led by that old Morocco hand, Philippe Petain. With Spain being ruled by that even older Morocco hand, Franco, the allies feared that Spain might enter the war on the Axis side through Spanish Morocco. Harvard anthropologist Carlton Coon was then serving in the Office of Strategic Services (OSS), the forerunner of the Central Intelligence Agency. He had a deep knowledge of, and had written extensively about, the tribes and languages of Morocco. His job was to unleash the Riffian tribes against the Spanish again if Franco made any move toward entering the war. He made secret contact with some of Abd el-Krim's old commanders. "During these meetings," Coon later wrote, "we laid plans for the revolt of the Riffians if needed, and plotted the landing of troops, the dropping of parachutists, the delivery of guns, the cutting off of raids and garrison, etc. We laid on a system of signals by which the Riffians were to assemble and seize various key positions, and await our arrival."[90] Fortunately for the allies, Franco remained neutral and the plans to raise revolt in the Rif were shelved.

Moroccan nationalists were not alone in hoping that Franklin Roosevelt's neo-Wilsonian Atlantic Charter would hasten their independence. That charter asserted the right of all peoples to choose their own form of government. As Wilson had done in 1919, here was another American president supporting self-determination. During the Casablanca Conference, when Roosevelt met with Winston Churchill to discuss the war, the American president asked his son and aide-de-camp, Elliott, "Why does Morocco, inhabited by Moroccans, belong to France? Or take Indochina ... Should that belong to France? By what logic and by what custom and by what historical rule? When we have won the war, I will work with all my might and main." Roosevelt said that the United States would not accept any plan that furthered "France's imperial ambitions."[91] When Roosevelt made his Flag Day speech on June 14, 1943, the Americans had it loosely translated into Moroccan Arabic until it sounded like something out of the Koran, "We are all of us children of the earth. Grant us that simple knowledge: If our brothers are oppressed, then we are oppressed. If they hunger, we hunger. If their freedom is taken away, our freedom is taken away …"[92] But Roosevelt died before war's end, and his commitment to anti-colonialism died with him.

After World War II, nationalism came to a boil in French Morocco. When France was embroiled in trying to hang on to its empire in neighboring Algeria in 1956, the French found it prudent to grant Morocco its independence. Spain abandoned its claim to its protectorate, and Morocco was united and free.

As for Abd el-Krim, he lived quietly in his Réunion exile until after World War II, when he petitioned the French to allow him and his family to settle in France. The French agreed, but when his ship was passing through the Suez Canal in 1947, Egyptian police boarded the ship and took the family to Cairo, where King Farouk gave them political asylum. Because Abd el-Krim's revolt had been against the Sultan of Morocco, and not just the Spanish, Morocco took a long time before it recognized Abd el-Krim as an early freedom fighter for independence. Eventually, the sultan invited Abd el-Krim to return, but he refused and never saw his homeland again. He did, however, live to see the entire North African littoral liberated from European colonialism. He died in Egypt in 1963.[ix]

---

ix In the 1980s Abd el-Krim's son, Said, told the American ambassador to Egypt, Frank Wisner, that an American diplomat and friend of North African independence movements, Hooker Doolittle, had been involved with his father's escape from French control. Abd el-Krim's daughter, Aisha, remembered that there was an American diplomat on the pier when the family disembarked in Port Said, but she was too young to remember his name.[93] The author has been unable to find any further confirmation of American involvement in the affair.

Today, in the once sacred city of Chaouen, now called Chefchoauen, where Christians were once forbidden, and where American pilots flying for the French once dropped bombs, foreign tourists wander the narrow streets looking for bargains among the twisting alleys of this upland town with the mountains of the Jibala rising in the background. The ancient Jewish community that brought out its keys to show the Spanish in 1920 began leaving the country with the birth of Israel and is now all but extinct.

Alhucemas (Al-Hoceima) has grown from a small fishing village of a century ago into a thriving town with modern hotels and tourist beaches. Nearby Ajdir, once Abd el-Krim's capital, is now a suburb. The Spanish fortress offshore, looking much as it did in Abd el-Krim's day, is still an outpost of Spain manned by Spanish soldiers. The headland where Abd el-Krim fired at Spanish planes from a cave, now resounds with jackhammers, as new apartment buildings march across the landscape. The beach, where the Spanish and French made their amphibious landing, is a destination for Moroccans and tourists alike, with a Ferris wheel and an expensive restaurant jutting out into the water. Seagulls wheel above in the skies that were once filled with circling Spanish warplanes.

At Ait Kamara, all that remains of Abd el-Krim's headquarters are roofless mud-brick walls disintegrating slowly into the red, garbage-strewn earth. Modern villas are springing up around the ruin like mushrooms after a rain. There is no plaque to commemorate what once transpired there. Further on, overlooking the battlefield of Anual, on the side of a gentle slope inside a walled enclosure of eucalyptus trees, there is a marble plaque to remind visitors that here a Spanish army died running in panic from Abd el-Krim's Riffians a century ago. There is a verse from the Koran in flowing Arabic script explaining how even a small band of holy warriors can defeat a superior force with the help of Allah. The desperate cries of dying men have long been silenced here, and the only sound is the rustling of leaves in the trees. Unlike Culloden, Waterloo, or Gettysburg, there are no other monuments to mark where various units stood and fought. The red earth ravines that hid hundreds of Riffians waiting in ambush are still obvious to the eye, but nothing else remains on these silent fields to remind what happened here. A farmer appears and volunteers the unsolicited information that this is where General Silvestre met his end. The locals have not forgotten.

At the local prefecture I am gently warned that it is not wise to ask questions about Abd el-Krim in today's Rif. The memory is still raw of violent demonstrations in 2017 in which present-day Riffians raised the flag of the Republic of the Rif in defiance of the Moroccan government. Although the government is making great efforts to integrate the Rif region into modern Morocco, after years of neglect and hostility, folk memories linger among the hill peoples of that brief period of independence of the Rif which the rest of the world has long forgotten.

Throughout the world like the voice of a prophet has gone the word of Woodrow Wilson, strengthening the weak, giving courage to the struggling. And the Chinese people have listened and they too have heard ... They looked for the dawn of this new Messiah; but no sun rose for China.

—Shanghai student pamphlet, May 1919

CHAPTER FOUR

Sun Yat-sen

THE "TRAGEDY OF DISAPPOINTMENT" fell hard and fast in East Asia, half a world away. Nowhere did President Wilson's words and actions raise more hopes than in China, and nowhere did the disappointment have a longer-lasting effect. One can draw a straight line between Wilson's perceived perfidy and China's emergence as an enemy instead of a friend of the United States in the century ahead. When the news reached China of how the Shantung Question had been resolved, the fury and sense of betrayal was instantaneous. Most Chinese, and many Americans too, believed that Wilson had abandoned his ideals at China's expense. Ceding the German concessions to Japan, China's number one exploiter was galling in the extreme. China had been an ally in the Great War, and Chinese blood had been spilled. Should an ally lose territory in a post-war settlement? The great reservoir of goodwill that Wilson and his ideals had inspired in China now burst like a breached dam with unforeseen consequences for both America and China downstream. Wilson had unwittingly helped radicalize the most populous country on earth. The effects are still being felt a hundred years later. There now began a thirty-year struggle between competing economic and political models for China, ending in a Communist victory in 1949.

Wilson's Shantung decision bewildered the Chinese. Secret treaties that the British and French had made with Japan, unequal treaties imposed on China, and gunboat diplomacy—everything Wilson had indicated he was against—were trumping self-determination and consent of the governed. A Chinese student caught the mood of May 1919. "When the news of the Paris Peace Conference finally reached us we were greatly shocked. We at once awoke to the fact that the foreign nations were still selfish and militaristic and that they were all great liars. I remember the evening of May 2nd, very few of us slept. I and a group of my friends talked almost the whole night. We came to the conclusion that we could no longer depend on the principles of any of the so-called leaders like Woodrow Wilson ... We couldn't help feel that we must struggle."[1] A student pamphlet put it even more bitterly:

> Throughout the world like the voice of a prophet has gone the word of Woodrow Wilson strengthening the weak and giving courage to the struggling. And the Chinese people have listened and they too have heard. They have been told that their four-thousand-year-old doctrine that peace is the greatest of all aims of a nation has become the slogan of mankind ... They have been told that secret covenants and forced agreements would not be recognized. They looked for the dawn of this new Messiah; but no sun rose for China. Even the cradle of the nation (Shandong) was stolen.[2]

The American ambassador to Peking, Paul Reinsch, recalled that "probably nowhere else in the world had expectations of American leadership at the Paris Peace Conference been raised so high as in China. The Chinese trusted America; they trusted the frequent declarations of principle uttered by President Wilson, whose works had reached China in its remotest parts."[3] George Creel's Committee for Public Information (CPI), which the Wilson administration had established in 1917 as its propaganda organ, had been remarkably successful promoting Wilson's ideals among the Chinese. Although few Chinese could read, those who could were the decision-makers. Creel used modern advertising techniques that have now become ubiquitous in American politics but were then brand-new. The

China
Map drawn by Julia L. Greenway

message itself—self-determination and the rights of weak nations against the bullying of great powers—fell on welcoming ears all over the world, but especially in China. American propaganda "cast Wilson's principles as the embodiment of American idealism, self-sacrifice and ... a new, fairer, more democratic world order, which were to be realized through America's triumphant successes in the war and consequent increasing power and prestige in international affairs."[4] Wilson's speeches, translated into the vernacular, were distributed widely. They were supplemented by lantern slides and amplified by the new medium of radio. Twenty thousand sepia photographs of Wilson were distributed; black and white, being associated with funerals, was avoided. One hundred thousand posters and 50,000 Wilson buttons were distributed in a formidable American propaganda campaign that was just what the Chinese wanted to hear.

When the World War I ended in November 1918, the Chinese organized street parades in celebration. Sun Yat-sen, China's greatest proponent of democracy, wired Wilson, "You have done the greatest service to civilization and democracy since the world began."[5] Scarcely six months later, these words were turning to dust in Sun's mouth. Wilson was no worse than his British and French counterparts, but the Chinese had expected more from America and especially from Wilson. The philosopher John Dewey, in China on the lecture circuit, wrote, "It is even plainer here than at home that if the United States was not going to see its 'ideals' through, it shouldn't have professed any."[6] A Chinese newspaper in Japanese-controlled Shantung scolded Chinese who had fallen under Wilson's spell. "Shallow people ... imagining that they are filled with the spirit of America, they rush to support this theory [democracy] singing the praises of America and hailing Mr. Wilson as the savior of the world. The evils of democracy are that it destroys the national idea, elevates the white races, and spreads the Christian religion ... By advocating the right of self-determination and preaching equality and fraternity," America has "incited the Koreans to revolt ... But why does she not set free Hawaii, the Philippines, and her other dependencies?"[7]

The stage was set for an incident that would give its name to an emerging cultural upheaval: the May Fourth Movement, the conception, if not the birth, of modern China. On the morning of that day, when news of the Shantung decision reached China from Paris, student representatives from thirteen colleges met at Peking University, a hotbed of revolutionary thought, to draw up five resolutions. The first was to protest the Shantung settlement. The second was to "awaken the masses all over the country" to China's plight.[8] The third was to hold a mass protest meeting in Peking. The fourth proposed forming a Peking student union, and the fifth called for protest demonstrations that very afternoon. In defiance of police orders, the students poured out of their red brick building onto Shantung Street—today called May Fourth Street—and marched to the great open space of T'ien-an Men (Tiananmen), meaning Heavenly Peace, near the Forbidden City where Chinese emperors had traditionally resided. The students joined up with 3,000 or so other students, and carrying funeral banners bearing the names of the most pro-Japanese members of the Chinese government, they headed for the Legation Quarter where the foreign embassies were housed.

They handed out pamphlets along the way, written in the simplified vernacular, protesting the assault on China's territorial integrity. Upon being blocked by police, the students went to the house of Tsao Ju-lin (Cao Rulin), the pro-Japanese minister of communications who had negotiated and signed the Japanese demands made on China concerning Shantung, to which the Chinese had capitulated. Luckily for him he was not at home, but the students set fire to his house anyway. There were violent clashes with police. Thirty-two students were arrested, and one died of his injuries.

Demonstrations spread quickly throughout China. Japanese goods were boycotted, and the movement took on a decidedly nationalistic and anti-foreign tone. A twenty-six-year-old future leader of China was working in the library of Peking University at the time, the still politically uncertain Mao Tse-tung (Mao Zedong). He would later say that in 1919, he began to take a more "direct role in politics. After the May Fourth Movement I had devoted most of my time to student political activities."[9] Having fully awakened to the injustices perpetrated upon them, the Chinese would never be the same again. What the historian Erez Manela called "The Wilsonian Moment," when China might have followed in the path of western democracy, was over.[10] In 1919 Wilson was far better known in China than the rising star in Russia, Vladimir Ilyich Ulyanov, known by his alias, Lenin. After May Fourth many of China's intellectuals looked toward Marxism and the new Soviet Union for nationalistic and anti-colonial inspiration, rather than the ideals of Woodrow Wilson.

Perhaps the largest mass movement of Chinese intellectuals in China's history, the May Fourth Movement was not limited to nationalist demonstrations of outrage. As China scholar Jonathan Spence has written:

> It was an attempt to redefine China's culture as a valid part of the modern world. In the attempt, not surprisingly, reformers followed different avenues of thought and conduct. Some May 4th thinkers concentrated on launching attacks against reactionary or irrelevant 'old ways' such as Confucianism, the patriarchal family, arranged marriages, or traditional education … Some had a deep interest in traditional Western art and culture, while others looked to the avant-garde elements of that culture, such as surrealist and cubist paintings, symbolist poetry, graphic design, realist drama and new fashions in dress and interior decoration. Some thought to re-infuse Chinese traditional arts with a new spirit of nationalism by borrowing a select range of Western painterly techniques.[11]

Now that the old order had been discredited, it was time to look for other models. Western science and technology were praised and promoted as the way forward for China. The May Fourth reformers shared a central patriotic and anti-imperialist ideal. They wanted a "rejuvenated, unified China that would have the means to cope with the three great problems" of China: warlords, an exploitive, "feudal" landlord system, and foreign imperialism.[12] China's industrial base had been growing rapidly, and the May Fourth demonstrations unleashed strikes and boycotts, particularly of Japanese goods. Industrial unrest increased as trade unions and workers' associations bloomed. Some Chinese were drawn to Communism simply because they had heard the imperial powers were against it. Education, too, was expanding. By 1919 almost half a million students had received a college education, mostly in the eastern cities. New and reformist publications were multiplying. The influential journal *New Youth* had already been founded in Shanghai in 1915 by Ch'en Tu-hsiu (Chen Duxiu), a professor at Peking University. He would later be a founding member of the Chinese Communist Party. Its first issue had enjoined the youth of China to cast off old ways of thinking and conventions.

The Confucian universal state, inspired by the philosopher Confucius, who had set down practical codes for society 500 years before the birth of Christ, had been swept aside with the fall of the Ch'ing Dynasty. There were many ideas competing to replace it. Some thought Confucianism should simply be abandoned. Others, notably K'ang Yu-wei (Kang Youwei), thought that Confucius could be made relevant for the modern world. Educated women were just coming into their own in China. For many of them Confucius stood for an outdated patriarchy. Whatever one thought of Confucius, Western culture and Western thought were flooding into China as never before. "Destroy the aristocratic literature which is nothing but literary chiseling and flattery, and construct a simple, expressive literature of the people," wrote Ch'en Tu-hsiu.[13]

Politically, China was a mess. The feeble government in Peking had virtually no authority over the warlords and their regional fiefdoms around the country. Each had his own private army, and they fought each other, joining in convenient alliances, and then betraying each other when it seemed opportune. Some were little more than bandit chieftains. Periodically, one warlord would take control of Peking only to be driven out again by another with a more powerful army. The most important of these breakaway regimes was that of Sun Yat-sen, who was based in the southern city of Canton (Guangzhou). Neither a warlord nor a soldier, Sun was a single-minded idealist who of necessity became a skilled politician, diplomat, philosopher, and rebel who is regarded today as the founding father of the Chinese republic.

Sun is uniquely revered not only in Taiwan and by non-Communist Chinese, but by the Communist mainland as an honored harbinger of the modern state who fought against both imperialism and feudalism. Chou En-lai (Zhou En-lai), Maoist China's voice of reason, called Sun "the great hero of China's democratic revolution."[14] Sun was the perfect man for those restless times. Foreign-educated, English-speaking, and a Christian, Sun carried little baggage of China's past. For those who wanted a radical break with what had gone before, Sun was ideal. Charming, soft-spoken, and reticent, he inspired loyalty. He had a healthy ego and could be ruthless with his enemies, but he treated his friends and followers with politeness and compassion. Compared to the venal and power-hungry warlords, Sun seemed almost saintly. When he died he left little more than his books and a house or two. His dedication was to China, not the accumulation of personal wealth. Few leaders in history have suffered so many defeats without ever giving in.

Chang Chin-tung[i]—the name Sun Yat-sen came later—was born to peasant parents in a country village near Canton in 1866, two

---

i   Like many other Chinese, Sun had different names at different stages of his life. In Sun's case there were aliases for different countries as well. Sun Wen was a name he used often late in life. When in exile in Japan, Sun adopted the name of Nakayama Sho, meaning Central Mountain. Translated into Chinese, his Japanese name was Ch'ung Shan (Zhongshan), which is the name by which he is best known in today's China. Sun Yat-sen, however, is the Cantonese pronunciation, and that is the name best known in the West.

years after nineteenth-century China's most traumatic episode, the Taiping Rebellion. Led by a mystic who thought of himself as the younger brother of Jesus Christ, the rebellion lasted for fourteen years and nearly toppled the Ch'ing Dynasty that had ruled China since 1644. It cost the lives of between twenty and seventy million people. The rebels opposed both their Ch'ing Dynasty Manchurian overlords and the Confucian ethic that the Ch'ing had adopted as their own. They sought to overturn society and convert China to their idiosyncratic version of Christianity. The Taiping rebels were inadvertent modernizers groping for the means to bring change and progress to a hidebound society.

Although the Ch'ing Dynasty ultimately prevailed, the cries for change and modernization did not die. The following decades were ones of discontent. The Ch'ing seemed stuck in an outdated, pre-modern past. Westerners and Japanese exploited their weakness by taking control of much of China's wealth while defeating the Ch'ing in sporadic warfare in which China lost ever more territory and control of its own affairs.

Until the nineteenth century, the Ch'ing had ruled China relatively well. In the eighteenth century, China had been among the most powerful states in the world. But by the nineteenth century China had fallen behind technologically. The Chinese may have invented gunpowder, but the West invented better guns. And despite having adopted many of the customs of the majority Han Chinese, the Manchu Ch'ing were considered by many as foreigners—a feeling Sun was to exploit in later years. It was obvious to many that China had to change.

Sun was not of the Mandarin class. He never received a classic Chinese education. He was a man of the future, desperate to shake up China and bring modernity by any means. He thought China was as cripplingly bound to the past as the bound feet of his mother.[ii]

---

ii It was the custom for respectable women to have their feet bound as young girls. It impeded the foot's growth. Tiny feet were considered

As a revolutionary, Sun did not fit the mold of twentieth-century figures such as Mao, Fidel Castro, Ho Chi Minh, or even Abd el-Krim. He did not live in the forests or mountain redoubts. He was not a leader of guerrilla armies gathering strength in the hills. In fact, he lived outside of China in the early years, plotting his uprisings against the Ch'ing from safe havens abroad while his disciples ran the risks. Although he would take great risks later on in his attempts to reunite China, Sun was primarily a man of the lecture hall, a man who cultivated the overseas Chinese in North and South America, Southeast Asia, and in Europe. His most famous book, *Three Principles of the People*, would inspire a generation. When Sun did plan military coups they were inept, usually ending badly. Unlike Abd el-Krim or d'Annunzio, he was neither a military strategist nor a war hero nor a larger-than-life personality. He was modest and reserved; a man of persuasion, a man of ideas who was driven to never give up. Sun was also an opportunist whose flame did not burn morally pure. He was perfectly willing to join with criminals, bandits, anti-Manchu secret societies, even imperialist powers and finally with Communists—anything to further his causes: overthrowing the Ch'ing Dynasty and then uniting China. He was not averse to having men executed if they were standing in his way. Although he was given credit for leading the revolution that overthrew the monarchy in 1911, he was fundraising in America when it actually happened. Yet he was the man to whom China first looked to lead the country when the 4,000-year-old monarchy was swept away.

Sun was already showing signs of a rebellious nature at the age of thirteen. He went to live for a while with his well-off older brother

---

erotic, but rendered women hardly able to walk. Ending the practice was a target of modernizers.

in the Kingdom of Hawaii, then an independent nation. There he learned English and attended the same school that later educated Barack Obama.[iii] He studied medicine in Hong Kong, where he converted to Christianity. He eventually set up a practice in Western and traditional Chinese medicine in Canton, dutifully marrying, as was the custom, a girl his parents had picked for him named Lu Muchen (Lu Muzhen). Although he eventually had a son and two daughters by her, she never accompanied him on his travels. Sun looked upon himself as an outsider lacking a classical education, and craved respectability. But after being rejected for a job with a local governor, he turned his hand to his true calling, that of a revolutionary.

When the war with Japan broke out in the summer of 1894, a war that cost China the loss of Taiwan, Sun went to Hawaii to begin recruiting revolutionaries from within Hawaii's Chinese community. There he founded the Revive China Society, which eventually became the Kuomintang (Guomindang) or KMT, his political organization which still exists. The following year he began organizing a series of armed uprisings aimed at overthrowing the Ch'ing that would occupy him for the next sixteen years. He launched them from Hong Kong until the British asked him to leave; from Japan until he was expelled; from Hanoi until the French kicked him out; and then from Singapore and Malaya. All were badly planned and executed. All of them ended in failure, yet he persisted. He became a prodigious fundraiser, especially among the overseas Chinese, whom he won over to the cause of overthrowing the monarchy.

The Ch'ing Dynasty quickly took note of this new threat. In 1896, when Sun was in London, he was held captive in the Chinese Embassy. The plan was to smuggle him onto a China-bound ship for trial and certain execution for his revolutionary activities. The British

---

iii The Oahu School was run by American Congregationalists. It was later to be called the Punahou School. Barack Obama studied there from the fifth grade until high school graduation.

press howled when it found out that Sun was being detained, and the British foreign office intervened to obtain his release. Questions were raised in the House of Commons. The incident burnished Sun's reputation and put the Ch'ing government in a bad light.

Sun hammered on the point that foreign imperialism was overwhelming China. "We are being crushed by the economic strength of the powers to a greater degree than if we were a full colony of one nation," he said. "China is not the colony of one nation but of all, and we are not the slaves of one country but of all. I think we should be called a hypo-colony."[15] Countries with only one colonial master, like the Philippines under the Americans, could at least count on help in a crisis because the colonial power "is bound both morally and by treaty" to assist. "China, on the other hand, has many foreign masters but none of them have any obligation to us." And with their extraterritorial rights, a foreigner could shoot even a cabinet minister dead in the streets, and China "would have no jurisdiction over him."[16] On another occasion he spoke of China as a huge "piece of meat on a butcher's block," ready to be eaten by any "ravenous foreign tiger."[17] But when addressing European audiences he downplayed his anti-foreign, anti-imperialist views.

Sun sought support among Chinese students studying in Japan and in Europe who were becoming increasingly radicalized. No rival could match his peripatetic travels, and it seems to many of them that nobody knew how to handle the "foreign devils" better than Sun Yat-sen. His essay, *On the Preservation or Dismemberment of China,* cemented his reputation as the leading defender of the motherland against colonial predators. Students who had once scorned him for his lack of education began to see that "he was not the illiterate ruffian they had assumed him to be. They wanted the job done and here was the man with the contacts, tools and confidence to perform it."[18] Sun's Western, rather than classical Chinese, education became an advantage in the eyes of the students rather than a liability.

On October 9, 1911, revolutionaries not under Sun's direction accidentally exploded a bomb in the provincial capital of Wuchang on the Yangtze River. When the police arrived, they discovered a list of conspirators that identified a number of army personnel. The following day, as disloyal soldiers were being sought and rounded up, a sergeant in the 8th Engineering Battalion shot his officers and called upon his men to mutiny.

And mutiny they did, on October 10th, the "Double Ten," a day that has passed into history as the beginning of the end of the monarchy. The revolt spread to other units, and by the following day Wuchang was in rebel hands. Then the revolt sped to Hanyang and Hangkow (Hankou) until the three cities of Wuhan were in rebel hands. The revolt spread quickly to other cities and provinces across China. A young officer named Chiang Kai-shek was instrumental in taking over the city of Hangchow (Hangzhou). Garrisons in other cities followed suit. Generals were disobeying orders from Peking to contain the revolution. The desperate government in Peking turned to China's most powerful general, Yuan Shih-k'ai (Yuan Shikai), who had recently been fired, asking him to come back and head the army to save the Ch'ing. The wily Yuan bided his time to see which way the wind was blowing. When he finally agreed to serve, the Ch'ing anointed him as Prime Minister of China. His troops quickly recaptured Hangkow and Hanyang, but elsewhere China began falling apart, as province after province began declaring their independence from the central government. At this point, Yuan, who knew he had the backing of the foreign powers, began negotiating with the rebels.

Sun was in Denver, Colorado, when the news of the uprising reached him. Perhaps doubtful that this uprising would succeed while all of his had failed, Sun did not immediately return to China. Instead he headed for Washington. But the Taft administration wanted to remain neutral in the drama that was unfolding in China, so Sun went on to London. The British were backing strongman Yuan as the potential savior of China, so Sun went on to Paris. The best he could get there was a promise of neutrality in the struggle of the dying Ch'ing Dynasty against the rebels, but Western opinion was consolidating behind Yuan.

Having achieved virtually nothing diplomatically, Sun set sail from Marseilles to China, arriving in Shanghai on Christmas Day. Most of the rebel organizations were in Nanking (Nanjing), deadlocked between two rival candidates hoping to become the first president of the republic should the rebels prevail. Sun's arrival broke the deadlock. Sun was the obvious compromise candidate upon whom everyone could agree. On January 1, 1912, the Republic of China was officially declared with Sun as provisional president, even though they had not yet brought down the monarchy. His investiture was held at the tomb of the first Ming emperor, whose dynasty the Manchurian Ch'ing had displaced 300 years before. However, the new republic's writ didn't run very far. The Ch'ing were still in charge in Peking with the best army in China under Yuan. Most of the provinces that had declared their independence had yet to join the republic. There were now two power centers, one in Nanking and the other in Peking, with warlords in the countryside accountable to neither. The country seemed on the verge of civil war. Yuan argued that Peking now had a constitutional monarchy with a national assembly, which should satisfy the rebels, but the rebels insisted on an end to the monarchy. So a deal was cut to avoid further conflict. Sun and the rebels offered to hand over the republic's provisional presidency to Yuan Shih-k'ai if he would obtain the abdication of the monarchy and join the rebels.

On the day Sun was inaugurated as provisional president, he cabled Yuan in Peking saying that the presidency was waiting for him. Sun did not lack ego, but on the very same day he reached the pinnacle of power in the new republic he was offering it to somebody else. Why? Neither Sun nor his supporters, nor the rebel army units, had any assurances that they would not be crushed by the imperial forces under Yuan. So, they turned to Yuan, whom they thought they could control. The alternative was to risk everything. They also believed that Yuan was the one man who could remove the Ch'ing from the affairs of China. Accordingly, Yuan went to the Forbidden City, where the new Empress Dowager, the widow of the former emperor, was in charge. Threatened with the specter of Louis XVI and Marie Antoinette's beheadings at the hands of French revolutionaries, she agreed to a deal whereby Pu-yi (Puyi), the teenage emperor, would abdicate. He would keep his title and his household and could continue to live in the royal palaces funded by the republican government, but with no authority. Yuan would replace Sun as provisional president of China with the support of the rebels, the government in Peking, the business interests and the approval of the foreign imperialists. "So perished, with scarcely a struggle, a monarchical institution which had its beginnings in prehistoric times ... " as the sinologist Kenneth Scott Latourette wrote. "With almost no preparation, the Chinese were scrapping political institutions whose operations they were familiar with and were adopting from the West a form of government with which they were quite inexperienced. On second thought, however, it is clear that this offered some, perhaps the best, hope of avoiding prolonged civil war and possible foreign intervention." [19]

Sun wrote an article in *Strand Magazine* explaining, "Whether I am to be the titular head of all China, or work in conjunction with another, and that other is Yuan Shih-k'ai, is of no importance to me. I have done my work; the wave of enlightenment and progress cannot now be stayed ..."[20] But Sun was neither to lead China, nor work in conjunction with Yuan Shih-k'ai for very long. And his work was far from over. Sun had hoped to trade his resignation for a firm commitment to parliamentary rule, and for moving China's capital to Nanking, away from Yuan's power base in Peking and closer to his own in the south. Yuan would grant neither. He demanded that the new provisional government move to Peking, and Sun withdrew from the political scene to take up the role of elder statesman. He would remain titular head of his political organization, the Kuomintang, but the actual running of the party would be done by others.

A constitution was promulgated in March 1912, calling for the president to share power with the prime minister and the newly formed National Assembly. But Yuan Shih-k'ai, ever the authoritarian, was not about to submit to that. Yuan at first welcomed Sun with banquets and honors in Peking. Sun believed that railways were the key to China's future economic development, and so Yuan made him Director of Railways, a safe place to put a potential rival. Sun made a month-long visit to Japan, the only foreign power that took any interest in his plans. He was treated with the utmost respect, as if he were the chief of state he had briefly been. A private train was put at his disposal to travel around the country.

The new Republic of China held its first national election in December 1912, and Sun's Kuomintang Party won by a landslide. The party hoped to bind Yuan Shih-k'ai's ambitions with constitutional ropes, but Yuan was not to be bound. The party's rising star, Sung Chi'iao-jen (Song Jioren), was assassinated, and it was not hard to discern Yuan's hand in the murder. When Sun returned from Japan five days later, he called upon the southern provinces, his base of support, to resist Yuan's power grab. But his KMT associates were hesitant.

Yuan then took out a loan from a consortium of foreign powers without consulting parliament. Sun appealed to the powers not to grant the loan but to no avail. The imperial powers were putting their money on Yuan Shih-k'ai, who was well on his way to becoming dictator of China. The assassination of Sung and Yuan's bid for total control rang the alarm bell that ended Sun's recess from active politics. Abandoning his new role as senior statesman, Sun went back to the trade he knew best: revolution. Sun called for a second revolution against Yuan Shih-k'ai to preserve the republic. "This tyrannical and unconstitutional action (the loan) had added to the intent indignation aroused by the murder of Sung," Sun wrote. "A terrible revolution seems inevitable."[21]

The terrible revolution Sun called for, however, never materialized. The armed anti-Yuan uprisings of July 1913 were disorganized, anemic, and easily defeated. With another failure under his belt, Sun fled back to Japan along with hundreds of other anti-Yuan conspirators. He was no longer received as an honored guest, as he had been just months before, and had it not been for his old friends and supporters in Japan, he would not have been allowed to disembark. The Japanese government, like its European and American counterparts, was betting on Yuan Shih-k'ai, who promptly purged the KMT from parliament and then abolished parliament itself. Sun's hopes for democracy in China were now dead.

In 1914, with the European powers preoccupied by the bloodshed of World War I, the Japanese made their move. After invading and occupying the German concessions in Shantung, they submitted a list of twenty-one demands to Yuan. All but the most humiliating were accepted. Yuan also secretly agreed to let Japan keep what it had captured from the Germans when the war was over. It was an agreement that would later cause so much trouble for the Chinese delegation at the Paris Peace Conference. As news of Yuan's concessions became public, boycotts and demonstrations broke out across China. Then, in 1915, Yuan Shih-k'ai overreached, as dictators are wont to do. He decided to revive the monarchy, and like Napoleon Bonaparte before him, declared himself the new emperor. Considerable state funds were spent providing him with suitable costumes as the inheritor to the Dragon Throne. He was enthroned on New Year's Day of 1916. But he badly miscalculated his support, and his position began to crumble.

The foreign powers were hesitant, and once again provincial governors began to secede. As armed uprising in the west began to spread east, Yuan backed down and abdicated after only eighty-three days. His abdication did not mollify discontent, but by then Yuan was a very sick man. He died of uremia at the age of fifty-six in June 1916. With his death a power vacuum opened. It was quickly filled with chaos and bloodshed as China disintegrated into warring fiefdoms and competing generals fighting among themselves. China's warlord period had begun.

As for Sun, he married for a second time.[iv] Taking a second wife, or concubine, was not unusual in China at that time. Lu Muchen, of whom he had seen little since their marriage in 1884, did not object. Therefore, in October of 1915, Sun married his English-language secretary, the beautiful, well-spoken, and American-educated Soong Ching-ling (Song Quingling). She was half his age, the daughter of an old friend. Sun had earlier fallen in love with Ching-ling's older sister, but her father, from a wealthy Shanghai family, had been against it. This time he did not seek the father's permission, which shocked tradition-minded Chinese. Nor did he divorce Lu Muchen, which shocked his fellow Christians.

In 1917, when America joined the allies in World War I, China debated whether to follow America's lead. Sun argued for neutrality, arguing that since the allies were all the colonial powers that had subjugated China, maybe it would be better if the Central Powers won. But Sun lost that argument, and China went to war alongside the allies. Although thousands of laborers were sent to help the British and the French, China sent no soldiers, who were busy fighting each other. One warlord, who had all along been sympathetic to the Ch'ing, captured Peking and put Pu-yi back on the throne. But the restoration lasted only a few weeks before other warlords took Peking and deposed Pu-yi once again. By this time, as one historian put it, "the recurrence of civil war had become almost as regular as the return of spring."[22] The chaos led Sun to thinking he might move to Canton and create his own national government in

---

iv Ching-ling was either Sun's second or third wife depending on how you count it. For a quiet, reserved man he led a surprisingly lively love life. Sun had several affairs while living in Yokohama, Japan. In 1902, when he was thirty-six, he married a fourteen-year-old Japanese girl with her father's permission. She did not accompany him on his travels, but she had a daughter by him. He abandoned his Japanese family in 1906, and whether his Japanese wife was his second wife or a concubine is a matter of interpretation. His daughter was adopted by another Japanese family.

the south until he could gather enough strength to take Peking and unite the country. He pursued this strategy with the same intensity he had in ridding China of the Ch'ing Dynasty.

There was a clear contrast between Peking in the north, isolated, landlocked, facing the great desert of inland Asia; and Canton on the Pearl River in the south, leading to the sea and open for centuries to foreign influences. Thus, Canton became Sun's base for a rival republic. He persuaded members of the old parliament, that Yuan Shih-k'ai had dissolved, to join him. Disaffected elements of the Chinese Navy defected to Sun's cause and brought their warships south. The southern warlords, however, were not thrilled to have Sun set up shop in their midst, and the only military force Sun could count on was the garrison stationed in Canton itself. But for the moment he was safe.

Once again Sun took up his old game of trying to raise money for his regime from overseas sources. He tried to play the Japanese off against the Americans, but neither country would lend him money or recognize his government. Even though China had joined the allies against Germany, he sent emissaries to see if the Kaiser might loan him money in exchange for access to mineral wealth. But the Kaiser was enmeshed in the last desperate battles of World War I, and the war ended before Germany could even respond.

The southern warlords felt increasingly threatened by Sun's activities and soon made their displeasure known. Rather than risking a confrontation, Sun left for Shanghai, where he spent the next two years writing memoirs and political tracts. When the May Fourth Movement first burst with student strikes and riots all over China, Sun had been skeptical, still hoping that by playing the warlords off against each other he could unify China. But he soon came to see that the energy of the May Fourth Movement and the growing radicalization of students could be harnessed to his cause. So he joined in the May Fourth Movement's criticism of Japan, his erstwhile sponsor and host in exile.

Meanwhile, a Cantonese warlord and one-time supporter, Ch'en

Chiung-ming (Chen Jiongming), recaptured Canton. Sun returned to Canton in 1920, hoping to set up his southern government as a rival to Peking again. He was appointed "Extraordinary" President because there were not enough of his rump parliamentarians to reach a quorum. He hoped the foreign powers might switch their recognition of the Peking government to him. But now he was viewed abroad as a greedy politician who was hindering the unification of China with his breakaway Canton regime. Still, in comparison to blood-soaked and squabbling warlords, Sun stood as an honest man uncompromised by greed. Few could match his persuasive oratory, but the foreign imperialist powers were still backing Peking.

In the summer of 1921, Sun got permission from his rump parliament to mount a northern expedition to take Peking. He did not, however, ask Ch'en Chiung-ming for his approval. Sun raised an army and marched as far as Kweilin (Guilin), where he hoped to go on the offensive. But Ch'en believed in a federalist future for China in which warlords could come together in a unified country but still keep their fiefdoms intact. This was anathema to Sun. And so, with Ch'en refusing to back him and presenting a potential hostile force at his rear, Sun spent a humiliating winter in Kweilin before retreating back to Canton. It was yet another expedition ending in failure. Sun started negotiating with the quarreling warlords of the north. He was prepared to back anyone with an army who would back him. When this failed, he set off again in May 1922 on another northern expedition to capture Peking and restore constitutional government. No sooner had he left Canton, however, than Ch'en, whom Sun had fired as provincial governor, moved into the city with his troops. Sun rushed back and demanded that Ch'en and his troops evacuate Canton. He threatened to use poison gas artillery shells if his demands were not met. Warlords were not known to take orders from Sun or any other politician, and with his bluff called, Sun's house came under hostile fire. Ching-ling described the scene, "The enemy fired downhill at us from two sides, shouting 'Kill Sun Wen! Kill Sun Wen!' [one of his many aliases]. As day broke our men began firing their rifles and machine guns, while the enemy employed field guns."[23]

Sun and Ching-ling escaped the bombardment and made their way to a gunboat in the Pearl River. Sun contacted a trusted young officer, Chiang Kai-shek, who joined him. For five weeks, while battles raged between Ch'en's men and forces loyal to Sun, Chiang and Sun tried to negotiate with General Ch'en, but to no avail. With his forces losing, Sun reached out to the American consul for help. But the Americans held to their policy of strict neutrality, so he turned to the British, who got him out to Hong Kong on a British gunboat. From there he quickly embarked on a steamer to Shanghai. With his second Canton regime ending in failure, and fleeing for his life, Sun now found himself with no allies among any of the warlords. Japan and the European colonial powers, whom he had often denounced and at other times assiduously wooed, showed no interest in him now. There was America, perhaps a less greedy imperial power, but Sun was now thoroughly disillusioned with the United States. Still convinced he needed help from abroad, he turned his gaze toward two European powers who were on the outs as much as he: post-war Germany and the new Soviet Union.

Of the two, Russia was in the best position to help. In 1917, when the Bolsheviks first came to power, Sun had fired off a congratulatory cable to Lenin expressing the hope that revolutionary parties could work together for the betterment of the world. Communism may have terrified the West, but it was looking better and better to many in the East. Lenin was in no position to hold on to Tsarist Russia's colonial concessions, so, making a virtue of necessity, he renounced them all and denounced imperialism in all its forms everywhere. As another leading Bolshevik, Nikolai Bukharin, put it, "If we propound the solution of the right of self-determination for the colonies ... we lose nothing by it. On the contrary, we gain; for the national gain as a whole will damage foreign imperialism."[24]

Lenin had hoped that Marxism would spread throughout the industrialized countries of western Europe, and in 1919 it looked as if it might. In that year revolutionary waves were rising in Europe; Soviet workers' councils were sprouting up in both Germany and Austria; and Communist regimes had actually taken over in Hungary and in Bavaria. But those regimes soon collapsed and the Red tide began to recede. It became evident that Communism was not going to take hold in the West. In March 1919 Moscow created the Communist International, or Comintern, an organization designed to promote, incite, and coordinate Communist revolutions abroad.

Although China lacked the bourgeoisie and the industrial base for a classic Marxist revolution—only 0.5 percent of the Chinese population could be considered proletarian workers—Soviet Russia began looking eastward to spread its doctrine. Lenin had taken note that China had shed its monarchy before Russia had, and given China's proximity, what happened to China was of intense interest to the Bolsheviks. Having a friendly China on its border could counterbalance Japan's territorial ambitions. Even before the formation of the Comintern's Eastern Bureau in 1920, Bolshevik agents had been dispatched to China to help found a Soviet-style party. Their message was attractive: that Soviet Russia was the only country not taking advantage of China's weakness, and that Russia backed the emancipation of oppressed peoples everywhere. The Bolsheviks stood for the freedom, equality, well-being, and self-determination of all peoples, or so they said. It sounded very much like what they had been told about Wilson's ideals, but that was before Wilson's perceived betrayal of China in Paris.

With the advice and guidance of the Comintern, the fledgling Chinese Communist Party, the CCP, published its own manifesto in 1920. In July of the following year, meeting secretly in the Bower School for Girls in the tree-shaded French concession of Shanghai, the Communist Party convened its first Congress. The school was empty in the summer months, and the Chinese government did not have the authority to arrest in the French concession. Most of the meetings took place nearby in the house of one of the delegate's brothers. There were fifteen delegates at that first meeting, all of them men. Thirteen were Chinese, veterans of the May Fourth Movement. Their average age was twenty-six, and most were journalists or teachers.

It is fair to say that none had a firm understanding of either Marxism or Communism. Some had been attracted to anarchism, a movement that had gained traction among Chinese radicals and intellectuals. Russian agents were forever complaining about China's political immaturity. Thus, the Chinese delegates were joined by two Comintern agents sent by Russia to guide them. One was a Dutchman named Hendricus Sneevliet, alias "Maring," who had been an organizer for the Comintern in the Dutch East Indies (Indonesia today). The other was a Russian recently new to Bolshevism, Vladimir Nikolski. The two original founders of the party, Ch'en Tu-hsiu and his Peking University colleague, Li Ta-chao (Li Dazhao), who had organized the Marxist study group that evolved into China's Communist Party, were not present at that first congress. The thirteen that were present constituted a sizable proportion of the party's total membership in 1921. There were fewer than sixty party members in all of China. Among the attendees was the young radical from Hunan, Mao Tse-tung. Much would be heard of him in later decades, but Mao had little to say at that first congress. As he was to tell the writer Edgar Snow fifteen years later, in those early days of the party his mind was a "curious mixture of ideas of liberalism, democratic reformism, and utopian socialism."[25]

The congress did not last long in Shanghai for, to the dismay of all, a stranger walked in off the street during their deliberations. He left quickly, but none could be sure he was not an informer working for the French police. Fearing exposure, the delegates left quickly, making their separate ways to the train station. From there they traveled to a small lake near Shanghai, where the wife of one of the delegates provided a boat in which to resume the congress. A mahjong set was brought aboard, and whenever other boats passed by, the mahjong tiles were shuffled with loud clicks to give the impression that the delegates were only playing a game instead of charting the future of China. Among the topics discussed were overthrowing the capitalist class's state power, whether there should be a dictatorship of the proletariat, and whether they should follow Lenin's advice to join forces with Sun Yat-sen's KMT. The latter motion was rejected, as was the motion that the Chinese Communist Party should be subservient to the Comintern. A proposal to study how Bolshevism was working in other countries was also rejected. The absent Ch'en Tu-hsiu was elected General Secretary of the new party. As recently as 1919, Ch'en had believed that China should follow the path of democracy similar to the United States and Britain. But all of that had now changed, and Ch'en, along with many others, was turning toward Marxism for inspiration.

Not everyone agreed with what Russia wanted at the first congress. Four of the delegates would soon leave the party. But by the time of the second CCP Congress, a year later, the party was more aligned with Lenin. They voted to "act jointly with the democratic party (i.e. the Kuomintang) to establish a united front of democratic revolution ... to liberate the Chinese people from a dual yoke—the yoke of foreigners and the yoke of powerful militarists (i.e. the warlords) in our country—a war which is just as urgently needed as it is inevitable."[26] The CCP also voted unanimously to obey the Comintern in all matters. The party had come fully to Moscow's heel.

The next effort would be to sell a united front to Sun Yat-sen. Sun may have been a poor administrator, but he had a genius for inspiring others, and he was widely perceived as China's best hope. Although never a Communist, he thought of himself as a socialist and a nationalist. Sun had reached out to Moscow because no help was forthcoming from the Western powers. That help would become crucial. As the historian Conrad Brandt has written, "Without Soviet munitions and Soviet advice on party organization, China's 'Great Revolution' would certainly have been delayed; and without inspiration from Soviet dogma it would certainly have been less forceful."[27] The new Soviet government's anti-colonial stand put Woodrow Wilson's equivocations on colonialism to shame.

Moscow did not believe that China was historically ready for a Communist revolution, and neither did Sun. Therefore, the Comintern's decision that the CCP should join forces with Sun's KMT in their attempt to reunify China made sense to both parties. In 1923 the United Front was negotiated between Sun and the Comintern's Adolph Joffe, Russia's ambassador in Peking. Their joint statement set a prenuptial tone:

> Dr. Sun Yat-sen holds that the Communistic order or even the Soviet system cannot actually be introduced into China, because there do not exist here the conditions for the successful establishment of either Communism or Sovietism. This view is entirely shared by Mr. Joffe, who is of the further opinion that China's paramount and most pressing problem is to achieve national unification and attain full national independence, and regarding this great task, he has assured Dr. Sun Yat-sen that China has the warmest sympathy of the Russian people and can count on the support of Russia.[28]

From the start it was an uneasy alliance, with each of the players hoping to use the others for their own ends. The KMT wanted Russian support, arms and ammunitions; the Chinese Communists wanted to gain experience and credibility to eventually seize power; and the Soviet Union wanted an ally on its southeast border as a hedge against Japan. Yet there were some Russians, including Grigorii Zinoviev, who worried that there were elements in the KMT that "look, not without benevolence, to the side of America ... thinking that it will be from there that the blessings of democracy and progress will flow on revolutionary China."[29] The more conservative elements of the KMT were not pleased with the United Front either. They accused Sun of a "plot to borrow the body of the Kuomintang, but to infuse it with the soul of the Communist party."[30] Ch'en Tu-hsiu, the head of the Communist Party, was "skeptical of how useful or trustworthy" the KMT would be.[31] Stalin's rival, Leon Trotsky, believed the Communists should seize power as soon as possible, but Stalin insisted they follow the Communist dogma that a country like China needed to pass through a bourgeois-democratic phase of revolution before it was ready for state Communism. After all, it was the bourgeoise who were in the forefront of the anti-imperial cause. Lenin, and later Stalin, thought the Chinese Communists should piggyback on the bourgeoisie until the Communists were ready to take power by themselves. Stalin's famous answer to Trotsky was that once the KMT had served Moscow's purpose, it would be "squeezed out like a lemon and then flung away."[32,v]

As for Sun, he chose a different metaphor but was playing the same game as Stalin. "We may merely yoke up Soviet Russia and mount it," he said.[33] Sun made it very clear from the beginning that the CCP should not merge with the KMT in a marriage of equals. Communists could join the KMT only as individuals, not in a bloc. What Sun feared most was that Russia would funnel arms, ammunition, and military advisors through the CCP rather than through the Kuomintang. As a concession, Chen Tu-hsiu was made a member of the KMT's governing body.

Thus did Sun Yat-sen enter into a formal agreement with a foreign power for the first time, and for the first time a foreign power recognized him as an ally. The CCP, despite Sun's wishes, began acting as a bloc within the Kuomintang, something that Sun had to overlook if he wanted to keep Soviet arms and money coming.

---

v Stalin made this remark just before the KMT turned on the Communists, all but destroying the CCP in 1927. Trotsky attacked Stalin for his faulty judgment, and Stalin went to great lengths to expunge from the record any mention of his "lemon" speech. Communist agents on two continents razored out Stalin's remarks in libraries and archives. The journalist Harold Isaacs, however, found a source in New York that had kept back copies of the *Communist Daily Worker*, so Isaacs was able to reproduce Stalin's speech in his book, *The Tragedy of the Chinese Revolution*.

"We have lost hope of help from America, England, France, or any other of the great powers," he said. "The only country that shows signs of helping us ... is the Soviet government of Russia."[34] With that, the flow of Soviet money, guns, and ammunition began to flow toward Sun Yat-sen.

Even before Lenin's death, Joseph Stalin was rising in the party to take power in Russia. One of the Comintern agents sent to China was Mikhail Borodin, a man of exceptional talent and persuasive charm. Born Mikhail Gruzenberg to Jewish parents in rural Russia, Borodin had been a close ally of Lenin. He had been partially educated in America, having fled there after the failure of the 1905 revolution. He spoke English fluently with a Midwestern accent, although his first language had been Yiddish. Upon returning to Russia after the 1917 revolution, Borodin participated in the first Comintern congress in Moscow in 1919. He traveled widely on behalf of the Comintern. His penultimate assignment was in Scotland, where he was known as George Brown.[35] Following Sun Yat-sen's request for help, he was sent to China in 1923 as the head of a Comintern delegation. His cover was as a correspondent for the *Rosta News Agency*. Borodin spoke no Chinese, so he and Sun communicated in English. Unlike Sun, Borodin was a brilliant organizer, and with his help the KMT was soon being organized along Leninist lines. Borodin also established a reliable flow of Russian arms and ammunition to be sent from Vladivostok to Canton.

Borodin impressed many with his analytic powers, his unflappable demeanor, and his long view. The American journalist Vincent Sheean described him as a "large, calm man with the natural dignity of a lion or a panther and had the special quality of being in, but above the battle ... "[36] Sheean compared him to Abd el-Krim, whom Sheean had interviewed in Morocco before coming to China. Others, such as the head of Canton Christian College, Dr. James Henry, found Borodin "a very pleasant personality," sincere and deeply earnest.[37]

Sun fell immediately under Borodin's spell, and Borodin knew how to play to Sun's ego. Even though he wasn't buying Borodin's Communist strategy, Sun was impressed with Borodin's tactical skill. When Ch'en Chiung-ming's forces started advancing again on Canton in November 1923, Borodin criticized the KMT for not mobilizing the masses. He began organizing peasants and workers to resist. Organizers were sent out on bicycles, horse carts, and on foot to rally the countryside against Ch'en. Borodin even suggested land confiscation, but Sun reminded him that the overseas Chinese, on whose resources Sun had for so long depended, would never put up with anything as confiscatory as that.

Workers were offered a minimum wage and an eight-hour work day, which was radical in China. Before the end of November, Ch'en's men had been checked, and Sun's third Canton government saved. Sun was willing to give Borodin the credit, telling visitors "his name is Lafayette," after the French aristocrat who helped save George Washington.[38] "Now we can have a good friend, who has come from Russia ..." Sun told his colleagues. "He is to train our comrades ... If we want our revolution to succeed, we must learn the methods, organization and training of the Russians."[39] From then on mobilizing the masses, Soviet-style, became KMT doctrine. However, Sun was firmly opposed to both land confiscations and the Communist emphasis on class warfare. Sun hoped that the Chinese revolution would be a death sentence for European and Japanese imperialism in China.

Borodin's private opinion of Sun was less than flattering. In confidential reports to Moscow, Borodin described Sun as politically unsophisticated, and often prone to showing bad judgment. Sun, in Borodin's opinion, saw himself as a latter-day Confucius—"the hero and the others the mob."[40] But Borodin knew that his effectiveness in China depended on his rapport with Sun. Borodin's task was to build up both the Kuomintang and the Communist party so that eventually the latter could replace the former. The important thing for Sun was that Russian weapons keep arriving. They were far superior to the weapons manufactured locally. The Russians made sure that the forces supporting Sun were better fed, better led, and better organized than their opposition. So Sun defended Borodin and supported the inclusion of the CCP, despite the opposition of the KMT's right wing.

Desperate for funds, Sun took the bold step of threatening to seize the customs house in Canton and take the revenues. His excuse was that foreigners controlled the customs, and revenues were being sent to his enemies in Peking. Sun even made an appeal to the Americans, reminding them of the Boston Tea Party and their own protests against unjust taxation in colonial times. But once again the Americans were not buying, and along with other foreign powers, they sent sixteen warships up the Pearl River to assert foreign dominance. In addition to American, British, French, and Japanese warships, the flotilla included an Italian torpedo boat and a Portuguese warship from nearby Macau. But the largest contingent was American. This was gunboat diplomacy at its most naked, only this time it was aimed directly at Sun Yat-sen. Faced with such overpowering force, he had to back down.

Although Sun had lost his confrontation with the foreign powers, the propaganda value of being bullied by imperialists was invaluable. "Among Chinese his prestige soared," wrote one biographer. "In Canton, newspapers and mass meetings denounced gunboat diplomacy. Even some officials of the Peking government could not help admiring Sun's stand against foreign interference. More than any previous time in his life, he spoke for China and for the students of the May 4th Movement."[41] The gunboats of the West drove Sun even further into the welcoming arms of the Soviet Union.

A curious incident occurred at this time. A group of off-duty American naval officers from the ships sent to intimidate Sun were drinking in Canton's Anglo-French concession. At the bar was one of Sun's cohorts, and the naval officers asked if they could meet this Dr. Sun Yat-sen whom they had heard so much about, and whose plans they had come to thwart. Sun agreed to see them, and the next day a meeting was arranged at Sun's headquarters. Sun charmed the

American officers. Upon leaving, one of them said, "Doctor, I am right glad we know where you live. If we have to bombard Canton City, we'll take care nothing comes in your direction." Sun is said to have replied, "Gentlemen, I must remind you that it is your duty to obey orders, however contrary to your personal feelings."[42]

In January 1924, the Kuomintang's first national congress was held in Canton. Sun defended the inclusion of the Communists, praising their organizational skills, while simultaneously arguing that industrialization in China was not advanced enough to warrant class struggle. It was not a question of who was using whom. The Communists and Sun were using each other to achieve their goals. To be sure, the Communists had not put all their efforts into Sun's KMT. The Soviets were also trying to establish good relations with the Peking regime as well.

An important development for Sun was the establishment of the Whampoa (Hangpu) Military Academy in Canton, with Borodin's help, in the spring of 1924. Russian instructors were sent from Moscow, and Sun's protégé, Chiang Kai-shek, who had just returned from military training in Russia, was put in charge. Sun badly wanted his own army to free him from reliance on warlords. Although he would continue from time to time to enlist help from warlords, his dependence on them was now greatly reduced. Soviet Russia's Far East Commander, General Vasily Blücher, known in China as Galin, was named as Chiang Kai-shek's chief of staff. The CCP's Chou En-lai was named deputy head of the political department at Whampoa. Chiang and Chou retained a curious respect for each other all through the years of enmity that lay ahead.

At this time, Sun gave a series of lectures on the need to save China, spelling out his political philosophies. He called upon a nationalist spirit to resist the rapacious imperialists who were gobbling up the world. He repeated his allegations that Wilson had once offered hope, but after his decisions in Paris and the unjust peace treaty, that hope had been extinguished. Only the Soviet Union remained China's friend. Sun strongly preferred a democratic China, but, for him, Russia was as a raft to a drowning sailor in a sea of foreign imperialism. It was not a time to criticize the raft. The united front with the Communists remained intact, although rivalry between right and left factions of the KMT was growing. In one of his lectures, Sun tried to smooth over these differences, arguing that although heartless capitalism in the West had undoubtedly brought forth a Marxist response, China was not in a situation that would make class warfare inevitable. Therefore, Communism was not appropriate for China, he argued. Naturally this brought rebukes from the left wing of the KMT and from Borodin.

In another speech, Sun provided the intellectual justification for his collaboration with the Communists by quoting Abraham Lincoln. The goal of government of the people, by the people, and for the people meant that all would share in the benefits of society. As always, Sun was willing to trim his sails to suit any prevailing wind just as long as the boat kept moving forward toward the reunification of China, preferably with him at the helm. As the right wing of the party showed more and more unease with the Communists, Sun assured them that Moscow backed him, personally, rather than the Communist Party. But there could be no denying that he had let the Communists in the door.

Here we should pause to consider Sun's philosophy for governing, for during this time Sun published his final work, *Three Principles of the People,* summarizing his political thinking that had been developing for twenty years. His guiding principles were nationalism, democracy, and the livelihood of the people. On one level, Sun's principles are a "hodgepodge: Chinese cultural pride is mixed with Leninist anti-imperialism, Montesquieu's Laws rubbing shoulders with Lincoln's precepts and socialism … goes hand in hand with Marxism and traditional Chinese utopian thinking," as historian Marie-Claire Bergère puts it.[43] Much is borrowed from European and American thought, but then, as now, China was wrestling with what to take from the West without adopting Western civilization. Even during Mao Tse-tung's near-isolation from the rest of the world, one could see big posters proclaiming, "Let Foreign Things Serve China" in Chinese cities.[44] For Sun, nationalism was of the blood, meaning race, not soil. There were too many overseas Chinese for Sun to restrict Chinese nationalism to those living in China. And within the borders of China there were many minorities—Mongols, Manchurians, Tibetans, Turkic Muslims, not to mention the animist hill tribes of southern China. That said, Sun's emphasis was on the majority Han population, roughly 400 million in Sun's time. The minorities accounted for approximately ten million, and could be absorbed within a majority Han nation, Sun believed, but to be truly Chinese was to be part of a 4,000-year-old culture, not just a nationality that could be put on or taken off like a coat.

Echoes of that thinking can be heard in China today in its relationship toward Tibet and its Muslim minorities. Sun, like China's leaders today, invoked a sense of danger from the outside world. In Europe one race could contain many countries, while in America one country could contain many races. But "China has been developing a single state out of a single race."[45] What Sun had initiated as an anti-Manchu campaign had developed into a more inclusive, anti-imperialist nationalism focused on foreign concessions, unequal treaties, and extraterritoriality.

If Sun was slow to recognize the wave of nationalism brought on by Woodrow Wilson's Shantung decision in Paris, he was now making up for lost time. "This world tendency has flowed from theocracy on to autocracy and from autocracy now on to democracy, and there is no way to stem the current," Sun said.[46] But democracy had to be the servant of nationalism if imperialism was to be defeated.

Sun disagreed with those students who called for a Western-style democracy. In Sun's view, European monarchs had interfered with every facet of European life, thus causing a counter-reaction. But in China, except for collecting taxes, the state had not interfered with people's lives. To illustrate, Sun recalled an ancient Chinese poem:

When the sun rises, I toil;
When the sun sets, I rest;
I dig wells for water;
I till the fields for food;
What has the Emperor's power have to do with me?[47]

Today's China has become a surveillance state, interfering in the most minute affairs of its people, but not then.

Sun conceded that the needs of the state should trump individual liberty. "The revolution cannot be said to aim at liberty. If we declare that we are fighting for liberty we shall remain a loose sheet of scattered sand," Sun said, borrowing a metaphor from the Confucian classics. "We shall never be unified, we shall never attain the desired end of our revolution … On no account should we give greater liberty to the individual … in order to make the nation free, we must each sacrifice our personal freedom."[48] The absence of a strong state and strong institutions, Sun felt, was the reason for the chaos after the fall of the Manchus. Chinese leaders ever since have limited individual rights in favor of a strong state, fearing that to do otherwise would lead to chaos and the disintegration of the country. Memory of the warlord period still shapes the politics of China today.

Commenting on the United States, Sun said, "Wealth and power have not come only from independence and self-government of the original states, but rather from the progress in unified government which followed the federation of the states."[49] Sun believed that citizens had to trust their government and give it freedom to maneuver, just as a chauffeur must be trusted and empowered to drive a car. China needed a guided democracy run by experts, at least in the beginning. Sun was short on specifics, and we can never know how China would have developed if Sun had been able to put his principles into effect. Taiwan offers a clue: a government established on Sun's principles that developed over the years from a one-party state to a pluralistic democracy. Sun's concept of tutelage was very different from Communism's dictatorship of the proletariat. Nevertheless, modern China has achieved all that Sun wanted in terms of material well-being, unity, and national power.

As for Sun's third principle, promoting the people's livelihood, he recommended combining socialism and economic development. Performing intellectual acrobatics, Sun sought to bring Communism in line with Confucian theories of Great Harmony. Contrary to what his Russian advisors were saying, Sun maintained that class war was "not the reason for social evolution ... The principle force in human evolution was cooperation, not conflict."[50] He firmly believed that the interests of capitalists and workers could be reconciled. He believed that China's poverty problem was simply poverty itself rather than a failure to redistribute wealth. Although he did say that land should belong to those who worked it, the process had to be gradual, free from the violent immediacy of Bolshevism—land reform, not land confiscation. As for the problems posed by industrialization, Sun believed that the Americans had been more successful in mitigating them than the Soviets. Capitalism should be restrained, not eliminated. China's path to a constitutional republic should be in three stages, Sun believed. In the beginning, democracy would be deferred in favor of a military dictatorship. Ancient wrongs, such as foot-binding and bureaucratic corruption, would be eliminated. China would then have six years of guided democracy with local elections in the provinces. Once the practice of democracy was learned, and only then, could China emerge as a full-fledged democracy.

Sun was forced to abandon his lecture series when influential businessmen of Canton began objecting to high taxes and the threat of organized labor. The business community formed its own militia and began smuggling guns and ammunition into the city, as Sun himself had once done. Sun's men were able to confiscate the arms shipments, but Sun was so strapped for money that he even contemplated selling the confiscated arms back to the militias. Sun wanted to mount yet another military expedition to overthrow the

Peking regime and unify the country, but his more cautious allies were not with him. Chiang Kai-shek refused to allow his military cadets to participate, and his Communist allies protested as well. They wanted Sun to consolidate his base in Canton before he pursued the reunification of China. And they were not wrong. Canton's businessmen organized a general strike and called for Sun's ouster and a return to warlord control, which they thought would be better for business. The left wing of the KMT, led by Borodin, called for a strong response and Sun acquiesced. In August 1924 the business quarter was looted and set on fire. The business community in both Canton and Hong Kong now believed that Sun had completely gone over to the Communists.

In 1924, with control of Peking changing hands once again, Sun was invited to attend a conference of reconciliation in the Chinese capital. Seeing an opportunity, Sun announced he would attend. His colleagues feared for his safety, but Sun's reputation as a man of determination and principle had extended beyond his Canton base. Accompanied by his wife, Ching-ling, and Borodin, Sun traveled to Peking in stages, stopping in Shanghai and then Japan, his old home in exile. Japan had long since given up on Sun, and was dealing exclusively with whatever government ruled in Peking, which it alternatively bullied and financed. Sun may have deplored Japanese imperialism, but he always left the door open for Japan to have a change of heart. During his stop over, Sun made a speech calling for Japan to forgo its imperialist designs on China and join a pan-Asian effort to dislodge Western imperialism from the region. Although Japan would later use this speech to justify its own Asian Co-Prosperity Sphere in World War II, the Japanese were not amenable to Sun's program. Disappointed once again, Sun left Japan for China.

It was not just disappointment that afflicted Sun at this time, however. A cancer was growing deep in his liver, causing him intense pain. When his ship arrived in port he was immediately confined to bed. On New Year's Eve 1924, Sun traveled by special train to Peking and was rushed to a Rockefeller Foundation-supported hospital in the capital. Surgeons operated, but determined that the cancer was beyond their ability to treat. He was released from the hospital to spend his last days in the house of Wellington Koo, the young Chinese who had argued so passionately in China's cause at the Paris Peace Conference. Supporters and KMT leaders rushed to Peking to be at Sun's bedside. Drafts of his final political testaments were written and read back to him. But how much he could take in at this point, so close to death, is debatable. With his wife guiding his failing hand, he signed his final testament:

> For forty years I have devoted myself to the cause of the people's revolution but with one end in view, the elevation of China to a position of freedom and equality among the nations. My experiences during these forty years have firmly convinced me that to attain this goal we must bring about a thorough awakening of our own people, and ally ourselves in a common struggle with those peoples of the world who treat us on the basis of equality ... Above all, ... the abolition of unequal treaties should be carried into effect with the least possible delay. This is my heartfelt charge to you.[51]

Just before he died, Sun signed a fawning letter to the Central Committee of the Soviet Union, stressing that a strong bond between their two nations would liberate oppressed peoples of the world. Whether he was sufficiently conscious to read and understand these documents, or whether his wife and other guiding hands took up the reins of his legacy as he lay dying, will never be known. But either way the deification of Sun had already begun by the time he died on March 12, 1925. In death, Sun's failures and defeats were forgotten in the enthusiasm to anoint him as the father of his country. Chinese, both at home and overseas, outdid themselves in posthumous praise. He had become in death the most popular public figure in China. Nobody had worked harder to rid China of despotism, or to reunite the country. Sun was temporarily interred in the Temple of the Azure Clouds in the Western Hills near Peking until an elaborate mausoleum could be built for him on the Purple

Mountain of Nanking, near the tombs of the Ming Dynasty emperors. His bones reside there to this day.

Moscow, too, was anxious to co-opt Sun's legend. Borodin was quick to recommend the opening of a Sun Yat-sen Communist University of Toilers of China, dedicated to the training of Chinese revolutionaries in propaganda and political agitation. The university was opened within seven months of Sun's death. Hundreds of Chinese students were enrolled, but ironically, the curriculum neglected to include the writings of Sun Yat-sen himself.

Toward the end of May 1925, riots erupted throughout China protesting against the Japanese in general, and specifically against British troops in Shanghai for opening fire on striking workers, killing eleven and injuring many more. "There were echoes of May Fourth in the way that May 30th also became a symbol and a rallying cry," writes sinologist Jonathan Spence, "but now—in 1925—conditions are different ... Both the Kuomintang and the CCP, or a combination of the two, stood ready to channel the rage and frustration of the Chinese into their own party organizations. Indigenous nationalism could now call on Soviet organizational expertise to build for meaningful political action. Perhaps that was Sun Yat-sen's true legacy."[52]

Sun had no successor, and his death triggered quarrels within the KMT between left and right factions. Party leadership fell to Wang Ch'ing-wei (Wang Jinwei),[vi] whose rebel credentials were established when he tried to assassinate Pu-yi's father. Wang was soon overshadowed by Chiang Kai-shek, who was rising in prestige

---

vi During World War II, Wang Ch'ing-wei continued his rivalry with Chiang Kai-shek by collaborating with the Japanese. He became head of Japan's puppet regime in Nanking. He justified his collaboration on the grounds that he was defending China against Communism and Western imperialism. He died before the war's end from wounds sustained in an assassination attempt, thus cheating retribution at the hands of either the Nationalists or the Communists.

and power. In March 1926, in an incident known as the Canton Coup, Chiang Kai-shek became alarmed when a warship under the control of the leftist faction began moving suspiciously as if it might be planning an attack. Chiang declared martial law and arrested prominent members of the CCP. For a moment it looked as if the United Front was finished. Stalin, however, still had faith, and against the advice of Leon Trotsky, patched up the quarrel between the two Kuomintang factions. Compromises were made and the United Front remained in force. Chiang's open hostility worried the Communists in the coalition, and some argued that the CCP should withdraw from the United Front then and there. But Stalin remained resolute. As scholar Conrad Brandt has observed, Stalin saw everything through the lens of class warfare, and "did not register Chiang Kai-shek as a man of flesh, blood and will, but merely as the organic particle of a class layer, to be shed in the next molting season of revolution. Stalin never suspected that this particle hid his own likeness."[53]

In June 1926, Chiang Kai-shek was named commander-in-chief of the new National Revolutionary Army (NRA), composed of his own troops and those of friendly warlords. The Western press soon began calling Chiang "Generalissimo," or G-Mo for short, a title that stuck for the rest of his life. In July of that year, Chiang launched his own northern expedition to re-unite China. He would succeed where Sun had failed. Capturing town after town as he marched north, he picked up defecting warlord battalions along the way. Many Chinese cities and towns in those days were still surrounded by walls, and Chiang's troops proved adept at charging these walls with ladders and climbing up and over them under fire, as they had been trained to do at the Whampoa Military Academy. By 1927 the NRA had reached the Yangtze, and by March it had captured Nanking on the river's south bank. NRA soldiers and civilians rioted, killing foreigners, including two Britons and the American vice president of Nanking University. The British and Americans promptly sent warships steaming up river to shell the town, land Marines, and evacuate foreigners.

Further upstream the warlords stoutly defended Wuhan's three cities, publicly beheading commanders who failed to stem the NRA tide. By autumn the three cities were in Chiang's hands—fifteen years after the Wuhan mutinies that had brought down the Ch'ing Dynasty. With the unifying presence of Sun Yat-sen no longer there to provide the glue, the United Front began to come apart. The recent events in Canton had put both KMT factions at sword's point. With Borodin's help, and with the Widow Sun's approval, the Communist faction set up a government in exile in Hangkow where they began using the class war tactics of which Sun had disapproved. After attempting a reconciliation with the CCP, Chiang set up a rival headquarters, first in Hangchow, then in Nanking.

It was there that the left-leaning American journalist Vincent Sheean interviewed Chiang Kai-shek, and found him "much to my surprise, sensitive and alert," and intending to carry out the whole program of Sun Yat-sen's three principles. Sheean reported that Chiang spoke in revolutionary cliches, "'wicked gentry, foreign imperialism.'"[54] But Sheean failed to draw him out on any differences he may have had with the left wing of his party. Chiang was too shrewd to show his hand on what was about to happen. Chiang's victories gave some warlords second thoughts about opposing him, and the same could be said about the British.

It was in the treaty port of Shanghai, however, where Chiang had allies among the city's criminal gangs, that matters came to a head. In late March 1927, as Chiang's army approached Shanghai, the Communist-inspired labor unions, led by Chou En-lai and Ch'en Tu-hsiu, rose up against the local warlord, declared a general strike and took over the key points in the Chinese city. The workers had strict orders not to interfere with foreigners in their concessions, and the workers obeyed. Chiang Kai-shek's troops marched in the next day, and at first Chiang praised the striking workers, leading them into a false sense of security. The Communist Party ordered the strikers to give up their weapons, with which they had armed themselves by raiding police stations, while Chiang calmed the business

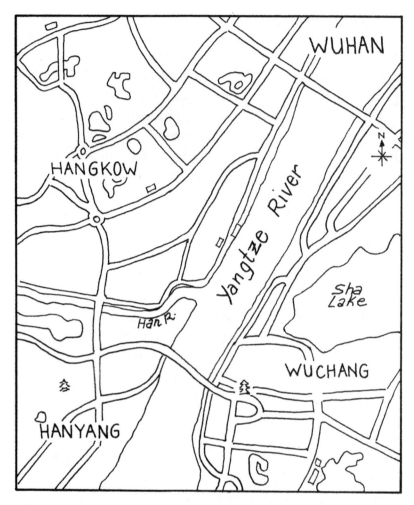

The three cities of Wuhan where the revolution of 1911 began, and where leftist factions of the Kuomintang set up headquarters during the final northern expedition to reunite China.
Map drawn by Julia L. Greenway

owners and industrialists. Then Chiang met with his criminal associates, especially those of the infamous Green Gang, to plan the next step. Lastly, he transferred out of the city army units that he suspected might sympathize with the workers.

Before dawn on April 12, 1927, Chiang Kai-shek and his allies struck. Moving in on the working-class sections of the Chinese city, away from the foreign concessions, Chiang's men rounded up Communists and their sympathizers, slaughtering them in the hundreds—perhaps thousands. An accurate count was never possible. Chou and Ch'en managed to escape in time, but the alliance between the KMT and the Communists, that Sun Yat-sen had brokered with Stalin's blessing, was now dead.

In an effort to rid China of the Communists once and for all, the anti-Communist purges spread to other cities across China. Even Chiang's warlord enemies in Peking joined in the anti-Communist howl. They invaded the Soviet Embassy, hauled out the CCP's co-founder, Li Ta-chao, and nineteen others who had sought asylum there, and executed them by garrote.[vii] The other co-founder, Ch'en Tu-hsiu, even though he escaped death, was drummed out of the Communist party for originally agreeing to the United Front, even though the Front was Communist doctrine at the time. Mao would later put the blame for the whole debacle on Borodin, and especially Ch'en, whose "wavering opportunism deprived the Party of decisive leadership and a direct line of its own at a moment when further compromise clearly meant catastrophe ... A new line was adopted by the Party," Mao told the author, Edgar Snow, some years later, "and all hope of cooperation with the Kuomintang was given up for the present, as it had already become hopelessly the tool of imperialism."[55]

---

vii   A garrote is an execution device whereby the victim is seated on a chair with a post for a back, with a hole aligned with the neck. A wire is inserted through the hole, around the victim's neck, and then slowly tightened until death by strangulation.

Stalin, who was ultimately to blame for the CCP's near destruction, now ordered the party to fight back. In Ch'ang-sha (Changsha), Mao organized his Autumn Harvest Uprising, and in Canton Communists attempted to take control of the city. But everywhere Chiang's armies proved too strong. In Hangkow, Madame Sun Yat-sen denounced Chiang in the strongest terms, but the rival government in that city was about to end. In a farewell to the Yangtze, before he fled for his life, Borodin wrote, "If a diver were to be sent to the bottom of this yellow stream he would rise again with an armful of shattered hopes."[56] Sun's widow, Borodin and those Chinese Communists who could get away fled to Moscow. In December Sun Ching-ling heard the bitter news that her younger sister, Mei-ling (Meiling), had married none other than General Chiang Kai-shek, who was now about to co-opt Sun's legend for himself. This was especially galling to Ching-ling because Chiang had proposed to her after Sun's death, a proposal she firmly rejected. The lemon had been squeezed, but not in the way Stalin had predicted.[viii] As Mao would later say, "The long open struggle for power now began."[57]

Chiang Kai-shek resumed his Northern Expedition in April 1928, and before the year's end had captured Peking, declaring that China was at last united. But it was not. The seeds of that lemon Chiang thought he had effectively squeezed had found their way into the soil and soul of China. The Communists famously made their 7,000-mile retreat to the mountain fastness of Yenan (Yanan), near the Great Wall of China—an epic retreat that has passed into legend as a Chinese Dunkirk. And from there, sometimes cooperating with the KMT against the Japanese and sometimes not, the Chinese Communists began their even longer twenty-two year struggle for

---

viii Trotsky, who had long opposed the United Front, lost out in his own power struggle with Stalin. He was exiled in 1929, and in 1940 Stalin had him murdered in Mexico.

control of China. After the Japanese surrender, Mao's forces went on to fight a four-year civil war against Chiang Kai-shek's American-backed Nationalists, until Chiang fled with what was left of his army to Taiwan. On October 1, 1949, Mao Tse-tung stood on the Gate of Heavenly Peace, near where the May Fourth demonstrators had gathered thirty years before, and in front of the assembled thousands proclaimed, "The Chinese People have stood up ... nobody will insult us again."[58]

Madame Sun Yat-sen returned to China to stand beside Mao in victory in 1949. She survived the Cultural Revolution, and died in 1981 with the title of Honorary President of the People's Republic of China.

Borodin was sharply criticized for the China fiasco, but was protected by Stalin, and became editor of the English language *Moscow News*. After World War II, however, he ran afoul of Stalin's growing paranoia, especially concerning Jews. He was arrested in 1949 and died in a Soviet labor camp in 1951.

Today, in Shanghai's former French Concession, the pink and gray house where the Communist Party of China held its first congress is now a museum where the faithful come to see life-size statues of the sixteen original delegates. A policeman stands in the actual room where the meeting took place, lest an overzealous comrade tries to take a splinter from the true table or from the chairs on which they sat. The nearby Bower School for Girls is no more, but a plaque describes how the Communist delegates stayed there in 1921. The building today houses a museum store, a joint venture with Disney. In the window there is a silhouette of Mickey Mouse.

As for the much-maligned Woodrow Wilson, once celebrated by his countrymen and recipient of the Nobel Peace Prize, he is looked down upon by some today as a failure, and even a hypocrite. No American president has fallen so far from grace. Even his old alma mater, Princeton where he served as president, has removed his name from its public policy school and one of its residential colleges in protest of his views on race. Yet for all his failures, he predicted with razor-sharp accuracy that another and more terrible war could come if a league of nations did not stand together to prevent it. World War II came because the democracies failed to take concerted action to prevent it, not because Wilson's vision was faulty.

Sun Yat-sen's own appraisal of Wilson's place in history was simply put: "Wilson's proposals, once set forth, could not be recalled." The colonized people of the world, along with the small and weak, were "doomed to disappointment by the results of the Peace Conference" in 1919, Sun said. But they were "stirred with a great new consciousness; they saw how completely they had been deceived by the Great Powers' advocacy of self-determination and began independently and separately to carry out the principle of the self-determination of peoples" on their own. That was Wilson's true legacy.

Endnotes

Chapter One

1. Arthur Link, *Woodrow Wilson: Revolution, War, and Peace* (AHM Publishing, Arlington, IL, 1959), 5.
2. Patricia O'Toole, talk at the Tavern Club, Boston, MA, April 18, 2018.
3. Wilson speech, June 27, 1917.
4. Wilson speech, February 11, 1918.
5. Ibid.
6. V.I. Lenin, "The Rights of Nations to Self-Determination" *Lenin's Collected Works*, Vol. 20, (Progress Publishers, Moscow, 1972), 393.
7. Wilson speech, January 8, 1918.
8. Wilson speech, February 11, 1918.
9. Ibid.
10. Wilson speech, January 8, 1918.
11. Wilson speech, April 2, 1917.
12. Winston Churchill, *The Aftermath* (Charles Scribner & Sons, New York, 1929), 124.
13. Robert Lansing, *The Peace Negotiations: A Personal Narrative* (Houghton Mifflin, Boston, 1921), 97, 98.
14. Margaret MacMillan, Paris 1919: *Six Months That Changed the World* (Random House, New York, 2002), 97, 98.
15. Link, 5.
16. George Creel, *The War, the World and Wilson* (Harper & Brothers, New York, 1920), 160.
17. Ibid, 159.
18. John Maynard Keynes, *The Economic Consequences of the* Peace (Harcourt, Brace and Howe, New York, 1920), 38, 39.
19. A. Scott Berg, *Wilson* (G. P. Putnam, New York, 2013), 17.
20. Keynes, 43.
21. MacMillan, 27.
22. Stephen Bonsal, *Suitors and Suppliants: The Little Nations at Versailles* (Kennihat Press, Port Washington, 1946), xii.
23. Patricia O'Toole, *The Moralist: Woodrow Wison and the World He Made* (Simon & Schuster, New York, 2018), 92.
24. Berg, 592.
25. Keynes, 43.
26. Ray Stannard Baker, *What Wilson Did at Paris* (Doubleday, Page, New York, 1920), 5, 6.
27. E. J. Dillon, *The Inside Story of the Peace Conference* (Harper & Brothers,

New York, 1920), 4, 5, 6.
28. Erez Manela, *The Wilsonian Moment: Self-Determination and the International Origins of Anticolonial Nationalism* (Oxford University Press, New York, 2007) 200.
29. Bonsal, 267, 268.
30. Ibid, 26.
31. Baker, 52.
32. Bonsal, 42.
33. Baker, 68, 69.
34. Ibid, 77.
35. Russell H. Fifield, *Woodrow Wilson and the Far East* (Archon Press, Hampden, CT, 1969), 295.
36. Bonsal, 97.
37. Edward House, *What Really Happened in Paris* (Charles Scribner & Sons, New York, 1921), 295.
38. Bonsal, 97.
39. Ibid, 101.
40. Ibid, 112.
41. Ibid, 104.
42. Ibid, 104.
43. Ibid, 102.
44. Baker, 119.
45. H. James Burgwyn, *Italian Foreign Policy in the Interwar Era* (Praeger, Westport CT, 1977), 13.
46. Ibid, 13.
47. Fifield, 295.
48. Ge-Zay Wood, *The Shantung Question* (Fleming H. Revell, London, 1922), 27, 28.
49. Pankaj Mishra, *From the Ruins of Empire: The Revolt Against the West and the Remaking of Asia* (Farrar, Straus & Giroux, New York, 2012), 1.
50. Ibid, 1.
51. Ibid, 1.
52. Ibid, 2.
53. Sun Yat-sen, *China and Japan: Natural Friends—Unnatural Enemies* (Shanghai 1941). Now in Library of Congress.
54. Admiral Alfred von Tirpitz, *My Memoirs* (Hurst & Blackett, London, 1919) Vol. II, 83.
55. Winston Churchill, *The World Crisis, 1911–1914* (Thornton, Butterworth, London, 1927), 262.
56. Wood, 68.
57. Fifield, 61.
58. Ibid, 85.
59. Ibid, 10.
60. *Encyclopedia Britannica: A Dictionary of Arts, Sciences, Literature and General Information,* Eleventh Edition, Vol. II (The Encyclopedia Britannica Company, New York, 1911), 172.

61. MacMillan, 327.
62. Charles Drage, *Two Gun Cohen* (Jonathan Cape, London, 1951), 124.
63. Fifield, 42.
64. Paul Johnson, *A History of the Modern World: From 1917 to the 1980s* (Weidenfeld & Nicholson, London, 1983), 198.
65. Drage, 125.
66. Bruce Elleman, *Wilson and China: A Revised History of the Shandong Question* (Routledge, Taylor and Francis Group, London, 2015), 42.
67. Stephen G. Kraft, *V.K. Wellington Koo and the Emergence of Modern China* (University Press of Kentucky, Lexington, 2004), 51.
68. MacMillan, 333, 334, 336.
69. Kraft, 51.
70. MacMillan, 331.
71. Ibid, 331.
72. Bonsal, 229.
73. Ibid, 234.
74. Rudyard Kipling, "The White Man's Burden" *McClure's Magazine* (February 1899) .
75. Bonsal, 229.
76. Ibid, 263.
77. Anthony Reed, *The World on Fire: 1919 and the Battle with Bolshevism* (W.W. Norton, New York, 2008), 160.
78. Fifield, 219.
79. Ibid, 220.
80. Ibid, 220.
81. Ibid, 119.
82. Berg, 568.
83. Fifield, 274.
84. Ibid, 272, 273.
85. Bonsal, 285.
86. Fifield, 228, 229.
87. William Bullitt and Sigmund Freud, *Woodrow Wilson: A Psychological Study* (Houghton Mifflin, Boston, 1967), 268.
88. Ibid, 268.
89. Ibid, 269.
90. Ibid, 269.
91. Fifield, 3.
92. John Milton Cooper, *Breaking the Heart of the World: Wilson and the Fight for the League of Nations* (Cambridge University Press, Cambridge, 2001), 88 .
93. Bonsal, 293.
94. Cooper, 125.
95. Ibid, 135.
96. Creel, 163.

Chapter Two

1. John Woodhouse, *Gabriele d'Annunzio: Defiant Archangel* (Oxford University Press, Oxford, 1998), 323.
2. Margaret MacMillan, *Paris 1919: Six Months That Changed the World* (Random House, New York, 2002), 11.
3. Woodhouse, 316.
4. Woodrow Wilson, *A History of the American People,* Vol. V (Harper Brothers, New York, 1902), 212, 213.
5. *New York Times,* November 19, 2017.
6. Wilson, 212, 213.
7. R.J. Bosworth, *Mussolini's Italy: Life Under the Dictatorship, 1915–1945* (Penguin Books, London, 2005), 95.
8. Lucy Hughes-Hallett, *Gabriele d'Annunzio: Poet, Seducer, and Preacher of War* (Anchor Books, New York, 2014), 5.
9. Ibid, 5.
10. Paolo Valesio, *Gabriele d'Annunzio: The Dark Flame* (Yale University Press, New Haven, 1962), 117.
11. Ibid, 175.
12. Gabriele D'Annunzio, translated by J.G. Nichols, "The Rain in the Pinewood" and "First Dithyramb" in *Halcyon* (Fyfield Books, London, 2003).
13. Henry James, *French Writers, Other European Writers, Literary Criticism* Vol. II (Library of America, New York), 908, 910.
14. *Encyclopedia Britannica: A Dictionary of Arts, Sciences, Literature and General Information* Eleventh Edition, Vol. II (The Encyclopedia Britannica Company, New York, 1911), 78, 79.
15. Romie Scott, "The Sex-Obsessed Poet Who Invented Fascism" post on *Atlas Obscura,* December 4, 2015 at 06.50; www.atlasobscura.com; obscura392.rssing.com.
16. Elizabeth Lunbeck, "The Allure of Trump's Narcissism," *Los Angeles Review of Books,* August 2007.
17. Hughes-Hallett, 30.
18. Ernest Hemingway, edited by Nicholas Gerogiannis, *88 Poems* (Harcourt Brace Jovanovich, New York, 1979), 128.
19. Valesio, 41.
20. Wilfred Owen, *Complete Poems* (Blackthorne Press, Pickering, 2013), 14.
21. Robert Greene, *The Art of Seduction* (Penguin Books, New York, 2002), 23.
22. Michael Ledeen, *The First Duce: D'Annunzio at Fiume* (Johns Hopkins University Press, Baltimore, 1977), 15.
23. Ibid, 62.
24. Igor Zic, *A Short History of the City of Rijeka* (Adamic, Rijeka, 2007), 133.
25. Greene, 23.
26. Ledeen, 68.
27. Ibid, 67.
28. Ibid, 69.

29. Ibid, 76.
30. Hughes-Hallett, 5.
31. Ibid, 27.
32. Ledeen, 102.
33. Ibid, 103.
34. Sir Osbert Sitwell, *Noble Essences* (Little Brown, Boston, 1950), 135.
35. Woodhouse, 346–347.
36. Hughes-Hallett, 419.
37. Ledeen, 69.
38. Hughes-Hallett, 419.
39. Ibid, 420.
40. Ibid, 4.
41. Ledeen, 138.
42. Ibid, 171.
43. Sitwell, 140.
44. Laura Fermi, *Mussolini* (University of Chicago Pres, Chicago, 1961), 217.
45. William Pfaff, *The Bullet's Song: Romantic Violence and Utopia* (Simon & Schuster, New York, 2004), 186.
46. Fermi, 218.
47. Ibid, 170.
48. Woodhouse, 318.
49. Sitwell, 137.
50. Woodhouse, 315.
51. Hughes-Hallett, 422.
52. Ibid, 438.
53. Woodhouse, 338.
54. Hughes-Hallett, 465.
55. Ledeen, xv.
56. Sitwell, 140.
57. Pfaff, 177.
58. Hughes-Hallett, 463.
59. Ibid, 463.
60. Ibid, 442.
61. Ibid, 542.
62. Ledeen, 201.
63. Ibid, 201.
64. Benito Mussolini, *My Autobiography* (Charles Scribner's Sons, New York, 1928), 123.
65. Sitwell, 129.

H.D.S. Greenway

Chapter Three

Editorial note: We were not able to obtain Abd el-Krim's signature but this is his full name translated to the Arabic: Abd al-Karim al-Khattabi.

1. Robert Lansing, *The Peace Negotiations: A Personal Narrative* (Houghton Mifflin, Boston, 1921), 97.
2. *Time,* August 17, 1925.
3. Erez Manela, *The Wilsonian Moment: Self-Determination and the International Origins of Anticolonial Nationalism* (Oxford University Press, Oxford, 2007), 175.
4. Vincent Sheean, *An American Among the Riffi* (Century, New York 1926), xx, xxi.
5. Walter B. Harris, *France, Spain and the Rif* (The Naval & Military Press, Uckfield East Sussex, 1927), 85. Reprinted by The Imperial War Museum, London, 2014.
6. David S. Woolman, *Rebels in the Rif: Abd el-Krim and the Rif Rebellion* (Stanford University Press, Stanford, 1968), 218.
7. Ibid, 77.
8. Ibid, 74.
9. Barbara Tuchman, "Perdicaris Alive or Raisuli Dead" *American Heritage* (August 1959).
10. Sebastian Balfour, *Deadly Embrace: Morocco and the Road to the Spanish Civil War* (Oxford University Press, Oxford, 2002), 56.
11. C. R. Pennell, *A Country with a Government and a Flag: The Rif War in Morocco, 1921–1926* (Middle East and North African Studies Press, Outwell, Wisbech Cambridgeshire, 1986), 83.
12. C. R. Pennell, "Ideology and Practical Politics: A Case Study of the Rif War in Morocco, 1921–1926" *International Journal of Middle East Studies,* Vol. 14, No. 1, February 1982 (Cambridge University Press, Cambridge, 1982), 21.
13. Ibid, 30.
14. Woolman, 88.
15. Ibid, 86.
16. Pennell, *A Country* ... , 81.
17. Woolman, 89.
18. Rupert Furneux, *Abdel Krim: Emir of the Rif* (Secker & Warburg, London, 1967), 67.
19. Woolman, 90.
20. William R. Polk, *Crusade and Jihad: The Thousand-Year War Between the Muslim World and the Global North* (Yale University Press, New Haven, 2001), 141.
21. Balfour, 74.
22. Woolman, 95.
23. Wikipedia, "Battle of Annual."
24. José E. Alvarez, *The Betrothed of Death: The Spanish Foreign Legion During*

the *Rif Rebellion, 1920–1927* (Greenwood Press, Westport, 2001), 6.
25. Woolman, 96.
26. Harris, 35.
27. Alvarez, 20.
28. Ibid, 19.
29. Al Maghreb al Aska, February 23, 1923, American Legation Museum, Tangier.
30. Woolman, 116.
31. Ibid, 116, 117.
32. Ibid, 117, 118 .
33. Harris, 121.
34. Woolman, 124.
35. Webb Miller, *I Found No Peace: A Journey through the Ages of Extremes* (de Coubertin Books, London, 2011), 135.
36. Furneaux, 96.
37. Sheean, *An American ...* , 249.
38. Woolman, 138.
39. Balfour, 100.
40. Woolman, 141.
41. *Spectator,* October 25, 1924.
42. Woolman, 141.
43. Balfour, 42.
44. Sheean, *An American ...* , 313.
45. Woolman, 152.
46. Sheean, *An American ...* , 227.
47. Woolman, 160.
48. Sheean, *An American ...* , 166.
49. Ibid, 168.
50. Ibid, 171.
51. Ibid, 173.
52. Ibid, 173.
53. Ibid, 174.
54. Ibid, 175.
55. Ibid, 175.
56. Ibid, 177.
57. Ibid, 178.
58. Ibid, 180, 181.
59. Ibid, 182.
60. Ibid, 185.
61. Ibid, 186.
62. Ibid, 233, 235.
63. Ibid, 243.
64. Woolman, 168.
65. Rom Landau, *Moroccan Drama, 1900–1955* (American Academy of Asia Studies, San Francisco, 1955), 92.
66. Sheean, *An American ...* , vii.

67. Max Boot, *Invisible Armies: An Epic History of Guerrilla Warfare from Ancient Times to the Present,* (Liveright Publishing, New York, 2013), 183.
68. Landau, 123.
69. Woolman, 169.
70. Furneaux, 110.
71. Woolman, 168.
72. Furneaux, 148.
73. Colonel Paul Ayers Rockwell, "American Fighters in the Rif War" *Aviation Quarterly,* Vol 5, No. 2, 1979.
74. Harris, 300, 301.
75. Rockwell.
76. Wikipedia, British Manual of Military Law.
77. Balfour, 127.
78. Ibid, 132.
79. Ibid, 132.
80. Ibid, 124.
81. Furneaux, 197.
82. Ibid, 197.
83. Woolman, 190.
84. Vincent Sheean, *Personal History* (Garden City Publishing, New York, 1937), 138.
85. Woolman, 193.
86. Harris, 317.
87. Woolman, 207.
88. Landau, 149.
89. Ibid, 152, 153.
90. Carlton Coons, *A North African Story* (Gambit, Ipswich, 1980), 20.
91. Elliott Roosevelt, *As He Saw It* (Duell, Sloan & Pearce, 1946), 115, 116.
92. Coons, 14, 15.
93. Interview conducted by Alan Berger for the author.

Endnotes

Chapter Four

1. Erez Manela, *The Wilsonian Moment: Self-Determination and the International Origins of Anticolonial Nationalism* (Oxford University Press, Oxford 2007), 186, 187.
2. Hans Schmidt; "Democracy for China, American Propaganda and the May Fourth Movement" *Diplomatic History,* Vol. 22, Winter 1998, 16.
3. Ibid, 2.
4. Ibid, 8.
5. Ibid, 13.
6. John Dewey, *Letters from Japan* (London 1920) as quoted by Schmidt, 7.
7. Tsinan Jib Bao, excerpted and translated in *Miller's Review* May 31, 1919, as quoted by Schmidt, 18.
8. Jonathan Spence, *The Search for Modern China* (W.W. Norton, New York, 1990), 311.
9. Edgar Snow, *Red Star Over China: The Classic Account of the Birth of Chinese Communism* (Random House, New York, 1938), 137.
10. Manela, xi.
11. Spence, *The Search ...* , 312, 313.
12. Ibid, 313.
13. J.A.G. Roberts, *A Concise History of China* (Harvard University Press, Cambridge, MA, 1999), 221.
14. Tjio Kayloe, *The Unfinished Revolution: Sun Yat-sen and the Struggle for Modern China* (Marshall Cavendish Editions, Singapore, 2017), 334.
15. Sun Yat-sen *Lecture #3,* as quoted in Paul Johnson, *A History of the Modern World* (Weidenfield & Nicholson, London, 1982), 198
16. Charles Drage, *Two Gun Cohen* (Jonathan Cape, London 1954), 124.
17. Kayloe, 67.
18. Harold Z. Schiffrin, *Sun Yat-sen and the Origins of the Chinese Revolution* (University of California Press, Berkeley, 1970), 364.
19. Kenneth Scott Latourette, *The Chinese, Their History and Culture* (MacMillan, New York, 1957), 401, 402.
20. Sun Yat-sen, "My Reminiscences" *Strand Magazine,* Vol. 1, 1912, as quoted by Kayloe, 228
21. Tang Leang-Li, *The Inner History of the Chinese Revolution* (Hyperion, Westport, CT, 1997), 112.
22. Latourette, 406.
23. Marie-Claire Bergère, translation by Janet Lloyd, *Sun Yat-sen* (Stanford University Press Stanford, CA, 1998), 303
24. Liu Jianyi, *The Origins of the Chinese Communist Party and the Role Played by Russia and the Comintern* (Doctoral dissertation, University of York, March 2000), 35.
25. Snow, 132.
26. Jianyi, 343.
27. Conrad Brandt, *Stalin's Failure in China, 1924–1927* (W.W. Norton New York 1966), vii.

28. Spence, *The Search* ... , 335.
29. Brandt, 28.
30. Kayloe, 280.
31. Spence, *The Search* ... , 337.
32. Harold Isaacs, *The Tragedy of the Chinese Revolution,* Second Revised Edition (Stanford University Press, Stanford CA, 1961), 162.
33. Bergère, 323.
34. Harold Z. Schiffrin, *Sun Yat-sen: Reluctant Revolutionary* (Little Brown Boston 1980), 238.
35. Ibid 241.
36. Vincent Sheean, *Personal History* (Garden City Publishing, New York, 1937), 203, 204.
37. Jonathan Spence, *To Change China, Western Advisors in China* (Penguin New York, 1980), 188.
38. Schiffrin, *Sun Yat-sen* ... , 241, 242.
39. Ibid, 244.
40. Ibid, 241.
41. Ibid, 246.
42. Drage, 117.
43. Bergère, 354.
44. Observed by author.
45. Bergère, 354.
46. Ibid, 371.
47. Stephen Chen, Robert Payne, *Sun Yat-sen: A Portrait* (Asia Press Books, John Day Company, New York, 1946), 176.
48. Ibid, 134.
49. Bergère, 373.
50. Ibid, 384.
51. Kayloe, 299.
52. Spence, *The Search* ... , 341.
53. Brandt, 10.
54. Sheean, *Personal* ... , 198.
55. Spence, *To Change* ... , 204.
56. Snow, 149.
57. Ross Terrill, *Mao: A Biography* (Harper & Row New York 1980), 198.
58. Sun Yat-sen, translated by F.W. Price, *Three Principles of the People* (Soul Care Publishing, Vancouver, 2011). Originally published by The Commercial Press Ltd, Shanghai, 1929.

Appendix

The Fourteen Points, January 8, 1918

1. Open covenants of peace, openly arrived at, after which there shall be no private international understandings of any kind but diplomacy shall proceed always frankly and in the public view.

2. Absolute freedom of navigation upon the seas, outside territorial waters, alike in peace and war, except as the seas may be closed in whole or in part by international action for the enforcement of international covenants.

3. The removal, so far as possible, of all economic barriers and the establishment of an equality of trade conditions among all the nations consenting to the peace and associating themselves for its maintenance.

4. Adequate guarantees given and taken that national armaments will be reduced to the lowest point consistent with domestic safety.

5. A free, open-minded, and absolutely impartial adjustment of all colonial claims, based upon a strict observance of the principle that in determining all such questions of sovereignty the interests of the populations concerned must have equal weight with the equitable government whose title is to be determined.

6. The evacuation of all Russian territory and such a settlement of all questions affecting Russia as will secure the best and freest cooperation of the other nations of the world in obtaining for her an unhampered and unembarrassed opportunity for the independent determination of her own political development and national policy and assure her of a sincere welcome into the society of free nations under institutions of her own choosing; and more than a welcome assistance also of every kind that

she may need and may herself desire. The treatment accorded Russia by her sister nations in the months to come will be the acid test of their good will, of their comprehension of her needs as distinguished from their own interests, and of their intelligent and unselfish sympathy.

7. Belgium, the whole world will agree, must be evacuated and restored without any attempt to limit the sovereignty which she enjoys in common with all other free nations. No other single act will serve as this will serve to restore confidence among the nations in the laws which they have themselves set and determined for the government of their relations with one another. Without this healing act the whole structure and validity of international law is forever impaired.

8. All French territory should be freed and the invaded portions restored, and the wrong done to France by Prussia in 1871 in the matter of Alsace-Lorraine, which has unsettled the peace of the world for nearly fifty years, should be righted, in order that peace may once more be made secure in the interests of all.

9. A readjustment of the frontiers of Italy should be effected along clearly recognizable lines of nationality.

10. The peoples of Austria-Hungary, whose place among the nations we wish to see safeguarded and assured, should be accorded the freest opportunity to autonomous development.

11. Rumania, Serbia, and Montenegro should be evacuated; occupied territories restored; Serbia accorded free and secure access to the sea; and the relations of the several Balkan states to one another determined by friendly counsel along historically established lines of allegiance and nationality; and international guarantees of the political and economic independence and territorial integrity of the several Balkan states should be entered into.

12. The Turkish portion of the present Ottoman Empire should be assured a secure sovereignty, but the other nationalities which

are now under Turkish rule should be assured an undoubted security of life and an absolutely unmolested opportunity of autonomous development, and the Dardanelles should be permanently opened as a free passage to the ships and commerce of all nations under international guarantees.

13. An independent Polish state should be erected which should include the territories inhabited by indisputably Polish populations, which should be assured a free and secure access to the sea, and whose political and economic independence and territorial integrity should be guaranteed by international covenant.

14. A general association of nations must be formed under specific covenants for the purpose of affording mutual guarantees of political independence and territorial integrity to great and small states alike.

The Four Principles, February 11, 1918

1. First, that each part of the final settlement must be based upon the essential justice of that particular case and upon such adjustments as are most likely to bring a peace that will be permanent.

2. Second, that peoples and provinces are not to be bartered about from sovereignty to sovereignty as if they were mere chattels and pawns in a game, even the great game, now forever discredited, of the balance of power; but that

3. Third, every territorial settlement involved in this war must be made in the interests and for the benefit of the populations concerned, and not as a part of any mere adjustment or compromise of claims amongst rival states; and

4. Fourth, that all well defined national aspirations shall be accorded the utmost satisfaction that can be accorded them without introducing new or perpetuating old elements of discord and antagonism that would be likely in time to break the peace of Europe and consequentially of the world.

The Four Ends, July 4, 1918

1. The destruction of every arbitrary power anywhere that can separately, secretly, and of its single choice disturb the peace of the world; or, if it cannot be presently destroyed, at the least its reduction to virtual impotence.

2. The settlement of every question, whether of territory, of sovereignty, of economic arrangement, or of political relationship, upon the basis of the free acceptance of that settlement by the people immediately concerned, and not upon the basis of the material interest or advantage of any other nation or people which may desire a different settlement for the sake of its own exterior influence or mastery.

3. The consent of all nations to be governed in their conduct towards each other by the same principles of honour and of respect for the common law of civilized society that govern the individual citizens of all modern states in their relations with one another; to the end that all promises and covenants may be sacredly observed, no private plots or conspiracies hatched, no selfish injuries wrought with impunity, and a mutual trust established upon the handsome foundation of a mutual respect for right.

4. The establishment of an organization of peace which shall make certain that the combined power of free nations will check every invasion of right and serve to make peace and justice all the more secure by affording a definite tribunal of opinion to which all must submit and by which every international readjustment that cannot be amicably agreed upon by the peoples directly concerned shall be sanctioned.

The Five Particulars, September 27, 1918

5. The impartial justice meted out must involve no discrimination between those to whom we wish to be just and those whom we do not wish to be just. It must be a justice that plays no favorites and knows no standard by the equal rights of the several peoples concerned.

6. No special or separate interest of any single nation or any group of nations can be made the basis of any part of the settlement which is not consistent with the common interest of all.

7. There can be no leagues or alliances or special covenants and understandings within the general and common family of the League of Nations.

8. There can be no special selfish economic combinations within the League and no employment of any form of economic boycott or exclusion except as the power of economic penalty by exclusion from the markets of the world may be vested by the League of Nations itself as a means of discipline and control.

9. All international agreements and treaties of every kind must be made known in their entirety to the rest of the world.

Bibliography

Ahmed, Akbar; *The Thistle and the Drone: How America's War on Terror Became a Global War on Tribal Islam* (Brookings Institution Press, Washington, D.C., 2013).

Alvarez, José E.; *The Betrothed of Death: The Spanish Foreign Legion During the Rif Rebellion, 1920–1927* (Greenwood Press, Westport, 2001).

Anderson, Scott; *Lawrence in Arabia: War, Deceit, Imperial Folly and the Making of the Modern Middle East* (Doubleday, New York, 2013).

Bailey, Thomas A.; *Woodrow Wilson and the Lost Peace* (Macmillan, New York, 1944).

Baker, Ray Stannard; *What Wilson Did at Paris* (Doubleday, Page, New York, 1920).

Balfour, Sebastian; *Deadly Embrace: Morocco and the Road to the Spanish Civil War* (Oxford University Press, Oxford, 2002).

Berezin, Mabel; *Making the Fascist Self: The Political Culture of Interwar Italy* (Cornell University Press, Ithaca, 1997).

Berg, A. Scott; *Wilson* (G. P. Putnam, New York, 2013).

Bergère, Marie-Claire, translation by Janet Lloyd, *Sun Yat-sen* (Stanford University Press, Stanford, California, 1998).

Bolton, John; *The Room Where It Happened, A White House Memoir* (Simon & Schuster, New York, 2020).

Bonsal, Stephen; *Suitors and Suppliants: The Little Nations at Versailles* (Kennihat Press, Port Washington, New York, 1946).

Bonsal, Stephen; *Unfinished Business* (Simon Publications, Safety Harbor, Florida, 2001). Originally published 1944.

Boot, Max; *Invisible Armies: An Epic History of Guerrilla Warfare from Ancient Times to the Present* (Liveright Publishing, New York, 2013).

Bosworth, R. J. B.; *Italy: The Least of the Great Powers* (Cambridge University Press, Cambridge, 1979).

Bosworth, R. J. B.; *Mussolini's Italy: Life Under the Dictatorship, 1915–1945* (Penguin Books, London, 2005).

Brandt, Conrad; *Stalin's Failure in China, 1924–1927* (W.W. Norton, New York 1966).

Bullitt, William and Freud, Sigmund; *Thomas Woodrow Wilson, Twenty-Eighth President of the United States: A Psychological Study* (Houghton Mifflin, Boston, 1967).

Burgwyn, H. James; *Italian Foreign Policy in the Interwar Era* (Praeger, Westport, Connecticut, 1977).

Cantlie, James and Jones, C. Sheridan; *Sun Yat-sen and the Awakening of China* (Fleming H. Revell Company, London, 1912).

Chang, Jung and Jon Halliday; *Mao: The Unknown Story* (Knopf, New York, 2005).

Chen, Stephen and Payne, Robert; *Sun Yat-sen: A Portrait* (Asia Press Books, John Day Company, New York, 1946).

Churchill, Winston; *The Aftermath* (Charles Scribner & Sons, New York, 1929).

Churchill, Winston; *The World Crisis, 1911–1914* (Thornton, Butterworth, London, 1927).

Coons, Carlton; *A North African Story* (Gambit, Ipswich, 1980).

Craft, Stephen G.; *V. K. Wellington Koo and the Emergence of Modern China* (University Press of Kentucky, Lexington, 2004).

Creel, George; *The War, the World and Wilson* (Harper & Brothers, New York, 1920).

d'Annunzio, Gabriele, translated by J.G. Nichols; "Rain in the Pinewood" and "First Dithyramb" in *Halcyon* (Fyfield Books/Carcanet, London, 2003).

d'Annunzio, Gabriele, translated by Lara Raffaelli; *Pleasure* (Penguin Classics, New York, 2013).

Dillon, E.J.; *The Inside Story of the Peace Conference* (Harper & Brothers, New York, 1920).

Donaldson, Robert H. and Nogee, Joseph L.; *The Foreign Policy of Russia, Changing Systems, Enduring Interests* (M.E. Sharp, Armonk, New York, 1998).

Drage, Charles; *Two Gun-Cohen* (Jonathan Cape, London, 1951).

Elleman, Bruce; *Wilson and China: A Revised History of the Shandong Question* (Routledge, Taylor and Francis Group, London, 2002).

Encyclopedia Britannica: A Dictionary of Arts, Sciences, Literature and General Information Eleventh Edition, Vol. II (The Encyclopedia Britannica Company, New York, 1911).

Fairbank, John King; *The United States and China* (Harvard University Press, Cambridge, 1971).

Fermi, Laura; *Mussolini* (University of Chicago Press, Chicago, 1961).

Fifield, Russell H.; *Woodrow Wilson and the Far East* (Archon Press, Hampden Connecticut, 1969).

BIBLIOGRAPHY

French, Paul; *Betrayal in Paris, How the Treaty of Versailles Led to China's Long Revolution* (Penguin Books, Melbourne, 2014).

Furneux, Rupert; *Abdel Krim: Emir of the Rif* (Secker & Warburg, London, 1967).

Gerwarth, Robert; *The Vanquished, Why the First World War Failed to End* (Farrar, Straus & Giroux, New York, 2016).

Greene, Robert; *The Art of Seduction* (Penguin Books, New York, 2002).

Harris, Walter B.; *France, Spain and the Rif* (The Naval & Military Press, Uckfield East Sussex, 1927) reprinted by The Imperial War Museum, London, 2014.

Hemingway, Ernest; edited by Nicholas Gerogiannis, *88 Poems* (Harcourt Brace Jovanovich, New York, 1979).

Hodgson, Godfrey; *Woodrow Wilson's Right Hand Man, the Life of Colonel Edward M. House* (Yale University Press, New Haven, 2006).

House, Edward; *What Really Happened at Paris* (Charles Scribner & Sons, New York, 1921).

Hughes-Hallett, Lucy; *Gabriele d'Annunzio: Poet, Seducer, and Preacher of War* (Anchor Books, New York, 2014).

Isaacs, Harold; *The Tragedy of the Chinese Revolution,* Second Revised Edition (Stanford University Press, Stanford, California, 1961).

Jacobs, Dan N.; *Borodin: Stalin's Man in China* (Harvard University Press, Cambridge, 1981).

James, Henry; *Literary Criticism: French and Other European Writers, Prefaces to the New York Edition* Vol. II (Library of America, New York, 1984).

Jianyi, Liu; *The Origins of the Chinese Communist Party and the Role Played by Russia and the Comintern* (Doctoral dissertation, University of York March 2000).

Johnson, Paul; *A History of the Modern World: From 1917 to the 1980s* (Weidenfeld & Nicholson, London, 1983).

Karnow, Stanley; *Mao and China from Revolution to Revolution* (MacMillan, New York, 1972).

Kayloe, Tjio; *The Unfinished Revolution: Sun Yat-sen and the Struggle for Modern China* (Marshall Cavendish Editions, Singapore, 2017).

Keynes, John Maynard; *The Economic Consequences of the* Peace (Harcourt, Brace and Howe, New York, 1920).

Khalil, Osamah F.; *America's Dream Palace: Middle East Expertise and the Rise of the National Security State* (Harvard University Press, Cambridge, 2016).

King, Wunsz; *China and the League of Nations: The Sino-Japanese Controversy* (St. John's University Press, New York, 1965).

Kipling, Rudyard; "The White Man's Burden," *McClure's Magazine* (February 1899).

Kissinger, Henry; *Diplomacy* (Simon & Schuster, New York, 1994).

Knock, Thomas J.; *To End All Wars: Woodrow Wilson and the Quest for a New World Order* (Oxford University Press, Oxford, 1992).

Landau, Rom; *Moroccan Drama, 1900–1955* (American Academy of Asia Studies, San Francisco, 1955).

Lansing, Robert; *The Big Four at the Peace Conference* (Houghton Mifflin, Boston, 1921).

Lansing, Robert; *The Peace Negotiations: A Personal Narrative* (Houghton Mifflin, Boston, 1921).

Latourette, Kenneth; *The Chinese, Their History and Culture* (MacMillan, New York, 1957).

Ledeen, Michael; *The First Duce: D'Annunzio at Fiume* (Johns Hopkins University Press, Baltimore, 1977).

Lenin, V. I.; "The Rights of Nations to Self-Determination" *Lenin's Collected Works*, Vol. 20, (Progress Publishers, Moscow, 1972).

Link, Arthur; *Woodrow Wilson: Revolution, War, and Peace* (AHM Publishing, Arlington, Illinois, 1959) .

Lunbeck, Elizabeth; "The Allure of Trump's Narcissism" *Los Angeles Review of Books* (August 2007).

MacMillan, Margaret; *Paris 1919: Six Months That Changed the World* (Random House, New York, 2002).

Manela, Erez; *The Wilsonian Moment: Self-Determination and the International Origins of Anticolonial Nationalism* (Oxford University Press, New York, 2007).

Miller, Webb; *I Found No Peace: A Journey through the Ages of Extremes* (de Coubertin Books, London, 2011).

Mishra, Pankaj; *From the Ruins of Empire: The Revolt Against the West and the Remaking of Asia* (Farrar, Straus & Giroux, New York, 2012).

Mussolini, Benito; *My Autobiography* (Charles Scribner's Sons, New York, 1928).

O'Toole, Patricia; *The Moralist: Woodrow Wilson and the World He Made* (Simon & Schuster, New York, 2018).

Owen, Wilfred; *Complete Poems* (Blackthorne Press, Pickering, 2013).

Paxton, Robert; *The Anatomy of Fascism* (Knopf, New York, 2004).

Pennell, C. R.; *A Country with a Government and a Flag: The Rif War in Morocco, 1921–1926* (Middle East and North African Studies Press, Outwell, Wisbech Cambridgeshire, 1986).

Pennell, C. R.; "Ideology and Practical Politics: A Case Study of the Rif War in Morocco, 1921–1926" *International Journal of Middle East Studies* Vol. 14, No. 1, February 1982 (Cambridge University Press, Cambridge, 1982).

Pfaff, William; *The Bullet's Song: Romantic Violence and Utopia* (Simon & Schuster, New York, 2004).

Polk, William R.; *Crusade and Jihad: The Thousand-Year War Between the Muslim World and the Global North* (Yale University Press, New Haven, 2001).

Pomfret, John; *The Beautiful Country and the Middle Kingdom: America and China, 1776 to the Present* (Henry Holt, New York, 2016).

Rand, Peter; *China Hands: The Adventures and Ordeals of the American Journalists Who Joined Forces with the Great Chinese Revolution* (Simon & Schuster, New York, 1995).

Read, Anthony; *The World on Fire: 1919 and the Battle with Bolshevism* (W.W. Norton, New York, 2008).

Roberts, J.A.G.; *A Concise History of China* (Harvard University Press, Cambridge, Massachusetts 1999).

Rockwell, Colonel Paul Ayers; "American Fighters in the Rif War" *Aviation Quarterly*, Vol. 5, No. 2, 1979.

Roosevelt, Elliott; *As He Saw It* (Duell, Sloan & Pearce, 1946).

Rubenstein, Joshua; *Leon Trotsky: A Revolutionary's Life* (Yale University Press, New Haven, 2011).

Sands, Philippe; *East West Street: On the Origins of Genocide and Crimes Against Humanity* (Vintage Books, New York, 2017).

Schiffrin, Harold Z.; *Sun Yat-sen and the Origins of the Chinese Revolution* (University of California Press, Berkeley, 1970).

Schiffrin, Harold Z.; *Sun Yat-sen: Reluctant Revolutionary* (Little Brown, Boston, 1980).

Schmidt, Hans; "Democracy for China: American Propaganda and the May Fourth Movement" *Diplomatic History*, Vol. 22, No. 1, Winter, 1998, Oxford Academic.

Scott, Romie; "The Sex-Obsessed Poet Who Invented Fascism" post on *Atlas Obscura*, December 4, 2015 at 06.50; www.atlasobscura.com; obscura392.rssing.com.

Seagrave, Sterling; *The Dragon Lady: The Life and Legend of the Last Empress of China* (Vintage Books, New York, 1993).

Seymour, Charles; *The Intimate Papers of Colonel House* (Houghton Mifflin, Boston, 1926).

Sheean, Vincent; *An American Among the Riffi* (Century, New York, 1926).

Sheean, Vincent; *Personal History* (Garden City Publishing, New York, 1937).

Sitwell, Sir Osbert; *Noble Essences* (Little Brown, Boston, 1950).

Smith, Gene; *When the Cheering Stopped: The Last Years of Woodrow Wilson* (Bantam Books, New York, 1965).

Snow, Edgar; *Red Star Over China: The Classic Account of the Birth of Chinese Communism* (Random House, New York, 1938).

Spence, Jonathan; *To Change China, Western Advisors in China* (Penguin, New York, 1980).

Spence, Jonathan; *The Gate of Heavenly Peace: The Chinese and Their Revolution, 1895–1980* (Viking Press, New York, 1981).

Spence, Jonathan; *The Search for Modern China* (W.W. Norton, New York, 1990).

Sun, Yat-sen; *China and Japan: Natural Friends—Unnatural Enemies* (Shanghai, 1941). Now in Library of Congress.

Sun, Yat-sen; *Memoirs of a Chinese Revolutionary* (AMS Press Inc., New York, 1970). First printed 1927.

Sun, Yat-sen; translated by F.W. Price, *Three Principles of the People* (Soul Care Publishing, Vancouver, 2011). Originally published by The Commercial Press Ltd, Shanghai.

Tang, Leang-Li, *The Inner History of the Chinese Revolution* (Hyperion, Westport, Connecticut, 1997).

Taylor, Jay; *The Generalissimo: Chiang Kai-shek and the Struggle for Modern China* (Harvard University Press, Cambridge, 2009).

Terrill, Ross; *Mao: A Biography* (Harper & Row, New York, 1980).

Tirpitz, Admiral Alfred von; *My Memoirs,* Vol. II (Hurst & Blackett, London, 1919).

Tooze, Adam; *The Deluge: The Great War, America and the Remaking of the Global Order, 1916–1931* (Penguin Books, New York, 2014).

Tuchman, Barbara; "Perdicaris Alive or Raisuli Dead" *American Heritage* (August 1959).

Valesio, Paul; *Gabriele d'Annunzio: The Dark Flame* (Yale University Press, New Haven, 1962).

Wells, H.G.: *The War That Will End War* (Duffield & Co., New York, 1914).

Wengian, Gao; *Zhou Enlai: The Last Perfect Revolutionary* (Public Affairs, New York, 2007).

Wilson, Woodrow; *A History of the American People Vol. V* (Harper Brothers, New York, 1902).

Willoughby, Westel W.; *China at the Conference: A Report* (Johns Hopkins Press, Baltimore, 1922).

Bibliography

Wood, Ge-Zay; *The Shantung Question: A Study in Diplomacy and World Politics* (Fleming H. Revell, London, 1922).

Woodhouse, John; *Gabriele d'Annunzio: Defiant Archangel* (Oxford University Press, Oxford, 1998).

Woolman, David S.; *Rebels in the Rif: Abd el-Krim and the Rif Rebellion* (Stanford University Press, Stanford, 1968).

Zic, Igor; *A Short History of the City of Rijeka* (Adamic, Rijeka, 2007).

Acknowledgments

THE IDEA FOR THIS BOOK came from Harvard historian Erez Manela's *The Wilsonian Moment: Self-Determination and the International Origins of Colonial Nationalism*. I wondered if there were other stories to tell about the fallout from Woodrow Wilson's decisions at the Paris Peace Conference in 1919. I am in debt to Margaret MacMillan's *Paris 1919: Six Months That Changed the World*. On the Fiume incident, the gold standard has to be Lucy Hughes-Hallett's *Gabriele d'Annuzio: Poet, Seducer, and Preacher of War*. I am also indebted to Columbia University's Dr. Hisham Aidi, who helped me understand the politics of the Rif in today's Morocco. My thanks, also, to Abd el Majid Hatim Khattabi, who helped me find the neglected ruins of his relative, Abd el-Krim's, headquarters in Ait Kamara in the Rif. Most helpful of all was my friend, Igor Zic, museum curator, historian, and author in Rijeka, who knows everything there is to know about his city and Croatia. My thanks, also, to Stephen Kinzer who suggested the title of this book.

I could not have written this book without the Harvard University Library system and its vast store of research material.

My thanks, also, to Jock Herron, Ingrid Mach, and Linda Chadwick of TidePool Press; to John Williams, agent; David Richwine, copy editor; and to Julia Greenway for the maps included in this book.

Index

Note: Page numbers in *italics* refer to images and drawings. Numbers followed by "*m*" indicate a map.

A

Abandonistas 98, 102, 105, 106, 109, 118
Abarran 93
Abbesses in Transit 76. *See also Vittoriale*
Abd el-Krim x, 79, 82, 133
   career and leadership x, 88–90, 92, 98–99, 101, 103, 107, 109, 111–115, 117–121, 125–128, 132–133, 148, 165, 173
   character 82, 84, 87–89, 93, 109, 111, 113–115, 118–119, 121, 126, 128, 148
   family 92, 129
      Aisha (daughter) 133
      father 88, 89
      Mhamed (brother) 82, 88–90, 102, 109–110, 115–116, 119, 127, 129
      Said (son) 133
   threat of assassination 109, 113, 128
Adriatic Sea and littoral 19, 46, *47m*, 49, 57
Afghanistan 84, 87, 117, 121
Africa 7, 85
African-Americans 70, 100
Africanistas 98, 100, 102, 106, 107, 129, 131
Ait Kamara 112, 113, 134
Ajdir 88, 107, 111, 112, 113, 115, 125, 126, 134
Alfonso XIII, King 91, 98, 102, 105, 107, 123, 129, 130
Algeria 110, 116, 117, 118, 128, 130, 133
Alhucemas Bay (Al-Hoceima) 102, 125, 126, 128, 134
allies 6, 10, 12, 15, 25, 27, 36, 39, 71, 124. *See also* specific countries
al-Qaeda 92
alteration of stock 48
Ambris, Alceste de 69
Amekran River 93

American aid 60
American exceptionalism 10, 41
American idealism 142
American sovereignty 39
Amritsar (India) 85
anarchism xi, 13, 34, 37, 61, 161
Andrea Doria 72
Anual 94, 96, 99, 107, 109, 123, 134
anti-colonialism ix, x, xi, 8, 23, 62, 63, 71, 82, 84, 87, 89, 93, 130, 133, 144, 163. *See also* colonialism
anti-Semitism 61, 85
Arditi 58, 59, 61, 71, 75
Arizona 6
Armenia 12
Art of Seduction, The (Greene) 57
Asian Pro-Prosperity Sphere 173
Atlantic Charter 132
Australia 7, 14, 24, 25
Austria 7, 15, 17, 18, 160
Austro-Hungarian Empire ix, 3, 7, 10, 15, 18, 19, 23, 46, 49, 50, 51, 55, 71
authoritarianism 71
autocracy 170
Autumn Harvest uprising 180
Axis 132. *See also* Germany, Italy, Japan
Azerbaijan 12
Azerkan, Mohammed 80, 103, 104

B

Baccara, Luisa 68
Baker, Ray Stannard 12, 13, 15, 36, 37
Balfour, Arthur 14, 25
Balfour, Sebastian 91, 96, 109, 123
Balkan countries 13, 15, 46
Balkan Kingdom 17
Baltic islands 13, 15, 17
Barcelona 104
Bavaria 160
Beffa di Buccari 56

Beijing. *See* Peking
Belgium 33
Beni Urriaguel tribe 88, 89, 110, 125, 128
Ben Tieb 95
Berber tribes vi, 86, 87, 92, 98, 99, 101, 104, 107, 109, 110, 116, 118, 119, 121, 123, 124, 128, 132
Berenguer, Dámaso 91, 93, 94, 99, 123
Bergen, Candice 90
Bergère, Marie-Claire 169
Big Four 11, 15, 19, 28, 33, 35. *See also* France, Great Britain, Italy, United States
bin Laden, Osama 87
Blad el-Makhzen 87
Blad es-Siba 87
Blücher, Vasily (Galin) 168
Boers 108
Bokhara 13
Bolsheviks 8, 10, 13, 14, 27, 35, 63, 123, 159, 160, 162, 172
Bonaparte, Napolean 58, 155
Bonsal, Stephen 11, 13, 17, 18, 34, 36
Boot, Max 117
Borodin, Mikhail 165, 166, 169, 173, 175, 177, 179, 180, 181
Boston Tea Party 167
Bower School for Girls 160, 181
Boxer Rebellion 22
Brandt, Conrad 162, 176
Brenner Pass 17
British Empire. *See* Great Britain
British Manual of Military Law of 1914 123
Brooke, Rupert 54
Brown, George 165. *See also* Borodin, Mikhail
Brownshirts 74
Bryan, William Jennings 29
Buccari, Bay of 56
Budapest 49
Bukharin, Nikolai 159
Bulgaria 10
Bullitt, William 37
Bureau of Native Affairs (Morocco) 88
Burma 70
Byron, Lord 57

C

Cairo 133
Canada 14
Canary Islands 131
Canton Christian College 165
Canton Coup 176
Canton (Guangzhuo) 29, 146, 149, 156–158, 165–168, 173, 177
Cao Rulin (Tsao Ju-lin) 143
capitalism 171, 172
Carnaro, Bay of 63, 72
Caroline Islands 22
Casablanca 129
Casablanca Conference 132
Casetta Rossa 56, 58, 75
Castro, Fidel 116, 148
Catalonia 70, 104, 105
Central Intelligence Agency 132
Central Powers 3, 4, 27, 36. *See also* Austro-Hungarian Empire, Germany, Ottoman Empire
Cerva d'Oro (Golden Deer) 69
Ceuta 85, 86, 89, 111, 113, 114
Chang Chin-tung 146. *See also* Sun Yat-sen
Ch'ang-sha (Changsha) 180
Chaouen (Chefchaouen) 91, 106–109, 122, 134
Charter of Carnaro 69, 71, 75
Ch'en Chiung-ming (Chen Jiongming) 158, 159, 166
Ch'en Tu-hsiu (Chen Duxiu) 145, 161, 162, 163, 164, 179
Chiang Kai-shek vi, 151, 159, 168, 173, 175, 176, 177, 179, 180
Chicago Tribune 44
China 7, 20, 21, 26, 27, 29, 30, 31, 37, 38, 70, 81, 100, *141m*
  agreements and treaties 48, 140, 143, 155, 163–165, 170, 174
  allies 139, 156, 157, 167, 168
  birth of modern xi, 143, 144, 145, 147
  coolies 27. *See also* China: laborers
  feudal land system and reform 145, 146, 155, 158, 172, 173
  foreign imperialism xi, 145, 146, 149, 150, 159, 162, 167, 169, 170, 173, 175, 177
  laborers 48, 156, 166, 172
  navy 157
  parliamentary rule 153–155, 157, 158
  railroads 22, 29, 33, 36, 154
  revolts and revolution 151, 154–157, 162, 164, 171, 172, 175
  Shantung sovereignty 20, 25, 30, 35, 38, 142, 170

INDEX

strikes 145, 157, 173
unification xi, 144, 157, 158, 163, 169, 171, 173, 176, 180
warlords xi, 145, 146, 152, 155–159, 162, 168, 171, 176, 177
China, Republic of 152, 154, 172
Chinese-Americans 70
Chinese Communist Party (CCP) xi, 145, 160–164, 166, 167–169, 173, 175–177, 179–181
  Congress 160, 162, 181
Chinese Embassy (London) 149
Chinese Labour Corps 27
Chinese Republic 26
Ch'ing (Ching) Dynasty 21, 30, 145, 147, 149, 151, 152, 156, 157, 177
Chou En-lai (Zhou En-Lai) 146, 168
Christianity 26, 71, 84, 85, 92, 134, 142, 147, 149
Ch'ung Shan (Zhongshan) 146. *See also* Sun Yat-sen
Churchill, Winston 6, 24, 123, 132
city-state 51, 62, 72
civilization of indigenous people x, 103, 104, 109, 116, 123
Cixi (Tz'u Hsi). *See* Tz'u Hsi (Cixi)
Clemenceau, Georges ii, 11, 14, 18, 19, 35, 45, 50, 58, 60
colonialism 4, 5, 7, 15, 21, 22, 29, 31, 33, 37, 63, 81, 82, 84, 88, 89, 101, 103, 104, 109, 115, 117, 123, 140, 150, 156, 159, 163, 167, 182. *See also* anti-colonialism and specific countries
Columbia University 30
Comintern 160–163, 165
Commandante 61. *See also* d'Annunzio, Gabriele
Committee for Public Information 140
Communism 18, 35, 46, 139, 145, 159–161, 163, 164, 168, 175
Communist Daily Worker 164
Communist International 160. *See also* Comintern
Communist University of Toilers of China 175
concessions 20
  in China 22, 25, 27, 28, 30, 35, 36, 139, 147, 155, 159, 160, 167, 170, 177, 179
  Fiume xi, 19, 45
  Pacific Islands 24
  in the Rif 112

Confucianism 144, 145, 172
Confucius 21, 145, 166
Congregationalists 149
Congress of Deputies 98
Congress of Submerged Nationalities 12
Connery, Sean 90
constitutional monarchy 22
Coon, Carlton 132
Corps de Travailleurs Chinois 28
Creel, George 9, 41, 140
Croatia 15–17, 19, 45, 46, 49–51, 66, 71, 75
Croatia, Republic of x, 51
Cuba 8, 85, 91, 100, 105
Cudia Taharas 125
Culloden 134
Cultural Revolution 181
Curzon, Lord George 23, 31
Custer, George Armstrong 94, 95

D

Dalmatian coast 17, 49, 60, 72
Damascus 84, 120
d'Annunzio, Gabriele ix, 43
  career 51, 52, 54, 68, 148
  character 51, 53–56, 58, 60, 63–66, 68–70, 72–73, 76
  health 56, 68, 74
  homes. *See Casetta Rossa*, *Doll House*, *Vittoriale*
  policies 54, 55, 57, 60–61, 64, 69, 72, 73
Debussy, Claude 52
Decadent Movement 67
Declaration of Independence (United States) 5
democracy x, xi, 5, 8, 27, 66, 105, 130, 142, 144, 146, 155, 162, 163, 168–170, 172, 182
Democratic Party (United States) 3, 8
democratic reformism (China) 161
Desert Song, The (Romberg & Hammerstein) x, 84
Dewey, George 21
Dewey, John 142
dictatorship 61, 68, 74, 77, 105, 107, 154, 155, 162, 172
Diederichs, Otto von 21
Dillon, E.J. 12
Disperata, La 64, 71
Doll House 76
Dominican Republic 8

Doolittle, Hooker 133
Double Ten 151
Dowager Empress 22, 153. *See also* Tz'u Hsi (Cixi)
Dragon Throne 155
Duce 52, 61
Duse, Eleonora 53
Dutch East Indies 161

E

Egypt 7, 13, 23, 62, 71, 84, 130, 133
Eia, Eia, Eia, Alala 69
Emanuele Filiberto (ship) 50
Emmanuel, King 73
Entente powers 3, 26
Escadrille de la Garde Chérifienne (Squadron of the Sherifian Guard) 121, 122
Estella, Marquis of 105. *See also* Primo de Rivera, Miguel
ethnicity 4, 7, 16, 17, 19
ethnic prejudice 46, 48, 71

F

fanaticism 87
Farouk, King 133
Fascism x, xi, 51, 59, 61, 65, 66, 68, 71, 73, 74, 131
Fenice (Phoenix Theater) 69
Ferdinand, King 85
feudal land system 22, 145
Fez 88, 119, 129
Fiat Type 4 58, 76
Fiume ix, 15–19, 47, 49, 57, 58, 62–64, 66, 68, 69, 71, 73, 75
  Governor's Palace 49, 50, 59, 61, 64, 68, 72, 73, 75, 77
  National Council 49, 50, 68, 69, 70
Flag Day speech (F. Roosevelt) 133
Flumen 15. *See also* Fiume
foot binding 147, 172
Forbidden City 143, 153
Fourteen Points (Wilson). *See* Wilson, Woodrow: principles for peace
fragging 104
France 9, 13, 27, 36, 49
  agreements and treaties 14, 15, 17, 31, 35, 39, 45, 81, 86, 115, 118, 120, 125, 129, 139
  allies ix, 3, 23, 50, 60, 67, 131, 151, 167
  army 120, 124, 127, 129

colonialism x, 50, 82, 84, 86, 89, 96, 111, 113, 114, 116–118, 124, 132, 133
  concessions 160, 181
  fortifications in the Rif 115, 118–120, 124
  League of Nations 33
  navy 126
Franco, Francisco x, 100, 102, 107, 126, 127, 131, 132
Free State of Fiume 51. *See also* Fiume
French Flying Corps 122
French Foreign Legion 100, 110, 121
French Indochina 117, 132
French Morocco *83m*, 86, 106, 114–116, 118, 120, 124, 127, 132, 133. *See also* Morocco, Spanish Protectorate of Morocco
Furneaux, Robert 119
futurism 67, 68

G

Galese, Duke of 51. *See also* d'Annunzio, Gabriele
Galin (Blücher, Vasily) 168.
Gandhi, Mohandas 23, 88
Garda, Lake 47, 73, 76
Garden of Fascism, The (Mussolini) 74
Gardiner, A.P. "Percy" 112
Garibaldi, Giuseppe 16, 45, 67
Gate of Heavenly Peace 143, 181
Generalissimo 176. *See also* Chiang Kai-shek
Geneva (Switzerland) 38
Georges-Picot, François 14
Germany 9, 10, 13, 21, 23, 30, 36, 100, 160
  agreements and treaties 11, 18, 40
  allies 3, 24, 45, 131, 132, 157, 159
  colonialism 7, 11, 20, 22, 40
  concessions and reparations 6, 20, 25, 28, 31, 36, 139, 155
  Kaiser 21, 23
Gettysburg 134
Gibralter 86
Giolitti, Giovanni 72
Giovinezza (song) 59
G-Mo 176. *See also* Chiang Kai-shek
Gordon-Canning, Robert 112
Grayson, Cary 35
Great Britain (British Empire) 6, 9–11, 27, 49, 100
  agreements and treaties 14, 15, 17, 24,

31, 35, 36, 39, 45, 81, 139, 159
allies ix, 3, 23, 24, 50, 60, 67, 131, 132, 151, 167, 176
colonialism 7, 13, 14, 21, 22, 25, 62, 84, 86, 87, 96, 112, 113, 116, 117, 121
League of Nations 4, 33
Great Harmony (Confucius) 172
Great Powers 9, 28, 32, 182
Greece 20, 61, 70
Greene, Robert 57
Green Gang 179
Grey, Lord Charles 25
Gruzenberg, Mikhail 165. *See also* Borodin, Mikhail
Guam 22, 85
Guangzhuo. *See* Canton
Guevara, Che x, 82, 116
Guillin (Kweilin) 158
gunboat diplomacy 140, 167
Guomindang. *See* Kuomintang (KMT)

H

Hadjaz 12
Haiti 8
haka 111
Hammerstein, Oscar 84
Han Chinese 147, 170
Hangchow (Hangzhou) 177
Hangkow (Hankou) 151, 177, 180
Hangpu (Whampoa) Military Academy 168
Hanoi 149
Hanyang 151
Hard Head, The 64
Harding, Warren G. 40
Harris, Walter 108, 120, 122
Harrow School 23
Harvard University 85, 132
Hawaii 22, 31, 143
Hawaii, Kingdom of 149
Hay, John 90
Hearst newspapers 52
heliograph 94
Hemingway, Ernest 55
Henle, Richard 21
History of the American People (Wilson) 48
Hitler, Adolf x, 51, 52, 60, 61, 73, 74, 131
Ho Chi Minh x, 13, 81, 82, 88, 116, 148
Hollywood x, 84
Holm, Sir Ian 84

holocaust 61
Holocaust, City of the 61
Honduras 8
Hong Hsiu-ch'uan (Hong Xiuquan) 147
Hong Kong 21, 149, 159, 173
Horace 57
House, Edward 10, 11, 31, 34, 36, 38
Hughes-Hallett, Lucy 51, 73
Hughes, William "Billy" 25, 32, 33
Hunan 161
Hungary 7, 15, 48, 49, 56, 64, 160
hypo-colony 29, 150

I

Il Vulture Del Sole (d'Annunzio) 44
immigration 32, 46, 48
Immigration Act of 1924 48
imperialism 23, 27, 32, 67, 70, 81, 85, 98, 133, 143, 159. *See also* colonialism and specific countries
independence xi, 5, 81, 84, 86, 88, 95, 102, 104, 105, 109, 111, 114, 120, 126, 130, 133, 135, 163, 171
India 13, 14, 23, 25, 62, 70, 71, 84, 85, 116
Indian Ocean 129
Indochina 13
Indonesia 161
industrialization 22, 24, 32, 172
Inter-Allied Commission of Control 50
international law 30, 97
international organization 4. *See also* League of Nations
international peace-keeping 40, 142
international zone 86, 114
Iqueriben 94
Iraq 84, 117, 121
Ireland 13, 61, 71
Isaacs, Harold 164
Isabella, Queen 85
Ishii Kikujiro (Viscount) 26
Islam 25, 71, 82, 84, 87, 90–92, 94, 103, 106, 107, 109, 110, 118, 119, 130, 133, 134, 170
Islamic State 87, 92
isolationism 40
Istrian peninsula 15, 72
Italy 9, 20, 39, 48
agreements and treaties 45, 68, 81
allies 3, 23, 45, 55, 60, 73, 131, 167
colonialism 7, 14–16, 20, 40, 45, 55, 62, 67, 81, 84, 121, 123

concessions xi, 18
League of Nations 33, 34, 36
unification 16, 45, 67

J

Jakelfalussy, Count Zoltan 49
Jallianwala Bagh massacre 85
James, Henry 53, 165
Japan 6, 7, 13, 22–25, 27, 28, 31, 33, 35–38, 40, 100
   agreements and treaties 139, 143, 155, 173
   allies 167
   colonialism xi, 22, 24, 31, 38, 84, 147, 149, 159, 160, 173
Jazz Age 62
Jibala region 90, 99, 101, 106, 107, 109, 110, 113, 122, 129, 134
jihad 87, 90, 93, 118
Joffe, Adolph 163
Johns, E.B. 33
Johnson, Douglas 17
Judaism 91, 107, 134, 165, 181

K

Kabul 121
K'ang Yu-wei (Kang Youwei) 145
Keller, Guido 63, 64, 69, 77
Keynes, John Maynard 9, 10, 12
Khattabi, Mohamed ibn Abd al-Karim al-x, 82. *See also* Abd el-Krim
Kiaochow (Jiaozhou) Bay 21
Klems, Joseph 110, 111
KMT. *See* Kuomintang (Guomindang)
Koo, Vikyuin V.K. Wellington (Gu Weijun) vi, 30, 31, 38, 174
Korea 7, 12, 13, 21, 23, 70, 84, 142
Koschnitzky, Leon 70, 71
Kosovo 16
Ku Klux Klan 48
Kuomintang (Guomindang, KMT) 149, 153–155, 162–166, 168, 169, 173–176, 177, 178–180
Kurdistan 12
Kvarner Gulf 63. *See also* Carnaro, Bay of
Kweilin (Guillin) 158

L

Lafayette Escadrille 121
Lansing, Robert viii, 6, 16, 26, 37, 46, 82
La Scala orchestra 65
Latourette, Kenneth Scott 153

League of Nations xi, 4, 12, 13, 14, 20, 32, 33, 34, 36–40, 70, 74, 81, 182
League of Oppressed Peoples 70, 71
Ledeen, Michael 74
Le Duan 116
Legation Quarter 22, 143
legionnaires 59, 63, 71, 74, 75, 100, 126
Lenin, Vladimir xi, 5, 35, 40, 51, 144, 159, 160, 162, 165, 169
Letter to the Dalmations (d'Annunzio) 57
liberalism 161
liberty 160, 171
Libya 84, 121, 123
Lincoln, Abraham 169
Li Ta-chao (Li Dazhao) 161, 179
Little Big Horn 94
Lloyd George, David ii, 11, 16, 18, 19, 20, 25, 35, 45
Lodge, Henry Cabot 39
London, Treaty of. *See* treaties
Loyalists (Spain) 131
Lu Muchen (Lu Muzhen) 149, 156
Lunbeck, Elizabeth 54
Lyautey, Hubert 106, 116–119, 124, 126, 127

M

Macau 167
MacDonald, Ramsay 112
MacMillan, Margaret 29
Mafia 48
Makino, Baron Nobuaki 30
Malaga 104
Malaya 117, 149
Manchu 147, 148, 170, 171. *See also* Ch'ing Dynasty
Manchuria 22, 23, 26, 27, 170
Mandarin 147
Manela, Erez 85, 144
Manila Bay 21
Mao Tse-tung (Mao Zedong) x, xi, 82, 144, 148, 161, 169, 179–181
March or Die 84
Marconi, Guglielmo 65
Mariana Islands 22
Maria Theresa, Empress 49
Maring (Hendricus Sneevliet) 161
Martino, Giacomo de 17
Marxism 61, 71, 144, 159–162, 169
May Fourth Movement 143, 144, 145, 157, 161, 167, 175, 181

INDEX

May Thirtieth 175
Mediterranean Sea 46, 88
Melilla 85, 86, 88, 89, 91, 93, 94, 95, 96, 97, 99, 102, 103, 106, 108, 110, 111, 113, 114, 120, 123, 131
Mencius 21
Mexico 6, 8, 180
militarism 37
Millán-Astray y Terreros, José 100, 102
Miller, Web 106
Ming Dynasty 152, 175
mining 88, 102, 112
missionaries 21, 22, 26
modernization 22, 23, 24, 29, 61, 66, 67, 103, 116, 147, 148
monarchy 27, 114, 148, 151, 152, 153
Mongols 170
Monroe Doctrine 26, 31
Monte Arruit 96, 99
Montenegro 16, 71
Montenevoso, Prince of 51. *See also* d'Annunzio, Gabriele
Montesquieu's Laws 169
Moors 84, 85, 89, 93, 131
moral certitude 8, 10, 29, 35, 39
Morocco vi, 81, 82, *83m*, 85, 130, 133, 134, 135. *See also* French Morocco, Spanish Protectorate of Morocco
Morocco, Sultan of 86, 87, 89, 90, 114, 116, 119, 120, 121, 128, 133
Moscow News 181
Mukhtar, Omar 84
Muñoz, Diego Esteves 102
Muslim state 118. *See also* Islam
Mussolini, Benito x, xi, 40, 51, 52, 56, 57, 58, 59, 60, 61, 64, 65, 66, 67, 70, 73, 74, 75, 77, 131
mutiny 58, 63, 64

N

Nakayama Sho 146. *See also* Sun Yat-sen
Nanking 152, 153, 176
Nanking University 176
Napoleanic Code 70
National Assembly (China) 152, 154
national boundaries 11, 14, 17, 19
nationalism ix, x, xi, 19, 28, 59, 73, 85, 89, 92, 93, 111, 118, 130, 132, 142, 144, 168, 169, 170, 175
Nationalists (in Spain) 131
National Revolutionary Army (NRA) 176, 177, 181

naval alliance 24
Navarro, Philipe 96
Navy League 33
Nehru, Jawaharlal 23, 88
New Jersey 3
New Mexico 6
New Territories 22
New Youth 145
New Zealand 14, 24, 25
Nicolas II, Czar 21
Nicolson, Harold 11
Nies, Franz 21
Nietzsche, Friedrich 51, 54, 69
Nikolski, Vladimir 161
Nitti, Francesco 60, 68, 69, 72
Nobel Peace Prize 181
North China Daily 21
Northern Expedition 180
Northern Macedonia 16

O

Oahu School 149
Oath Swearers of Ronchi 58, 63
Obama, Barack 149
Office of Strategic Services (OSS) 132
oil spot (*tache d'huile*) theory 117
On the Preservation or Dismemberment of China (Sun Yat-sen) 150
Open Door policy 26
Operation Torch 132
Orlando, Vittorio 11, 16, 18, 19, 20, 34, 60
ornamentalism 64
Ornitorinco (Platypus) 69, 75
Ottoman Empire 3, 10, 14
Owen, Wilfred 57

P

Pacific Islands 7, 31
Pact of Rome 18
Palestine 82
Panama 8
pan-Islamic movement 111, 113
Paris Peace Conference ii, ix, xi, 7, 8, 10, 13, 17, 28, 29, 34, 37, 41, 45, 48, 50, 57, 67, 71, 81, 140, 143, 155, 168, 170, 174, 182
Pearl Harbor 38
Pearl River 159, 167
Peggy Guggenheim Collection 75
Peking (Beijing) vi, 22, 29, 145, 152, 153, 157, 158, 163, 167, 173, 179, 180

Peking University 143–145, 161
People's Republic of China 146, 181
Perdicaris, Ion 90
Persia 12, 70
Persia (ship) 63, 71
Petain, Philippe 124, 126, 127, 132
Pfaff, William 66
Philippines 8, 22, 31, 85, 100, 105, 143, 150
Pichon, Stephen 9
Plato 69
plebiscite 68
Poland 48
Polk, William 95
Port Said 133
Portugal 33, 85, 100, 167
Pound, Ezra 55, 70
presidio 85, 86, 89, 111, 114. See also Ceuta and Melilla
Price, Ward 118
Primo de Rivera, Miguel 105, 106, 107, 109, 115, 117, 118, 124, 125, 126, 127, 129, 130
Primo Line 106, 111, 125
Princeton University 3, 181
proletariat 162, 172
propaganda 19, 55, 73, 121, 142, 167, 175
protectorate 23, 81, 86, 103, 111, 113, 117
Puccini 52
Pueblo (Colorado) 39
Puerto Rico 85
Puglia (ship) 73, 76
Punahou School 149
Pu-yi (Puyi), Emperor 153, 156, 175

Q

Quindao. See Tsingtao (Quindao)

R

Rabat 130
racial equality 32, 33, 174
racial homogeneity 48
racism 7, 28, 32, 33, 50, 89, 142
radicalization 139, 150, 157
radio 65, 142
Raisuli (Raisuni, Ahmed er) 90, 99, 101, 107, 109, 113, 121
Randaccio, sacred banner of 59
Rebels in the Rif: Abd el-Krim and the Rif Rebellion (Woolman) vi

rebus sic stantibus 30
Red Cross 101
Regency of Carnaro 47*m*, 51, 61, 70. See also Fiume
Regulares 91, 96, 100, 111, 131
Reinsch, Paul S. 26, 31, 38, 140
Republican Party 3, 8, 38, 40, 90
Risorgimento 45
Réunion (island) xi, 129, 133
Revive China Society 149. See also Kuomintang
Riffian army (Riffi) 84, 87, 101, 103, 107–110, 115, 119, 123, 124, 127, 128, 132, 134, 135
Rif Mountains x, 81, 101, 107, 135
Rif, Republic of x, 81, 82, 83*m*, 92, 101, 102, 104, 112, 114, 126, 128, 135
  government 103, 112, 117
Rif War x, 82, 84, 85, 93, 98, 102, 104, 105, 127, 128, 130
  concessions and reparations 101, 103
Rijeka x, 51, 75, 77
Rockefeller Foundation (hospital) 174
Rockwell, Paul 122
Roman Catholicism 17, 92, 131
Roman Empire 15, 19, 53, 57, 60, 65, 67, 76
Romania 33, 71
romanization of names vi
Romberg, Sigmund 84
Ronchi 58, 63, 65, 75
Ronchi dei Legionari Airport 75
Roosevelt, Elliott 132
Roosevelt, Franklin D. 40, 132, 133
Roosevelt, Theodore 6, 8, 54, 90, 113
Rosta News Agency 165
Rostra 76
Royal Danieli Hotel 56
Rumania 7
Russia 14, 21, 23, 24, 36, 71, 100, 132
  allies 10, 23, 159
  revolution 8, 13, 27, 63, 87, 123, 144, 160, 165. See also Bolsheviks

S

Salafists 92, 93
Samarkand 13
Sardinian Grenadiers 50, 58
Scotland 165
Seapower (magazine) 33
self-determination ix, xi, 4, 5–7, 14, 41, 49, 85, 103, 182

INDEX

China 28, 31, 138, 142, 159, 160
Fiume 16, 17, 20, 45, 46
Italy 66
Korea 13
Rif Mountains x, 80, 81, 82, 104, 111, 112, 129, 132
Senegal 118
Serbia 15–18, 71
Serbia, Kingdom of 46, 71
Serbian Orthodox religion 17
Serbs, Croats and Slovenes, Kingdom of 16, 46, 49. *See also* Serbia, Croatia, Slovenia
Shanghai 145, 152, 157, 159, 160, 161, 175, 177
Shantung amendment 38
Shantung Question xi, 20, 26, 38, 139
Shantung (Shandong) 21, 22, 24, 25, 28, 30, 31, 33, 35, 36, 38, 139, 140, 143
Sharia law 92, 93, 118
Sheean, Vincent 85, 107, 109, 110, 112–115, 116, 126, 165, 177
Siberia 27, 64
Silvestre Line 97
Silvestre, Manuel 91, 93–95, 98, 135
Singapore 25, 149
Sinn Féin 61
Sitwell, Sir Osbert 62, 65, 67, 74
Slovenia 15, 16, 19, 46, 71
Smyrna (Izmir) 20
Sneevliet, Hendricus 161
Snow, Edgar 161, 179
socialism 61, 68, 71, 161, 169, 172
Soong Ching-ling (Song Quingling) 156, 158, 173, 174, 177, 180, 181
Soong Mei-ling (Meiling) 180
South Africa 14, 108
Sovietism 160, 163, 175
Soviet Union xi, 37, 40, 71, 86, 144, 159, 160, 172
   agreements and treaties 163, 164, 165, 166
   allies 163, 167, 168
   Central Committee 174
Spain 22, 81
   agreements and treaties 86, 103, 115, 120, 125, 129
   allies 131
   civil war x
   colonialism x, 82, 85, 88, 93, 94, 98, 99, 103, 107, 118, 122, 123
   navy 125, 127
   republic 130, 131
Spanish Army of Africa 91, 98, 100, 102, 117, 127, 130, 131, 134
   blockade 101, 111
   blockhouses and forts 91, 94, 96, 97, 98, 99, 100, 106, 111, 125, 134
   casualties 95, 96, 97, 101, 105, 106, 108, 109, 114, 125, 134
   conditions 91, 95, 96, 98, 100, 102
   corruption and cowardice 91, 93, 95, 96, 98, 99, 104
   prisoners 101, 102, 108, 113, 128
Spanish Civil War 131
Spanish Foreign Legion 100, 106, 123, 126, 131
Spanish Protectorate of Morocco 81, 83m, 86, 92, 103, 104, 111, 113, 115, 117, 120, 127, 129, 130, 132, 133. *See also* French Morocco, Morocco
Spectator (magazine) 108
Spence, Jonathan 144, 175
Squadristi 74
Squadron of the Sherifian Guard 121, 122
Stalin, Joseph 164, 165, 176, 180, 181
Starkie, Walter 66
State Bank of the Rif 112
St. Germaine, Treaty of. *See* treaties
Strand Magazine 153
Suez Canal 133
Sufis 92
Sung Chi'iao-jen (Song Jioren) 154
Sun Wen 146, 158. *See also* Sun Yat-sen
Sun Yat-sen vi, 23, 26, 29, 137
   career and leadership xi, 142, 146, 150–152, 154–158, 162, 164–165, 167–170, 172–173
   character 146–150, 158, 165–167, 169, 174
   family and wives 149, 156
   health 173
surveillance state 171
Sweeney, Charles 121
Sykes, Mark 14
Sykes-Picot agreement 14
Syria 82, 84, 120, 130

T

tache d'huile theory 117
Taft administration 151
Taiping Rebellion 147
Taiwan 22, 146, 149, 171, 181
Tangier 86, 102, 109, 114, 120

Tartary 12
Taza 129
Telegram del Rif 88
Telegraph 12
telephone system 107
Temple of the Azure Clouds 174
Tercio 100
terrorism 105
Tetuan 104, 108, 125, 126, 127
Texas 6
theocracy 170
Three Principles of the People (Sun Yat-sen) 148, 169
T'ian-an Men (Tiananmen) 143
Tibet 170
Time (magazine) x, 82
Times (of London) 63, 87, 99, 108
Tirpitz, Alfred von 24
Tizi Azza 101
Toscanini, Arturo 65
Tragedy of the Chinese Revolution (Isaacs) 164
Transjordan 130
treaties 27, 29, 30, 37, 104
 of London 15, 16, 17
 of Versailles 34, 37, 38, 39, 65, 80, 104
 peace 11, 18, 33, 38, 40
 of Rapallo 72
 of St. Germaine 50
 secret 14, 18, 25, 28, 35, 46, 139
Trieste 15, 18, 46, 55, 75, 77
Tripoli 82
Trotsky, Leon 164, 176, 180
Trump, Donald J. xi
Tsao Ju-lin (Cao Rulin) 143
Tsingtao (beer) 22
Tsingtao (Quindao) 22, 24, 30
Tsushima Strait 23, 24
Tunisia 117
Turkic people 170
Turks 14, 25
Tyler, John 3
Tyrol 18, 20
Tz'u Hsi (Cixi) 22, 153

U

Ujda 128
Ulyanov, Vladimir Ilyich (Lenin) 144
Union of Free Spirit Tending Towards Perfection 62
United Front 162, 163, 169, 176, 177, 179, 180

United Nations 33, 38, 40
United Press 106
United States 6, 9, 10, 30, 36, 38, 71, 104, 105, 117, 121. *See also* American topics
 agreements and treaties 45, 81
 allies ix, 23, 50, 60, 67, 131, 132, 156, 167, 176
 China, relationship with 27, 139, 140
 Civil War 32
 colonialism 8, 21, 22, 26, 31, 85, 86, 143
 Constitution 40
 Department of State 122
 League of Nations 33, 40
 propaganda 142
utopian state 61, 64, 69, 70, 72, 169

V

Valesio, Paolo 53
Venetian Republic 19, 53, 60, 67, 70
Venice 19, 56, 58, 73, 75
Versailles, Treaty of. *See* treaties
Vichy government 132
Viet Minh 124
Vietnam 13, 50, 104, 105, 117, 124
Virgil 66
Vittoriale 73, 76
Vladivostok 165
Vo Nguyen Giap 116

W

Wade-Giles system vi
Wang Ch'ing-wei (Wan Jinwei) 175
warfare
 air 99, 108, 110, 113, 120, 121, 123, 124, 126, 134
 atrocities 90, 94, 96, 98, 120, 122, 123
 colonial 121
 espionage 6
 European superiority 85
 grenades 110
 guerilla x, 82, 87, 95, 97, 99, 100, 101, 108, 111, 121, 123
 poison gas x, 82, 123, 124, 158
 submarine 6, 24
Washington Naval Conference of 1921–1922 38
Waterloo 134
Wei-hai-wei (Wehai) 22
Wergha River 119, 120, 121, 127
Western Hills region 174

INDEX

Whampoa (Hangpu) Military Academy 168, 176
White Australia policy 32
white man's burden 32, 33
Wilhelm II, Kaiser 21
Wilson, Edith 39
Wilsonian Moment 144
Wilson, Woodrow *ii*, 1
  career ix, 3, 9, 11, 20, 39, 41, 181
  character 2, 3, 4, 9, 12, 18–19, 26, 32, 35, 37, 39, 60
  health 34–35, 38–40, 65
  idealism 10, 84
  policies xi, 4–6, 8, 9, 11, 14, 19, 26, 31, 33–34, 36, 46, 49–50, 57, 63, 70, 81, 101, 103, 111, 132, 138–140, 163, 168, 170, 182
  prejudices 46, 48–49
  principles for peace
    Five Particulars 4, 187
    Four Ends 4, 186
    Four Principles 4, 185
    Fourteen Points ix, 4, 8, 14, 16, 18, 31, 37, 48, 71, 183
Wind and the Lion, The 90
Wisner, Frank 133
Woodhouse, John 46
Woolman, David vi, 97
World War I ix, 3, 6, 9, 12, 23, 24, 26, 27, 30, 46, 55, 62, 64, 81, 82, 84, 89, 90, 98, 103, 110, 121, 122, 123, 124, 139, 142, 155, 156, 157
World War II x, 33, 40, 75, 82, 124, 126, 131, 132, 133, 173, 175, 181, 182
Wuchang 151
Wuhan 151, 177, *178m*

X

Xauen (Chaouen), Count of 91. *See also* Berenguer, Dámaso
Xi Jinping xi

Y

Yale University 53
Yangtze River 29, 151, 176, 180
Yellow Sea 21
Yenan 180
Yuan Shih-k'ai (Yuan Shikai) 151, 152, 153, 154, 155, 157
Yugoslavia 16, 17, 18, 45, 46, 50, 51, 68, 71, 72, 75

Z

Zara 17
Zhongshan (Ch'ung Shan) 146. *See also* Sun Yat-sen
Zhou En-lai. *See* Chou En-lai
Zimmerman, Arthur 6
Zimmerman Telegram 6
Zinoviev, Grigorii 163

About the Author

H.D.S. GREENWAY was born in Boston, and educated at Yale, Oxford, and Harvard. After serving in the U.S. Navy, he was a foreign correspondent for *Time* magazine and the *Washington Post,* and served as foreign editor, national editor, and opinion page editor of the *Boston Globe.* Reporting from ninety-six countries, he was also a contributing columnist for the *International Herald Tribune* and *Global Post.* He lives with his wife, JB Greenway, in Needham, Massachusetts.